# Ethics and Research in Inclusive Education

D0219972

The recent move towards inclusive education has radically influenced the way educational research is conducted. Students need to become aware of the critical, ethical and legal responsibilities that arise from investigation in this new and expanding area.

Written from the perspective of inclusive education, rather than 'special education', this carefully edited collection of articles from a wide variety of sources will develop the student's ability to

- identify and respond to ethical dilemmas that occur within their particular research methodologies and settings;
- respond appropriately to the complex issues that are pertinent to their own work.

The contributions to this book draw upon examples of inclusive practices from around the world. Students taking postgraduate courses or diplomas in Inclusive Education will find this an invaluable read.

**Jonathan Rix**, **Katy Simmons** and **Kieron Sheehy**, are all lecturers in Inclusive and Special Education at the Centre for Curriculum and Teaching Studies, The Open University.

**Melanie Nind** was formerly a Senior Lecturer in Inclusive and Special Education at the Centre for Curriculum and Teaching Studies, The Open University, and is now Reader in Education at the University of Southampton.

# Companion Volumes

---

The companion volumes in this series are

**Curriculum and Pedagogy in Inclusive Education**
Values into practice
*Edited by Melanie Nind, Jonathan Rix, Kieron Sheehy and
Katy Simmons*

**Policy and Power in Inclusive Education**
Values into practice
*Edited by Jonathan Rix, Katy Simmons, Melanie Nind and
Kieron Sheehy*

This Reader is part of a course: *Researching Inclusive Education Values into Practice*
that is itself part of the Open University MA programme.

## The Open University MA in Education

The Open University MA in Education is now firmly established as the most
popular postgraduate research degree for education professionals in Europe, with
over 3,500 students registering each year. The MA in Education is designed particularly for those with experience of teaching, the advisory service, educational
administration or allied fields.

### Structure of the MA

The MA is a modular degree, and students are therefore free to select from a range
of options the programme which best fits in with their interests and professional
goals. Specialist lines in management, applied linguistics and lifelong learning are
also available. Successful study in the MA programme entitles students to apply for
entry into the Open University Doctorate in Education Programme.

*Open University supported learning*

The MA in Education programme provides great flexibility. Students study at their own pace, in their own time, anywhere in the European Union. They receive specially prepared study materials, supported by tutorials, thus offering the opportunity to work with other students. The University also offers many undergraduate courses. Within the area of Inclusive Education there is an undergraduate second level course *Inclusive Education: Learning from each other.*

*The Doctorate in Education*

The Doctorate in Education is a part-time doctoral degree, combining taught courses, research methods and a dissertation designed to meet the needs of professionals in education and related areas who are seeking to extend and deepen their knowledge and understanding of contemporary educational issues.

## How to apply

If you would like to register for this programme, or simply find out more information about available courses, please write for the *Professional Development in Education* prospectus to the Course Reservation Centre, PO Box 724, The Open University, Walton Hall, Milton Keynes MK7 6ZW, UK (Telephone +44 (0) 1908 653231). Alternatively, you may visit the Open University website http://www.open.ac.uk where you can learn more about the wide range of courses offered at all levels by the Open University.

# Ethics and Research in Inclusive Education

## Values into practice

Edited by
Kieron Sheehy, Melanie Nind,
Jonathan Rix and Katy Simmons

RoutledgeFalmer
Taylor & Francis Group

LONDON AND NEW YORK

The Open
University

First published 2005
by RoutledgeFalmer
2 Park Square, Milton Park, Abingdon, Oxon OX14 4RN

Simultaneously published in the USA and Canada
by RoutledgeFalmer
270 Madison Ave, New York, NY 10016

*RoutledgeFalmer is an imprint of the Taylor & Francis Group*

Typeset in Bembo by
Newgen Imaging Systems (P) Ltd, Chennai, India
Printed and bound in Great Britain by
TJ International Ltd, Padstow, Cornwall

*British Library Cataloguing in Publication Data*
A catalogue record for this book is available
from the British Library

*Library of Congress Cataloging in Publication Data*
A catalog record for this book has been requested

ISBN 0–415–352–053 (hbk)
ISBN 0–415–352–061 (pbk)

# Contents

# Acknowledgements

The following chapters are reproduced with the permission of Taylor & Francis Group, (www.tandf.co.uk/journals):

Chapter 2
Thinking about inclusion. Whose reason? What evidence?
Gary Thomas and Georgina Glenny

*International Journal of Inclusive Education (2002), 6, 4, 345–369*

Chapter 4
What a difference a decade makes: reflections on doing 'emancipatory' disability research
Colin Barnes

*Disability and Society (2003), 18, 1, 3–17*

Chapter 5
Research by children
Priscilla Alderson

*International Journal of Social Research Methodology (2001), 4, 2, 139–153*

Chapter 6
The ethical and methodological complexities of doing research with 'vulnerable' young people
Gill Valentine, Ruth Butler and Tracey Skelton

*Ethics, Place and Environment (2001), 4, 2, 119–125*

Chapter 7
Children with special needs, teachers with special needs
Ros Frost

From *Doing Practitioner Research Differently*, Marion Dadds and Susan Hart, RoutledgeFalmer (2001), 13–26

Chapter 8
'Do you get some funny looks when you tell people what you do?' muddling through some angsts and ethics of (being a male) researching with children
John Horton

*Ethics, Place and Environment (2001), 4, 2, 159–166*

Chapter 9
'This won't take long…': interviewing, ethics and diversity
Carol Vincent and Simon Warren

*Qualitative Studies in Education (2001), 14, 1, 39–53*

Chapter 11
The moral maze of image ethics
Jon Prosser

From *Situated Ethics in Educational Research*, edited by Helen Simons and Robin Usher, RoutledgeFalmer (2000), 116–132

Chapter 12
Rants, ratings and representation: ethical issues in researching online social practices
Michele Knobel

*Education, Communication and Information (2003), 3, 2, 187–210*

Chapter 15
Methodological challenges in researching inclusive school cultures
Melanie Nind, Shereen Benjamin, Kieron Sheehy, Janet Collins and Kathy Hall

*Educational Review (2004), 56, 3*

The following chapters are reproduced with the permission of Blackwell Publishing Ltd:

Chapter 10
'Parents as partners' in research and evaluation: methodological and ethical issues and solutions
Sheila Wolfendale

*British Journal of Special Education (1999), 26, 3, 164–169*

Chapter 13
Ethics in quasi-experimental research on people with severe learning disabilities: dilemmas and compromises
Mary Kellett and Melanie Nind

*British Journal of Learning Disabilities (2001), 29, 51–55*

Chapter 17
Reflections on interviewing children and young people as a method of inquiry in exploring their perspectives on integration/inclusion
Ann Lewis

*Journal of Research in Special Educational Needs (2001), 1, 3*

The following chapter is reproduced with the permission of Lawrence Erlbaum Associates, inc.:

Chapter 14
Owning the story: ethical considerations in narrative research
William E. Smythe and Maureen J. Murray

*Ethics & Behaviour (2000), 10, 4, 311–336*

The following chapter is reproduced with the permission of the Open University Press/Mc-Graw-Hill Publishing Company:

Chapter 18
Researching children's perspectives: legal issues
Judith Masson

*Researching Children's Perspectives*, edited by Ann Lewis and Geoff Lindsey, Open University Press (2003), 34–45

The following chapters are reproduced with the permission of the authors:

Chapter 3
Taking curiosity seriously: the role of awe and Wanda in research-based professionalism
Marion Dadds

*Educational Action Research (2002), 10, 1, 9–25*

Chapter 16
A guide to ethical issues and action research
Jane Zeni

*Educational Action Research (1998), 6, 1, 9–19*

# Chapter I

# Introduction

## Inclusive education and ethical research

*Kieron Sheehy*

This *Reader* is intended to support those embarking on educational research in the area of inclusive education. It is designed as a text for Master's level, and other advanced, students and teacher researchers. Research about inclusive education can raise complex ethical issues and the researcher needs to be aware of these and the ethical and legal responsibilities that arise from current research practices.

This book also hopes to contribute to a broader goal that is encapsulated within the following quotation.

> good quality research, which develops our theoretical and empirical knowledge of the world of education, is important, and if researchers are seen to conduct their activities unethically then this research is less likely to get done and will not be given the consideration it should receive. ... research, as with any other activity in a humane, open and democratic society, should be conducted within a framework of values. ...
>
> (Foster 1999)

Discussing examples and sharing our understanding of ethical issues is one way of working towards these goals. Good quality research helps us move our own understanding and educational practices forward, and, in doing so, also contributes to the wider activities of a democratic society. We would see research in inclusive education as part of this process, developing inclusive educational practices and thereby improving the educational experience of all learners.

## The context of inclusive education

The definition of inclusive education remains a contested ground; the term can mean different things to people who have varied investments in how it is constructed and enacted, and hence researched. This context is considered in the opening chapters (Gary Thomas and Georgina Glenny, Chapter 2, and Colin Barnes, Chapter 4) and sets the scene for examining subsequent issues.

The authors support the view that moving towards inclusive education should significantly influence how we approach research and it has been forcibly argued that inclusive education 'must signify new times for educational research' (Slee 1998: 440). A key part of such a change is developing an awareness of the ethical aspects of our research and the impact that these have in understanding and developing inclusive educational practices. This context means that certain issues and interactions are more likely to be acknowledged and to be seen as challenging for the researcher and those researched. It is these issues and interactions that are considered in the chapters. General ethical guidelines offer sensible advice but these are often inadequate in the field of inclusive education, either through lack of contextual information, detailed example or because the nature of educational research has expanded to encompass new fields and relationships. The chapters give examples of how issues that are 'beyond the guidelines' can be addressed.

Often research in the area of inclusion is a rearticulation of old ideas that fail to do justice to the 'new times' (Slee 1998) and one issue in the design of this *Reader* has been the degree to which it would concern itself with inclusive research, rather than research into inclusive education. If inclusive education is seeking to develop a situation where in 'learning for all' is achieved, then should the research process itself be in the hands of those researched and primarily for the benefit of this group? We would support this view, and recent changes in research practices have illustrated how this can be achieved. People with learning disabilities are moving beyond 'involvement' to begin directing research that influences on their lives (Walmsley and Johnson 2003). The Disability Activist movement has had a major impact in the UK on who represents and researches disability issues, and the application the social model of disability has contributed to and underpinned the construction of, inclusive educational practices (Open University 2004). The concept of pupils acting as researchers has recently emerged as an innovative practice in the area. One might argue that research practices can either support existing segregationist models of education and knowledge production, or support the development of inclusive educational practices.

This *Reader* includes material that considers the ethical issues surrounding working with children who are researchers and there are also several discussions of the ethical aspects of working co-operatively and in partnerships with different groups of people. However, the balance of the book is not about the ethics of being engaged in emancipatory inclusive research but rather about the ethical issues faced by those carrying out research in the context of, and for the development of, inclusive education. There is a danger that by adopting this stance we are simply reinstating old special practices in a new field and 'adjusting our language to fit newspeak' (Slee 1998). The approach we have taken in addressing this issue is a consideration of the relationship between the researcher and the researched – and hence reflexivity is a theme that runs throughout this book. The professional and academic interests, and power relations of the research situation are discussed and made visible by the examples offered. We also intend that the ethical practices and recommendations developed in this book act to support the voice and influence of those whose educational lives are being researched. This approach would not sustain essentialist views of disability, learning difficulty and diversity that have characterised much

Special Educational research. In contrast inclusive education is being developed from ideas about social justice and human rights. Gary Thomas and Georgina Glenny (Chapter 2) discuss how these values should provide the lead for new developments in inclusion. They argue that inclusive education should reinstate the importance of teachers' own experience, insights, and values and restore the significance of reflective practice. One way of doing this is described by Marion Dadds (Chapter 3). She offers a rationale for research-based professionalism and explores the problematic 'real life' contextual issues of using research as a means of developing one's practice. One criticism of using research to develop inclusive education problematises having a priori agenda for a particular form of social change. Colin Barnes (Chapter 4) tackles this issue in his discussion of emancipatory disability research and the social model of disability. Thus Part I provides perspectives on the theoretical and practical context of research.

## New voices and relationships

'New Voices and Relationships' (Part II) introduces examples of research perspectives that feature different groups of people. As we have mentioned, there is a growing movement to include pupils in projects as researchers themselves (Jones 2003). 'New Voices and Relationships' begins with an examination of the problems and advantages that arise when children are actively involved in this process. Priscilla Alderson (Chapter 5) offers an international perspective on children's and teenagers' activities at various stages of projects, their levels of participation, and their use of a range of research methods. She reviews some of the problems and advantages of children doing research. A significant issue when researching inclusive education is that common methodological and ethical dilemmas can become much more complex and significant when working with a 'vulnerable' group of children or youth. Gill Valentine, Ruth Butler and Tracey Skelton (Chapter 6) discuss this situation, in this case in discussions with self-identified lesbian and gay young people. The themes they identify have a relevance to a wide range of research situations, particularly where marginalised groups are being consulted.

An important aspect of research within the classroom is the personal experience of the teacher researcher and the challenging everyday ethical decisions that they need to make. In 'Children with special needs, teachers with special needs' (Chapter 7) Ros Frost gives a reflexive account of carrying out research in her own classroom. The personal experience of research is also highlighted in 'Do you get some funny looks when you tell people what you do? Muddling through some angsts and ethics of (being a male) researching with children' (Chapter 8). John Horton discusses aspects of research that are unpredictable and are not, and possibly cannot be, addressed though general guidelines and legal boundaries. He also draws out the importance of doing research with participants as opposed to 'on' them. Sensitivity to the relationship between the researcher and those researched is a theme that runs through the book. The multiple and intersecting factors that affect this relationship are discussed by Carol Vincent and Simon Warren (Chapter 9).

In the context of working with parents they consider the formation and development of relationships with their respondents. In doing this they explore factors such as differences and similarities of age, race, social class, language, and gender, and suggest how these factors influence the research process. Other ethical issues arise when working with 'Parents as Partners' and Sheila Wolfendale offers some solutions to these in Chapter 10. Many of the chapters illustrate how the ethical issues are context dependent and offer examples of how these have been addressed. Context in this sense includes the relationships with whom we are working and whose experiences we are researching and also the relationship with one's own professional and personal identity. Another important aspect of research context is the methodology that is chosen and this is discussed in Part III. Research approaches contain within them a model of what knowledge is, and how it is produced. Positivistic and constructivist research methods hence give rise to different ethical questions because of their methodology.

## Methods and practices

'Methods and Practices' (Part III) looks at a range of methodological contexts and highlights the ethical issues that emerge, in order to suggest potential ways forward. Overall the section focuses on newer methods and approaches, and those that have particular relevance to inclusive education. New technology brings new opportunities both, as a tool for conducting research with, as a topic of research itself and also as a context in which people interact. The ethical implications of using visual images and video in classroom-based research is discussed by Jon Prosser in Chapter 11. As with some other chapters it does not arise from within the literature typically associated with 'inclusion', but rather focuses on the method, one that is increasingly used within inclusive educational research (Mclarty and Gibson 2000). Similarly, Michele Knobel (Chapter 12) explores education-related research that is conducted online with reference to studies whose data is drawn solely from cyberspaces, as well as those that have an Internet-based investigation component (such as comparisons of in-class versus at-home activities). The world wide web and online life presents challenges to some constructions of inclusive education (Sheehy 2003) and researchers need to consider their research approach within this new terrain.

Whilst ethical guidelines for conducting research are relatively well established (BERA 2004; BPS 2004; SRA 2004) power relations and communication barriers can shape how we enact established ground rules such as informed consent. Melanie Nind and Mary Kellet discuss this in 'Ethics in quasi-experimental research on people with severe learning disabilities: dilemmas and compromises' (Chapter 13). The issues they discuss are pertinent to all situations where power relationships and communications barriers affect participants informed involvement. Whilst the degree to which this is achievable can be problematic in all research, Nind and Kellett, as researchers committed to inclusive education, illuminate these issues in an area that presents many challenges.

In the majority of situations people are able, and can be facilitated, to tell their own stories (Atkinson *et al.* 2000). The narrative study of lives has become established as a powerful way of understanding experiences of inclusion and exclusion. Yet the traditional principles of research ethics are not adequate for the complex and sensitive, ethical dilemmas that arise from this approach, for example, concerning issues of narrative ownership and the attribution of meanings to a person's life. William E. Smythe and Maureen J. Murray (Chapter 14) analyse this situation and make valuable recommendations about working with participants.

Research into inclusive education often seeks to capture and understand good practice. Chapter 15 in this part discusses one such attempt to research 'an inclusive school' using an ethnographic approach. Melanie Nind *et al.* describe the process of beginning the research and its subsequent progress. They highlight how the context of the research produced ethical and methodological dilemmas, unforeseen at the start of the investigation, and they discuss the extent to which these can be resolved.

Perhaps the two most commonly used methods within the field are action research and interviewing, and these are considered in Chapters 16 and 17. A framework of questions to support ethical practice for teachers and others using action research to developing their own practice is given by Jane Zeni (Chapter 16). The last chapter in this part discusses the use of a positivist approach wherein Ann Lewis considers ethical practice in interviewing and exploring the perspectives of children and young people. She focuses on the complexities of eliciting and interpreting children's views and discusses the merits of different ways of initiating and sustaining dialogue.

## The legal context

Underpinning the practice of educational research are legal issues. It is vital that the educational researcher is able to identify the legal requirements that are pertinent to their own research and this is the focus of the two chapters in Part IV. Judith Masson (Chapter 18) provides an important overview of research with children differentiating where appropriate between England/Wales and Scotland. The topics themselves have an international relevance and include identifying who has parental responsibility, legal viewpoints concerning confidentiality and the protection of participants. Masson concludes: 'Research with children which does not take on board legal dimensions is likely to harm both children and research' (see p. 241). Finally, 'Data protection issues in educational research' are considered by Clare Wood (Chapter 19). A relatively recent development, the Data Protection Act has significant implications for the way in which researchers work. This chapter considers the principles of good practice in relation to data issues, and highlight potentially problematic situations that educational researchers can find themselves in.

As the *Reader* illustrates undertaking research in inclusive education presents many complex ethical issues. There are some inevitable tensions between the viewpoints that we have included in the *Reader*. The way the researcher resolves these will be determined by the context of their work and their own beliefs about the role and purpose of research in inclusive education. We hope that you will find the ideas presented in the *Reader* both practically useful in your research and also thought-provoking. The manner in which research in inclusive education is conducted is important, and we would concur with Soltis's (1989) view.

> What purpose could be more worthy than to include in our educational research a concern for the good and the rights of those we investigate and the society of which we and they are a part.
>
> (Soltis 1989: 124)

## References

Atkinson, D., McCarthy, M., Walmsley, J. *et al.* (eds) (2000) *Good times, Bad Times, Women with Learning Difficulties Telling Their Stories*, Kidderminster, BILD Publications.

British Education Research Association (BERA) (2004) Ethical Guidelines http://www.bera.ac.uk/guidelines.html [accessed 21.02.04].

British Psychological Society (2004) Code of Conduct, Ethical Principles and Guidelines http://www.bps.org.uk/documents/Code.pdf [accessed 21.02.04].

Foster, P. (1999) Some critical comments on the BERA Ethical Guidelines. BERA Research Intelligence No 67 February. http://www.bera.ac.uk/ri/no67/ri67foster.html [accessed 21.02.04].

Jones, A. (2003) Involving Children and Young People as Researchers, in S. Fraser (ed.) *Doing Research with Children and Young People*, London, Sage Publications.

Mclarty, M.M. and Gibson, J.W. (2000) Using video technology in emancipatory Research. *European Journal of Special Needs Education*, Vol. 15, No. 2, pp. 138–148.

Open University (2004) E243 Inclusive Education Learning from Each Other. The Open University ISBN 0749253061.

Sheehy, K. (2003) New Technology and Inclusion: The World (Wide Web) is not Enough, in M. Nind, K. Sheehy and K. Simmons (eds) *Inclusive Education: Learners and Learning Contexts*, David Fulton Publishers, pp. 115–128, ISBN 184312-065-8.

Slee, R. (1998) Inclusive Education? This must signify new times for educational research. *British Journal of Educational Studies*, Vol. 46, No. 2, Dec, pp. 440–454.

Soltis, J.F. (1989) The ethics of qualitative research. *International Journal of Qualitative Studies in Education*. Vol. 2, No. 2, Apr–Jun 89, pp. 123–130.

The Social Research Association (SRA) (2004) Ethcial Guidelines http://www.the-sra.org.uk/ethics03.pdf [accessed 21.02.04].

Walmsley, J. and Johnson, K. (2003) *Inclusive Research with People with Learning Disabilities: Past, Present and Futures*, London, Jessica Kingsley.

# Part I

# A new context for educational research

# Chapter 2

# Thinking about inclusion.
# Whose reason? What evidence?

*Gary Thomas and Georgina Glenny*

## Introduction

There is a strand in the argument against inclusive education that goes like this: 'Inclusive education is all very well, and it is engendered by the kindest of motives, but there is a central problem: support for it springs from ideology rather than rational inquiry, and it is untested.' The assumption behind this position is that there is a body of rational, informed knowledge accessible to those who possess the right instruments for finding it, and that this is separate from the political, the partisan, the value-laden.

Academics, blessed with the best methods of rational inquiry, should stick to what they know in the debate about inclusive education – stick in other words to reason, informed by near certainties furnished by empirical study – and decline to meddle with the sentimental, the subjective, the sloppy and the politicized. It is that position which this chapter challenges.

Take one example of this kind of criticism of the inclusive position – in Wilson (2000) – which typifies many. Wilson begins with the acceptance that we all want to be kind and fair and that this is what motivates those who promote inclusive education. However, the argument proceeds, kind sentiments and high ideals are unsatisfactory as a basis for a large-scale change in educational policy, since on the one hand they are insufficiently clear or well defined, and on the other, evidence for them is unlikely to be of the right calibre to warrant any broad move in the direction indicated.

Because of lack of clarity, discussion about inclusion is taken to be 'vacuous or mistaken' (Wilson 2000: 298) – as are related notions, such as democracy in schools, or the elimination of competition between schools, or the elimination of selection. And because of the paucity of evidence in the area 'careful and profound empirical study' (Wilson 2000: 304) is necessary to establish the outcomes of inclusive endeavour.

There are some big assumptions here: that with the proper analysis, inclusion can in some way be disambiguated; that with appropriate grounding in evidence we shall know what is best. Without sentiment and with proper definition, it will be possible to discuss inclusion clearly, rationally and disinterestedly.

The view taken in this chapter is that the assumptions behind such a position are mistaken; it is that their acceptance during the twentieth century was responsible for many of the wrong turnings in the development of special education. We argue that it is time for a new epistemology in that part of education which concerns inclusion. It is time, in other words, for a reappraisal of the precepts, presumptions, tenets and methods of inquiry which stood behind the edifice of twentieth-century special education. An argument is made that the ways in which during the twentieth century the failure of children or the failings of schools were examined have proved wanting. We make the case that inquiry has proved wanting because key assumptions – about reason, about evidence and outcome – which led to notions of correct (or at least better) forms of pedagogy and schooling are illusory.

We are arguing, to put it more broadly, for a questioning and an untangling of what Charles Taylor (1984: 21) calls our 'inarticulate assumptions': we have to take a new stance towards our practices. Instead of just living in them and taking their implicit construal of things as they are, we have to understand how they have come to be, how they came to embed a certain view of things.

## Reason, ideology and rhetoric

Stanley Fish, makes the following case:

> whenever Reason is successfully invoked, whenever its invocation stops the argument and wins the day, the result will be a victory not for Reason but for the party that has managed (either by persuasion or intimidation or legerdemain) to get the reasons that flow from its agenda identified with Reason as a general category, and thereby to identify the reasons of its opponents as obviously *un*reasonable. Like 'fairness', 'merit' and 'free speech', Reason is a political entity, and never more so than when its claim is to have transcended politics.
>
> (Fish 1994: 18)

Proponents of this or that position, in other words, seek to bolster their stand by argument, by the invocation of what is supposed to be Reason. However, what is therein so proudly identified is inevitably merely one brand of reason; one set of reasons associated with one group's agenda.

By being logical, apolitical, clearheaded, tidy, parsimonious, consistent – by being supposedly rational – they seek to make their positions, their propositions and conclusions stand in a superior light. Part of this process involves the deliberate distancing from the political, the partisan, the value-laden, which is taken to infect the process of Reason.

[...]

This is an important matter to address, for criticism of inclusion often pivots on the notion that its proponents are motivated in large part by ideology rather than evidence. Proponents of reason and evidence, by contrast, are apolitical and motivated by a dispassionate concern for the truth.

In fact, of course, there is no one truth – only arguments which are what MacIntyre (1981: 8) calls 'incommensurable'. Rival arguments, he suggests, are each valid, and . . . the conclusions do indeed follow from the premises. But the rival premises are such that we possess no rational way of weighing the claims of one as against another. For each premise employs some quite different normative or evaluative concept from the others, so that the claims made upon us are of quite different kinds.

The mistaken belief is that one can in education unproblematically separate the disinterested from the interested, the apolitical from the ideological, the objective from the subjective, the reasoned from the irrational, the evidence-based from the arbitrary. It is a belief that in education there is a straightforward set of empirical questions for which answers can be supplied by empirical study.

A faith in this set of beliefs is bolstered by the manifest success of the investigative methods of natural science, at which educational researchers of a certain hue – whether they are looking at children's weaknesses or at schools' effectiveness – gaze enviously. In recent years, there has been a popular resurgence in the faith induced by science's success. It is almost a new form of scientism and it is based, interestingly, not on science's scepticism and doubt, but rather on the perception of almost magical understanding induced by the success of the natural sciences. Science, far from embodying what Haldane (1965) called 'the duty of doubt' has come to represent for many people, professional as well as lay, doubt's antithesis: faith.

There is no denying that the kind of rational and empirical epistemological world crafted by natural science is valuable in approaching some questions. Its success with certain kinds of question is palpable. However, whether it is valuable for all questions – and in our case, most educational questions – is open to debate. As Berlin (1979) points out, the sciences' espousal of and successful use of rationalism probably marks the major achievement of the human mind. But the problem arises, as he goes on to explain, from the assumption that 'the world is a single system which can be described and explained by the use of rational methods' (p. 81). It comes from the assumption that rationalism, 'while it may not lead to absolute certainty, attains to a degree of verisimilitude or probability quite sufficient for human affairs' (p. 88).

Education, possibly more than any other field of inquiry, is concerned with those 'human affairs', and if Berlin is right we cannot be guided in our notions of the form education should take by the methods of natural scientists. Many commentators have pointed to this fallacy: the expectation that the methods of natural science should be the methods of educational inquiry, attempting to impose, as Mouzelis (1995: 42) puts it, 'order and unity on the fragile, chaotic . . . character of the social'. The aim here is not to replicate that wide discussion. Rather it is to point to the interconnectedness of the questions we ask in education, particularly when thinking about inclusion: it is to point to the indissolubility of questions about inclusion, to stress that the political is mixed with the empirical, the subjective inseparable from the objective.

Even for natural scientists, political is mixed with empirical for some of the matters that they confront. As biologists Levins and Lewontin (1985: 4) point out, 'The denial of the interpenetration of the scientific and the social is itself a political act, giving support to social structures that hide behind scientific objectivity to perpetuate dependency, exploitation, racism, elitism, colonialism.' They go on to note that 'Of course the speed of light is the same under socialism and capitalism' but that questions which arise about *the way people live* cannot be answered without reference to an interrelated range of matters. Thus, the cause of tuberculosis may be shown empirically to be a *Bacillus*, yet epidemiologists tell us that the disease rarely takes hold where people's living and working conditions are adequate. In education, matters are no less complicated: the denial of the interpenetration of the social and the scientific (or at least what is supposed to be scientific) in considerations of teaching and learning has led us to forms of school organization which only too readily discriminate against certain children and segregate them.

[. . .] The crude questions asked about an event disguise the multiplicity of levels at which inquiry can occur.

The interpenetration of issues is no less complex when one comes to think of the ways in which questions about the social world are themselves constructed. Giddens (1994) notes that empirical information comes actually to create the social world – not merely reflect it or explicate it:

> Concepts . . . and the theories and empirical information linked to them, are not merely handy devices whereby agents are somehow more clearly able to understand behaviour . . . they actively constitute what that behaviour is and inform the reasons for which it is undertaken.
>
> (Giddens 1994: 42)

Giddens suggests that as we 'discover' new ways of making sense of phenomena, these explanations in turn become inseparable from the phenomena themselves. For example, the empirical and epidemiological information drawn on by the Warnock Committee in the UK in 1978 (DES 1978) did not merely hold a mirror up to some objective reality which could be used by educators. Rather, it actively generated a 'reality' that had to be responded to. As can be shown with the identification of reading difficulty (Thomas and Davis 1997), the construction of that reality meant that practitioners sought ways of conforming to it and confirming it, identifying one in five children, wherever their schools were situated. Such nominally empirical and theoretical knowledge comes to be used in practices which mark out pupils as being different. This has been particularly well discussed by those who have examined the nature of research into disability, for example, Barton (1992), Finkelstein (1992) and Zarb (1992).

Complexity is the hallmark of the questions that are asked about education. This is particularly the case with inclusion in education. It is the expectation that it will be possible to reduce those questions to simple propositions stripped of political, subjective or other unwelcome elements that leads to the notion that discourse about inclusion is in some way ideological. And it is the assumption that this *can* be done – that one *can* be objective and apolitical in these matters – which leads those who make such claims to assume that their own thinking is not infected by the ideology impostor. As Eagleton (1991: 2) notes, 'Ideology, like halitosis, is . . . what the other person has'.

Why is there this collection of allegiances to the empirical/rational dogma amongst special educators? It is a legacy not just of the structural and theoretical predilections of educational inquiry in general but in particular of a deficit-orientated thrust – or what Jordan *et al.* (1997) call a *pathognomonic* orientation – of special educators over the twentieth century.

Such a set of precepts sees some malady which has to be put right. Nowhere else in educational discourse does this fealty to one way of looking at things occur quite in the way that it occurs in special education. For example, when Hoggart (2001) discusses the shape of another part of the education system, the universities, and the desirability of more open access to them, he can make that argument clearly in a cultural and political context. It is only in special education and inclusion, where the delusions engendered by a scientistic and pathognomonic past have been so overwhelmingly influential, that there is a danger posed that the social, the political – the ideological – will infect proper rational debate.

It is our contention that far from bringing a feast of riches over the twentieth century, the approach of special education – pathognomonic, and supposedly theoretical, empirical – has been profoundly distorting to the shape of special education and currently to discussions of inclusion. Let us now look in a little more detail at this. What have been the fruits of the dominant approach – the *Weltanshauung* of special education?

## Evidence and experience

### Evidence

The consequences of the dominant approach are not impressive. (It is important to distinguish here between the fruits of the *approach* itself – our focus here – and the efforts of individual practitioners, which have been made with integrity and conscientiousness; no one would want to deny the latter.) It is a salutary thought that although there are some notable exceptions, academics in the fields most closely associated with education have seldom proffered incisive insights into the ideas which have shaped the ways in which we think about the schools children inhabit.

It would be a brave special educator who would venture to proffer for critical scrutiny a putative advance in practice-from-research which has occurred over the last one hundred years. Certainly there have been advances in thinking about the proper form education should take (such as those which occurred in the UK after the report of the Plowden Committee (DES 1967), recommending a more child-centred education), and there have been advances in thinking about the care and humane treatment of children and young people with physical or sensory impairments. However, these are advances that have arisen more from changes in the political and social climate than from research in special education.

The challenge we would put is to identify what beneficial effects have emerged in special education practice from a particular piece of research – about assessment, or pedagogy, or whatever – which have not, on evaluation, proved to be as good as the effects emerging from the next non-research-based method, effects emerging in other words from teachers' own intelligence and reflective practice. One of the problems about the practice which emerges from the dominant model of research is that it becomes over-concerned with correctives: methods, techniques – cures. The problem is that the correctives and cures which are derived from such research are shown empirically to have effects, and these effects are quite often dramatic. However, in the messy field of research about people and their social environments, where it is difficult if not impossible to delineate variables for inspection of their effects, new techniques can acquire potency for any number of reasons: the charisma of a pioneer; the energy of a dedicated research group; the support of a government, or the publicity machine of a publishing house (see Coles 2000 for a detailed analysis of the predilections and failings of the research machine in education). Thus, special education has come up with a panoply methods and techniques over the years, all of them claiming empirical justification: instrumental enrichment, Doman-Delacato, conductive education, Direct Instruction, behaviour modification, diagnostic/prescriptive teaching . . . the list goes on.

The problem is that the high expectations that early work arouses later prove not to have been fulfilled, as evaluation shows gains to slip away steadily over time and reflection reveals the pitfalls in having single-mindedly followed a particular path.

Direct Instruction, for example, rested in a hyperrational set of ideas about teaching and learning formal skills. Specifying exactly what should be taught, how it should be taught and how learning should be evaluated, early forays into its use showed great promise. Longer term evaluation, however, in the large US Follow-Through project (DeVault et al. 1977) indicated that the great benefits attributed to it may have been due as much to the generous resourcing allocated to it as to the specific pedagogic elements. More worryingly, recent analysis has indicated that on leaving school those children who were part of a Direct Instruction curriculum were significantly more likely to have been involved in crime, were less well adjusted and engaged in fewer community activities than those who partook at an earlier age in traditional nursery activities (Schweinhart and Weikart 1997).

Similarly, great hopes were placed in the potential of behavioural techniques both to help children learn and to help them behave appropriately. While there is no doubt that these techniques provided some assistance in thinking about pedagogy for some children, there can be equal certainty that they over-simplified the nature of learning and led, in widespread practice, to a kind of curricular desertification – as sensible, cautious thinking about educational aims was replaced with the certainties of behavioural analysis. [. . .]

Rueda and Mehan (1986), eschew simple deficit-orientated thinking, conceptualizing failure to learn in the social rather than in the individual context. They found that those children who fail to learn, far from lacking 'metacognitive skills', managed to do all the things they were not supposed to be able to do metacognitively: checking, monitoring, evaluating and so on. And they also used sophisticated planning in avoiding tasks expected of them. Rueda and Mehan conclude that supposedly context-free metacognitive activities are in fact context bound: it is almost as though the ability to use them is switched on or switched off by the surrounding social circumstances.

Like Rueda and Mehan, Hart (1996) rejects explanatory models that posit deficits as the causes of children's difficulties with schoolwork, and in particular, literacy. In a series of detailed case studies she makes a powerful case for a rejection of simplistic deficit notions such as 'weakness in phonics' being at the root of children's problems with reading and writing.

Talking of one boy's invented spellings (e.g. 'Britten' for 'Britain', 'earmy' for 'army' and 'sore' for 'sir'), she points not to the lack of learning, but rather to sophisticated understandings of phonics in the context of the boy's own way of speaking. She says, 'we can see him working out spellings using the hypotheses he had already formed about how the spelling system worked. Indeed, he had already made considerable progress in discerning its rules and patterns' (p. 80).

Present in the deficit → diagnosis → cure sequence is a surrender from the challenge that reflective teaching poses. To yield to such deficit thinking is to relinquish reflective thought in favour of a simplistic 'solution'. Such solutions of course have their allure, but such allure is illusory. In particular, these 'scientific' solutions look good to politicians, who are attracted by the possibility of the quick fix in preference to tackling the roots of poor literacy in poverty and inadequate funding for early childhood education (Coles 2000, Berlak 2001).

Despite the avowed unpopularity of the deficit approach in the last quarter of the twentieth century, it keeps returning to haunt special educators. Models of pedagogy persistently seek to find deficiencies in children. More recent variants of the approach seek to find deficiencies in schools, as Slee (1998) notes. The solution is invariably to discover new ways of teaching to correct the problem (or to exclude the child) or to impose ways of supposedly enabling schools to be more effective.

Why should the preference for such procedural routes persist? Skrtic (1991) points to the imperatives of the professional bureaucracy continually turning analysis back to the analytical predilections of established professions in education. Not unconnected to this, the Canadian educator Frank Smith talks in his *Book of Learning and Forgetting* (1998) about two models of learning – the official and the classical. The official, promulgated by early psychologists – and preferred by educational bureaucrats and politicians – sees learning as hard, rather like trying to squeeze something (learning) into a box (the brain) that is too small. The classical model, by contrast, sees learning as happening all the time, effortlessly. In schools, the official model still prevails, and in special pedagogy it is overwhelmingly the case that the official model (learning is about input and output) forms the tacit grounding for deficit models of learning failure.

In other words this official model, bolstered by the mock scientific ballast of a supposedly empirical approach, has come to displace the learned sensitivities of what Schön (1991) called the *reflective practitioner*. We explore this further below under 'Experience and humanity'.

Why too, one should ask, does faith in the traditional approach persist in the face of its less-than-outstanding success? The answer, as we explore in the next section, is because it provides explanations. The explanations are empty and illusory, but they suffice nevertheless for private satisfaction and for public consumption as explanations. For practitioners who have been encouraged to place reliance in the analytical tools of special education inquiry and have therefore lost confidence in their ability to analyse for themselves – lost confidence in the ability to teach reflectively – these explanations are bound to have much palliative appeal.

[. . .]

## Experience and humanity

The argument we are making is that the assays of psychologists, researchers and special educators have done little to provide direction and progress for children who have found it difficult to cope with or adapt to the systems of education with which they are confronted. [. . .] The thrust of their inquiries has been as resolute as it has been simplistic: to discover what is wrong, or in the most enlightened cases of the genre, what characterizes success. The latter has had its mark right to the end of the twentieth century, as social scientific method has sought to find the essence of the effective school, the effective teacher, the miracle pedagogies that gave rise to the Tiger economies of the South East Asia rim. (The fact that the economies were not so Tigerish after 1996 gives the lie to the causative imputations made to the simplistic association in the first place.) This seeking of pathology, this seeking of correction and its recent sequelae in the obverse, namely the seeking of the correct, has been the dogged thrust of special education endeavour. Whether it is a deficit in children, or more latterly a deficit in pedagogical technique or school organization, the thrust is the same. The questions are resolutely of one character.

It has been left to others – artists, novelists, philosophers, historians, journalists – to pose the most critical questions about the operation of institutions which care for and educate people who do not readily fit. Partly, this is because artists and those in the humanities come to social life with a different critical eye from social scientists. Although there are some notable exceptions, academics in the fields most closely associated with education have seldom proffered incisive insights into the ideas which have shaped the ways in which we think about the schools children inhabit.

The social commentary of the novels of Dickens did more, incomparably more, than the early special educators to reform understanding of the nexus of factors which contribute to unhappiness and failure at school. The effects of poverty, alienation, oppression, cruelty and a stultifying curriculum were well understood and explicated by Dickens and stand in sharp contrast to the scientistic contributions of his psychological contemporaries. Dickens's contemporary, journalist Henry Mayhew (1985), in a series of articles for the *Morning Chronicle* did more, by exposing their living conditions, to improve the lot of the London's child poor than his generation of educators. The tradition has, of course, continued. More recently, Ken Kesey's *One Flew Over the Cuckoo's Nest* and Christy Nolan's *Under the Eye of the Clock* have arguably done more to shape contemporary public policy on how people with differences are treated than all the academic research and writing of the last half-century. [. . .]

It is a freedom to make a 'close and detailed appreciation of what actually presents itself' which a loosening of grasp on the methodological dogmas of special education offers. If we are seeking to understand why one child is not reading, or why another refuses to go to school we should perhaps trust less in the epistemological shibboleths of twentieth-century special education endeavour and more in our own knowledge as people – trust in our experience and understanding of fear, interest, anxiety, friendship, perplexity, worry, loneliness and boredom. We know what it is to be confident, over-confident or to feel self-doubt or paralysing fear. We understand lying, openness and hypocrisy. We understand guile and the possibility of being deceived. We have self-knowledge, and this is surely our principal tool in helping us to understand others. As Joynson (1974: 2) puts it: 'Human nature is not an unknown country, a *terra incognita* on the map of knowledge. It is our home ground. Human beings are not, like the objects of natural science, things which do not understand themselves.'

Practitioners can use their understanding of these facets of being human, though, only if they feel confident in the knowledge that using them does not restrict their understanding – only if they feel that they are not missing out on some important empirical knowledge or missing some key theoretical insight. And it is most unlikely that anyone will have missed out on such knowledge or insight, for the models, theories and intellectual castles created in the field of special pedagogy have helped little in improving learning – helped little in understanding why children fail at school. This is unfortunate enough in itself, but the even more unfortunate corollary is that the existence of this kind of supposedly privileged knowledge has persuaded teachers in ordinary schools across the globe to think that they may not be sufficiently knowledgeable or sufficiently expert to help children who are experiencing difficulty: that they do not have sufficient technical expertise or theoretical knowledge to teach all children.

To say merely this, though, is to make the case too weakly: this privileged knowledge, these theories and models have, by satisfying Oakeshott's (1967: 2) 'irritable search for order' distracted attention from the ways in which we may use our common humanity to understand others, and use our common sense to make schools more humane, inclusive places.

When Foucault (1970: 49) said that 'knowledge [has] closed in on itself' he was referring to the codification of knowledge into disciplinary compartments. It would be a brave set of practitioners who would dare to move outside the professional edifices and procedural imperatives generated by those codifications. Procedural and professional responses and reflexes emerge from schools when problems with pupils arise, but these are often no more than what Skrtic (1991) calls 'symbols and ceremonies', distracting attention from more obvious and straightforward (but probably less prestigious, and certainly less immediately credible) action based on common humanity.

## Experience and humanity versus theory: teachers are people, not technicians

[. . .]

The legacy of positivistic science when transplanted to a focus on human beings was that we should deny what we know, as people, and put faith in a certain kind of disinterested knowledge. Behavioural psychologist B.F. Skinner (1972: 160) exemplified this denial and showed his contempt for our own knowledge of others when he said: 'What, after all have we to show for nonscientific or prescientific good judgment, or common sense, or the insights gained through personal experience? It is science or nothing.' Sadly, forty years of behavioural technology enable the question to be turned on its head: What has the supposedly scientific (some would say 'scientistic') approach to human behaviour given us that we did not already know? What has it caused us to disregard? To quote G.K. Chesterton, 'So far from being knowledge, it's actually suppression of what we know.' Indeed, it is worse than this, for it has not merely suppressed: it has distorted what we know and has, in the process, relegated our own personal knowledge. Take, for example, the notions of deficit and deprivation, which have been at the forefront of educational psychologists' analyses of school failure, presenting us with what Labov (1973) – in discussing the educational problems of children in ghetto schools – called 'the illusion of verbal deprivation' (p. 154). The analytic frames constructed by educational psychologists, in their fascination with deficit and disease, have distracted thought from more straightforward ways of explaining difference. As Labov continues, 'In the writings of many prominent educational psychologists, we find very poor understanding of the nature of language' – very poor understanding of 'the logic of nonstandard English' (p. 154).

Especially rooted in the analytical systems of psychology, the methods and predilections of special education provide an exemplar case of how explanatory frameworks can be misleading. Especially worrying is how these frameworks can seem to make us lose confidence in ourselves as teachers, and indeed, as people. Frank Smith's (1993) powerful narrative of his work on teaching at a South African university documents the resilience of belief among his teaching colleagues there in the canons of teaching and research method, and the way in which this belief had subverted their own self-confidence as teachers, and as people.

In a field like special education, there is the danger that 'theory' and 'profound empirical study' (Wilson 2000: 304) – particularly that of a respected social science such as psychology – may be used to add cachet to simple ideas or propositions. [. . .] But whether we are talking about children's behaviour in a classroom, or of the effectiveness of schools, there is no means in educational research of enabling what the philosopher of science Canguilhem (1994: 41) calls the 'elimination of the false by the true'. In what Hamilton (1998: 15) calls 'multivariate, nonlinear, adaptive systems' anything may happen. The technicist predilections of functionalist theory take no account of this: no account of these differences with the natural sciences. In those sciences there *is* an eventual elimination of false by true or at least (for those who balk at the starkness of false versus true) an elimination of less reliable knowledge by more reliable knowledge (Ziman 1991).

In rejecting one's own practical, tacit knowledge for the security of some scientistic notion of failure or of effectiveness, one rejects also the kind of knowledge which comes from friends and colleagues, alive and dead, who have not conformed to the scientistic archive with its fondness for technical inquiry methods and solutions. A consistent message – about stimulating interest, fostering security, gently enabling growth – comes through the work of the great educators: Pestalozzi, Froebel, Montessori, Rousseau. They were continued into the twentieth century by others such as John Dewey, Lev Vygotsky and John Holt. The reason that Vygotsky's ideas have been so interesting recently is that they have presented an alternative to the crystal-hard theorizations with which they were contemporary.

[. . .]

Vygotsky refreshingly returns to a kind of knowledge of learning which comes from our knowledge, as people, of what it is to learn.

That knowledge is, then, by no means new to us: it has not been revealed by some remarkable theoretical disclosure. It comes from Ryle's (1990) 'know how' which we gain of others (as learners, friends, deceivers, trusted colleagues, or whatever) and that knowledge arrives from our experience as teachers and as people. While Rousseau shocked the world with *Émile* (1762), he said only what confident teachers know (and probably have always known) about learning:

> Instead of keeping [*Émile*] mewed up in a stuffy room, take him out into a meadow every day; let him run about, let him struggle and fall again and again, the oftener the better; he will learn all the sooner to pick himself up. The delights of liberty will make up for many bruises. My pupil will hurt himself oftener than yours, but he will always be merry; your pupils may receive fewer injuries, but they are always thwarted, constrained, and sad. I doubt whether they are any better off.
>
> (Rousseau 1993: 49)

The contrast drawn by Rousseau seems remarkably prescient, and rather like a contrast between good nursery education and that which might be offered by Direct

Instruction, Doman Delacato or one of the other miracle methods of special ped-agogy. No miracle pedagogy has been discovered since his day, or is ever likely to be revealed by the theoretical endeavours of educators or psychologists. Nei-ther will the latter-day functionalist equivalents discover any formulae for imposing 'effectiveness'.

[...]

If, in other words, practitioners are immersed in the practice and observation of education, its traditions and literatures, there is no need for some external validation of their action, no need for theoretical explanation. The methodol-ogy, theory and disciplinary knowledge which have guided deliberation about the form special education should take have proved to be more knave than guide.

## Reinstating local inquiry and personal knowledge: toward social justice

### Valuing personal knowledge; valuing being human

We should invest less dependence in the grand theoretical edifices and rigid castles of metaphor constructed by special education's intellectual heroes. And we should place less faith in theory's methodological handmaidens. In education in general and special education in particular, there has been a tendency to displace value from the end to the means as the legitimacy and value of research is determined less by commonsense evaluations of its likely impact and more by notions such as 'reliability', imported from the natural sciences.

Not only does a focus on means rather than ends deliver a particular kind of knowledge, one that may well distort the sort of practice we feel that it is right to implement, it also may, in Andreski's (1972: 116) words, provide 'an alibi for timorous quietism'. It may, that is to say, distract attention from important yet challenging matters for the educator – away, in other words, from reflective practice, critical inquiry and innovation about the curriculum.

Thus, for example, with the kudos which learning theory invested in behavioural methods, more attention was devoted to the proper application of task analysis procedures, or the correctness of behavioural objective specification than was given to the question of what was actually wanted from an education of children for whom the procedures were devised. It was only when critical voices reached sufficient volume – from a number of directions (e.g. Stenhouse 1975; Wood and Shears 1986), and from the protestations of classroom teachers – that serious questions began to be asked about what was going on.

If one does not think small, one is in danger of being guided by the safety of prestigious theory, by the supposedly secure knowledge emerging from the findings of empirical inquiry.

We have made an argument here for a loosening of hold on the erstwhile theoretical knowledge behind special education, contending that less of our inquiry into children's difficulties at school – and, more importantly, less of our response to those difficulties – should be defined and tackled in the way that it hitherto has. An argument is made, if we are looking to the shape of an education system for the future, for more reliance by all in education – practitioners, planners, academics, researchers – on our own understandings of learning, and on ideas and ideals about equity, social justice and opportunity for all. In pursuing these ideals, in improving the education system, we should accept rather than deny the insights which emerge by virtue of being human – insights which emerge from our own knowledge of learning; our own knowledge of failure, success, acceptance or rejection. There is nothing to be lost in so doing, for as we noted earlier, there are no magic fixes or startling insights to emerge from the traditional knowledge-base of special education.

Oliver Sacks (1995) provides an excellent example of the change in research style for which we are arguing. He sets aside the methods of the scientific discipline, neurology, in which he was trained in favour of the tradition of the storyteller and the anthropologist. In so doing, he offers a set of sparkling insights and understandings into the worlds of a number of people who behave differently. Such insights have been largely curtained off from us by the understanding offered by traditional analyses. As part of Sacks's discourse on our understanding of difference – of the 'borders of human experience', as he puts it – he quotes Chesterton:

> I don't deny the dry [scientific] light may sometimes do good, though in one sense it's the very reverse of science. So far from being knowledge, it's actually suppression of what we know. It's treating a friend as a stranger, and pretending that something familiar is really remote and mysterious.
>
> (Sacks 1995: xvii)

When trying to understand people – *people*, as distinct from gases in a test tube – we each have to use our own humanity, recognizing our 'failings', our frailties, misunderstandings and prejudices.

[...]

It is special education which is the branch of education which has suffered most from assumptions that have been made in the twentieth century about the proper way to study the individual and social behaviour of human beings. If education as a field of study has always suffered from something of an inferiority complex about its academic status – borrowing its epistemological tenets and research methods only too readily from its clever cousins psychology and sociology – special education has suffered the inferiority complex even more profoundly. Not only have those tenets and methods been eagerly snapped up, but also special education has always seemingly been only too easily influenced by the prevailing cultural orthodoxy.

It has been vulnerable to such swaying in the wind since it has never had an intellectual homeland of its own – no core beliefs or understandings. It has thus been prey to passing intellectual fashion and transient cultural whim. It has occupied a place on the periphery of education where its *raison d'être* has been as a kind of service industry to mainstream education. There has been little in the way of intellectual lead. Where movement has happened it has taken place as a result of broader social movements. The knowledge produced by the scientific study of psychology and psychiatry have merely buttressed our everyday constructions about disability, difference or disorder.

The intellectual apparatus which has emerged ostensibly to add objectivity, humanity and disinterested 'science' to an analysis of social structures in fact does nothing of the kind. In the messy world of human beings and human relations, this intellectual apparatus does little other than provide in new words and garb what we already recognize and know.

Calls for a recognition of the validity of self-knowledge are not recent, though. It is Hans-Georg Gadamer who is credited with transforming the idea of 'hermeneutics' from one in which a person aimed to understand something in as disinterested and unprejudiced a way as possible to one where human preconceptions or prejudices are at the heart of understanding (Outhwaite 1990: 25). These preconceptions and prejudices, these 'sentiments, imaginings and fancies', as Oakeshott (1989: 65) put it, are what go to construct our understanding of others. To deny their significance in making sense of other people – their utterances, feelings, fears and failings – is to ignore the most important research tool at our disposal.

How is all this relevant for special education and how we think about an inclusive future? We quoted earlier from Oliver Sacks's *An Anthropologist on Mars* in which Sacks gave reasons for eschewing many of the procedural and methodological habits of his own discipline, neurology. Neurologists are like special educators in many respects: they try to help people who are, for whatever reason, uncomfortable, unhappy, disaffected, unable or unwilling to 'fit in'. Sacks's insight is that the methods which have been used to examine this discomfort or disaffection, while they can be successful up to a point, fail to address the real issues at stake, which are human issues. It is worth quoting from him:

> The exploration of deeply altered selves and worlds is not one that can be fully made in a consulting room or office. The French neurologist François Lhemitte is especially sensitive to this, and instead of just observing his patients in the clinic, he makes a point of visiting them at home, taking them to restaurants or theatres, or for rides in this car, sharing their lives as much as possible. (It is similar, or was similar, with physicians in general practice. Thus when my father was reluctantly considering retirement at ninety, we said, 'At least drop the house calls.' But he answered, 'No, I'll keep the house calls – I'll drop everything else instead.')
>
> (Sacks 1995: xvii–xviii)

Maybe we need to keep the house calls. To study and to think about the shape education should take for those who cannot or do not want to fit, maybe we should leave aside the investigative methods which have been developed by psychologists and educators during the twentieth century and look to new ways of understanding.

When children are excluded from the mainstream it is because someone feels that they will not fit. To examine why people do not fit, and to help organizations to enable them to fit we have to understand them as people and to understand the people in the organizations which accept or reject them. The reductionist and functionalist thrust of special education research has not in general led us to do this, and this has meant that special education has followed a particular route – one that has sought to analyse and fix instead of seeking to understand and include.

[. . .]

Our deliberations should undefensively and unapologetically put values first instead of embarrassedly trying to conceal those values behind some taken-to-be superior empirical knowledge.

If the latter is correct, where should we go for guidance on how to proceed? There is much to be said for reliance on what Marquand (1996) calls 'moral activism'.

### Moral activism: beyond redistribution

In talking about moral activism, Marquand (1996) draws a distinction between it and what he calls 'passive-hedonist' collectivism, which he takes to be the predominant characteristic of much searching for social justice in the twentieth century. This distinction is instructive for considerations about the nature of inclusion. It offers a way of thinking about inclusion more broadly than hitherto. It suggests that considerations of inclusion are about more than the righting of the oppression of individual groups (important though this is) and it is about more than redistribution of resources. Moral activism, as Marquand sees it, is about enabling people 'to lead purposeful, self-reliant and strenuous lives' in an individual sense, and about 'engagement with the common life of the society' (p. 21) in a collective sense. There is an extent to which without these considerations the agenda becomes dominated with the righting of wrongs perpetrated against a particular group, whether that group is defined by its disability, its language, its income, its gender, or its cultural or ethnic origin. The distinction is important in broadening considerations of inclusion, for injunctions to be more equal or to be fairer are insufficient without this moral dimension.

A good example as far as inclusion is concerned comes in interpreting the generally accepted axiom of John Rawls (1971) about the just distribution of resources. Rawls argued for the elimination of inequality through the redistribution of resources in his *Theory of Justice*, saying that in general there should be an equal distribution of social resources, but that there should be a bias in this distribution in favour of those who are 'disadvantaged'. This, however, is insufficient without a moral-activist dimension and the point becomes crystal clear in discussion of special education and inclusion. Rizvi and Lingard (1996) make the point that redistribution by itself is insufficient to achieve social justice. The thesis they propound is that redistributive logic on its own obscures and thereby perpetuates injustices in existing institutional organization. Emphasizing redistribution – what Slee calls being 'entrapped within a compensatory model of distributive justice' (Corbett and Slee 2000: 138) – could mean merely shifting resources into special education.

Roaf and Bines (1989) make an allied point: that an emphasis on *needs* in special education detracts from a proper consideration of the *rights* of those who are being educated. It is this emphasis on rights that a moral-activist stance encourages and it is central to thinking on inclusion. Following Marquand's reasoning, it is insufficient merely to appeal abstractly to some kind of Rawlsian justice for this may lead merely to formulaic, unguided attempts at redistribution. [. . .]

This is surely so in special education, where no claim could seriously be made that positive economic discrimination is not provided for children at special schools. The economic redistribution argument is not in other words sufficient on its own: it is the way resources are used that is more important. Fraser (1996) avers that more insidious and arguably equally powerful forms of injustice take the place of resource injustice. They arise from non-*recognition*, that is to say being rendered invisible by dominant cultural practice, and from *disrespect* – through routine malignment or disparagement. To illustrate her point, Fraser draws on the work of Charles Taylor (1992), who suggests that non-recognition or misrecognition can imprison someone

> in a false, distorted, reduced mode of being. Beyond simple lack of respect, it can inflict a grievous wound, saddling people with crippling self-hatred. Due recognition is not just a courtesy but a vital human need.
>
> (Taylor 1992: 25)

It is thus only through seeing injustice through the lenses of non-recognition and disrespect that redistribution makes any sense in the contemporary world. For existing inequalities between children – in their behaviour, in what they can do with their bodies, or in their cultural capital – cannot be compensated for simply by shifts in resources, by the physical and personnel resources they are given at school. Those inequalities lie importantly in opportunities to do the same as other children: to share the same spaces as other children and to speak the same language as other children. To be, in other words, part of the same culture. Reducing inequality is thus about more than providing money and better resources: it is about providing the chance to share in the common wealth of the school and its culture.

Without these additional dimensions, redistribution may remain hollow, leaving in place practices that demean and disempower people. It is this demeaning and disempowering to which so many who have passed through a special school system have referred (e.g. Rieser and Mason 1992).

Non-recognition and disrespect arise from the way that segregative systems handle existing inequalities between children. Exclusion from the wider culture is the consequence.

[. . .] To believe, then, that the kind of society we create emerges from the kind of education we provide has a long intellectual pedigree. The quest for comprehensive education and now inclusive education are part of that tradition. [. . .] In other words, there are gains in greater participation and comprehensiveness not just for the small minority who would formerly have gone to special schools, but there are perhaps more importantly reciprocal benefits – benefits for all.

Demonstration is a misnomer when thinking about inclusion. To be asked to show that inclusion works is like being asked to show that equality works. To promote inclusion involves judgements based on values, and there is no reason to be apologetic about this. As Amartya Sen (1996) puts it in the context of the dilemmas of making a socially just society, 'the choice of priorities is inescapably a judgmental exercise' (p. 21), and this is in the context of there always existing some conflict of interests to be resolved. To quote from Stanley Fish (1994): 'different interests will generate different notions of fairness' (p. 73).

That we should make judgements concerning these interests and these notions of fairness and come down on the side of x rather than y is surely what has to be accepted in our twenty-first-century discourse on the shape of inclusive education.

## Concluding comment

We have argued here for a loosening of hold on the erstwhile theoretical knowledge behind special education, contending that less of our inquiry into children's difficulties at school – and, more importantly, less of our response to those difficulties – should happen in the way that it has hitherto. If this argument is valid, and if we are looking to the shape of an inclusive education system for the future, it behoves all of us in education – practitioners, planners, academics, researchers – to put more reliance on ideals about equity, human rights, social justice and opportunity for all. In pursuing these ideals, in improving education, we should as practitioners and inquirers accept rather than deny the insights which emerge by virtue of human experience – insights which emerge from our own knowledge of learning, our own knowledge of failure, success, acceptance or rejection. There is nothing to be lost in so doing, for the evidence is that there are no magic fixes or startling insights to emerge from the traditional knowledge-base of special education.

## References

Andreski, S. (1972) *Social Sciences as Sorcery* (London: André Deutsch).

Barton, L. (1992) Introduction. *Disability, Handicap and Society*, **7**, 99.

Berlak, H. (2001) A short guide to understanding assessment policy, standardized achievement tests, and anti-racist alternatives. Available at [www.edjustice.org/pdf/raceassess.pdf].

Berlin, I. (1979) The divorce between the sciences and the humanities. In I. Berlin, *Against the Current* (London: Hogarth).

Canguilhem, G. (1994) The various models. In F. Delaporte (ed.), *A Vital Rationalist: Selected Writings from Georges Canguilhem* (New York: Zone).

Coles, G. (2000) *Misreading Reading: The Bad Science that Hurts Children* (Portsmouth: Heinemann).

Corbett, J. and Slee, R. (2000) An international conversation on inclusive education. In F. Armstrong, D. Armstrong and L. Barton (eds), *Inclusive Education: Policy Contexts and Comparative Perspectives* (London: David Fulton).

DES (1967) *Children and their Primary Schools (The Plowden Report)* (London: HMSO).

DES (1978) *Special Educational Needs.* Report of the Committee of Enquiry into the Education of Handicapped Children and Young People, Cmnd 7212 (London: HMSO).

DeVault, M.L., Harnischfeger, A. and Wiley, D.E. (1977) *Curricula, Personnel Resources and Grouping Strategies* (St Ann: ML-GROUP for Policy Studies in Education, Central Midwestern Regional Lab).

Eagleton, T. (1991) *Ideology* (London: Verso).

Finkelstein, V. (1992) Researching disability: setting the agenda for change. Available at [www.leeds. ac.uk/disability-studies/archiveuk/finkelstein/futures.pdf].

Fish, S. (1994) *There's No Such Thing As Free Speech* (Oxford: Oxford University Press).

Foucault, M. (1970) *The Order of Things: An Archaeology of the Human Sciences* (London: Tavistock).

Fraser, N. (1996) *Justice Interruptus: Rethinking Key Concepts of a 'Postsocialist' Age* (New York: Routledge).

Giddens, A. (1994) *Beyond Left and Right: The Future of Radical Politics* (Cambridge: Polity).

Haldane, J.B.S. (1965) The duty of doubt. In A.F. Scott (ed.), *Topics and Opinions* (London: Macmillan).

Hamilton, D. (1998) The idols of the market place. In R. Slee, G. Weiner and S. Tomlinson (eds), *School Effectiveness for Whom* (London: Falmer).

Hart, S. (1996) *Beyond Special Needs* (London: Paul Chapman).

Hoggart, R. (2001) Politics, anti-politics and the unpolitical: the universities in the second half of the twentieth century. In R. Hoggart (ed.), *Between Two Worlds* (London: Aurum), pp. 145–168.

Jordan, A., Lindsay, L. and Stanovich, P.J. (1997) Classroom teachers' instructional interactions with students who are exceptional, at risk and typically achieving. *Remedial and Special Education*, **18**, 82–93.

Joynson, R.B. (1974) *Psychology and Common Sense* (London: Routledge & Kegan Paul).

Labov, W. (1973) The logic of nonstandard English. In F. Williams (ed.), *Language and Poverty* (Chicago, IL: Rand McNally).

Levins, R. and Lewontin, R. (1985) *The Dialectical Biologist* (Cambridge, MA: Harvard University Press).

MacIntyre, A. (1981) *After Virtue: A Study in Moral Theory* (London: Duckworth).

Marquand, D. (1996) Moralists and hedonists. In D. Marquand and A. Seldon (eds), *The Ideas that Shaped Post-War Britain* (London: Fontana).

Mayhew, H. (1985) *London Labour and the London Poor* (London: Penguin).

Mouzelis, N. (1995) *Sociological Theory: What Went Wrong?* (London: Routledge).

Oakeshott, M. (1967) Learning and teaching. In R.S. Peters (ed.), *The Concept of Education* (London: Routledge & Kegan Paul), 156–176.

Oakeshott, M. (1989) Education: the engagement and the frustration. In T. Fuller (ed.), *The Voice of Liberal Learning: Michael Oakeshott on Education* (London: Yale University Press).

Outhwaite, W. (1990) Hans-Georg Gadamer. In Q. Skinner (ed.), *The Return of Grand Theory in the Human Sciences* (Cambridge: Canto).

Rawls, J. (1971) *A Theory of Justice* (Oxford: Clarendon).

Rieser, R. and Mason, M. (1992) *Disability Equality in the Classroom: A Human Rights Issue* (London: Disability Equality in Education).

Rizvi, F. and Lingard, B. (1996) Disability, education and the discourses of justice. In C. Christensen and F. Rizvi (eds), *Disability and the Dilemmas of Education and Justice* (Buckingham: Open University Press).

Roaf, C. and Bines, H. (1989) Needs, rights and opportunities in special education. In C. Roaf and H. Bines (eds), *Needs, Rights and Opportunities: Developing Approaches to Special Education* (London: Falmer).

Rousseau, J.-J. (1993) *Émile* [1762], trans. B. Foxley (London: J.M. Dent).

Rueda, R. and Mehan, H. (1986) Metacognition and passing: strategic interactions in the lives of students with learning disabilities. *Anthropology and Education Quarterly*, **17**, 145–165.

Ryle, G. (1990) *The Concept of Mind* (London: Penguin).

Sacks, O. (1995) *An Anthropologist on Mars* (London: Picador).

Schön, D.A. (1991) *The Reflective Practitioner: How Professionals Think in Action* (Aldershot: Avebury).

Schweinhart, L.J. and Weikart, D.P. (1997) Lasting differences: the high/scope preschool curriculum comparison through age 23. *Early Childhood Research Quarterly*, **12**, 117–143.

Sen, A. (1996) Social commitment and democracy: the demands of equity and financial conservatism. In P. Barker (ed.), *Living As Equals* (Oxford: Oxford University Press).

Skinner, B.F. (1972) *Beyond Freedom and Dignity* (London: Jonathan Cape).

Skrtic, T.M. (1991) The special education paradox: equity as the way to excellence. *Harvard Educational Review*, **61**, 148–206.

Slee, R. (1998) High reliability organizations and liability students – the politics of recognition. In R. Slee, G. Weiner and S. Tomlinson (eds), *School Effectiveness for Whom* (London: Falmer), 101–114.

Smith, F. (1993) *Whose Language? What Power? A Universal Conflict in a South African Setting* (New York: Teachers College Press).

Smith, F. (1998) *The Book of Learning and Forgetting* (New York: Teachers College Press).

Stenhouse, L. (1975) *An Introduction to Curriculum Research and Development* (London: Heinemann).

Taylor, C. (1984) Philosophy and its history. In R. Rorty, J. B. Schneewind and Q. Skinner (eds), *Philosophy in History* (Cambridge: Cambridge University Press), 17–30.

Taylor, C. (1992) *Multiculturalism and 'The Politics of Recognition'* (Princeton: Princeton University Press).

Thomas, G. and Davis, P. (1997) Special needs: objective reality or personal construction? Judging reading difficulty after the Code. *Educational Research*, **39**, 263–270.

Voltaire (1997) *Candide, Or Optimism* [1759], trans. N. Cameron (London: Penguin).

Wilson, J. (2000) Doing justice to inclusion. *European Journal of Special Needs Education*, **15**, 297–304.

Wood, S. and Shears, B. (1986) *Teaching Children with Severe Learning Difficulties: A Radical Reappraisal* (London: Croom Helm).

Zarb, G. (1992) On the road to Damascus: first steps towards changing the relations of disability research production. *Disability, Handicap and Society*, **7**, 125–138.

Ziman, J. (1991) *Reliable Knowledge* (Cambridge: Canto).

## Chapter 3

# Taking curiosity seriously

## The role of awe and Wanda in research-based professionalism

*Marion Dadds*

This chapter is written in two voices – the personal and the 'academic'. It draws on the author's reflective experience as a research co-ordinator in teacher education, trying to develop a research culture with colleagues in difficult national and institutional circumstances. These personal experiences are set against wider debates and issues about research-based professionalism. Wanda is a character the author created to illustrate the responses and reactions of colleagues, with whom she works, towards research-based work. Wanda is fictional, in that no one such character exists, yet she is also 'factual', in that the events and conversations illustrated through the character actually took place at some time, with someone, in the author's workplace over the period in which the chapter is set. The fiction is, thus, grounded in the data of the author's own 'reality', although some poetic licence has been applied in order to tell the story of Wanda with some theoretical coherence and validity.

> March 21st, 1998. The letter arrived from St Martin's, inviting me to interview. 'During the morning you will be asked to give a short presentation (10 minutes maximum) . . . The subject of the presentation is 'The role of research in teacher education'.
>
> Try as I may in the days running up to the event, I could not reduce my talk to less than 12. I took the risk of being thought verbose and stayed with my plan. Perhaps one day there would be chance to elaborate.
>
> April 21, 1998. I was led into a darkened room. Some seven or eight faces arranged in a semi-circle gazed at the lone chair. The Principal seated himself in the shadows, stop-watch to hand. 'I have a number of points', I heard myself declare, 'and some afterthoughts – if time allows'.
>
> The points fell out neatly, like bars from a chocolate dispensing machine. I covered, in the first few minutes, issues about research for new knowledge and understanding; research as a form of professional learning for ourselves and those with whom we share it. At a pace, I alluded to research as a form of professional improvement, underpinned by new self-understanding. The Cook's tour also raised issues about the role of research in challenging imposed

wisdom, or, what I chose to call, 'oppositional' research. In the short postscript, my points embraced issues about new, inventive methodologies if we are to be liberated to research creatively.

So there it was. My map of educational research in a twelve minute nutshell. On my way home, I felt stunned by my own audacity; to have clarified, neatened and made certain where no self respecting postmodernist would fear to tread.


As my new role as education research co-ordinator at St Martin's unfolded, I was to return time and again to those issues. It was inevitable that the dire circumstances of teacher education would help in the post-modern undoing of this tidy 12-minute package for it was, of course, far from tidy in practice.

Also, the relevance of the issues was augmented by the current national debates on research- and evidence-based professionalism. These discourses have already spread across other professions, most noticeably health and medicine. They have also been embedded within the practitioner research, action research and praxis movements for several decades (e.g. Hollingsworth 1997). The Teacher Training Agency has been offering research-based initiatives to the teaching profession for some four years. However, despite these trends, there has been no serious discussion at policy level of research-based professionalism in teacher education. Herein lies a great anomaly, for it is not clear how teacher educators can contribute to the development of teaching as a research-based profession if their own research development is not considered seriously as an essential part of this venture.

Moving in this direction is far from straightforward. Working conditions for teacher educators, as for teachers, are singularly unconducive to the systematic pursuit of research (Morrison 1998). Constant politically induced changes, power coercive strategies for reform, negating national climates of abuse have caused unprecedented levels of work overload and stress (Campbell 1999; Dadds 2001). It is miraculous that so many manage to surmount such adversity in order to produce quality research when research funding is shamefully inadequate. 'Unpaid slog sustains research', read the *Times Higher Education Supplement* headlines of the 12th May, 2000.

Many in post-1992 institutions like St Martin's have responded positively to the pressure to engage in more research that the Research Assessment Exercise (RAE) has generated. Yet, because they have not achieved high status in the RAE and funding arrangements may now be adversely reviewed (Bassey 1999), such institutions are in danger of becoming caught in the 'massacre of the innocents: the wiping out of those small research communities who have seen the vision of research, but failed to grasp its substance' (Bassey 1999: 23). This 'crisis of positionality' (Goodson 1999: 277) with funding may, indeed, put our newly developed research cultures at risk. Were such nascent cultures to be destroyed, the education service would be poorer for the loss, as would the schools that research in partnership with Higher Education institutions.

It becomes essential, therefore, in such hostile, fragile conditions for us to have sound justification for doing research. Part of this means considering what philosophies and methodologies might match our circumstances and desires. There is no reason, for example, for us to follow slavishly established research traditions that have emerged from far more favourable conditions than we can boast. So we need confidence to seek alternative approaches that are situationally sensitive and feasible; that nourish the rest of our work in beneficial ways. Small-scale, practice-related methodologies such as action research, narrative enquiry, case study, experience-based enquiry (e.g. Hart 1995; Ollerton 1997), critical-fictional research (Winter 1999) are available and are probably more appropriate. So, too, are collaborative methodologies that help teachers and teacher educators to research in partnership with each other, and with pupils, communities and other stakeholders so that we can, together, study educational contexts in ways that can feed both teaching and teacher education (e.g. Zeichner and Kler 1999). We are, in essence, working in an overloaded, 'hurry-along' (Dadds 2001) context, where time has to be used wisely. Research must support us in these conditions, not exacerbate the difficulties.

In addition, research is as politically important as ever it was, for these centralist, 'hurry-along' conditions have the tendency to mould us into obedient technical deliverers of others' political initiatives, engaging mostly in task-orientated work. Hurry-along reduces time for deeper thought and democratic critique as we seek to figure out the political game and learn how best to play it for the purpose of institutional survival.

However, giving priority to compliant thought and action may, ultimately, cause us to relinquish our traditional role as guardians of academic freedom, leading to ethic-less, fearful organisations which, by default, collude in the 'culture of silence' (Freire 2000: 9), thereby becoming intellectually impoverished. Hurry-along is dangerous for education if these are its consequences for we may become trapped inside this pressurised 'performance culture' (Campbell 1999) with no principled way out. So current bureaucratic and authoritarian excesses have to be counter-balanced by thoughtful inquiry if our work is to be truly educative.

What follows, then, is my justification for the continuing growth of a strong research culture in teaching and teacher education in today's political circumstances. Within this, I raise a number of issues, which I consider significant. These are sub-sumed under three broad themes: research for new knowledge and understanding, research for critique and research for improvement.

## Research for new knowledge and understanding

First and foremost, research can help us to create new knowledge and understanding of the complex professional worlds in which we work. This is its first function. 'An essential characteristic of research is that the enquiry should aim to increase knowledge', wrote Michael Bassey. 'Its purpose should be to make a claim to new knowledge: to tell someone something that they didn't know before' (Bassey 1995: 3).

As members of one of the caring professions, our work is a moral enterprise. What we believe, know and do as educators are consequential for others' lives – young people, families and their communities, student teachers. This brings with it a responsibility for us to be not simply practitioners, but ethically orientated scholarship practitioners (Zeichner 1998) seeking to underpin our work with well-developed theories from our own and others' research. This is one significant way in which we can engage in ethically based professional learning.

The now well-established practitioner research movement has highlighted for decades (e.g. Stenhouse 1975; Elliott 1993; Hollingsworth 1997) the need for practitioners themselves to be at the heart of the research process, identifying questions of significance for the learners in their care, conducting their own enquiries for their own professional purposes. Insider practitioner knowledge about the challenges of the classroom or seminar is seen to be crucial to setting a research agenda, which burrows into the ethical heart of teaching and learning. New professional knowledge, however, is not only a detached product of mind: the passions and humanity that are a natural part of professional work are inexorably locked into practice-based research. They are as significant as the more clinical logic and disengagement, which some take, erroneously, to be the sole indicator of good research. The past 20 years of research theory have done much to help us to re-think subjectivity and this is useful for practitioner research. Feminist scholars have reminded us that education involves 'connected knowing' (Belenky *et al.* 1986) within professional practices that are 'relational' (Noddings 1994). Human bonds are involved.

Good quality practice-related research strikes a balance between this subjective commitment and the more detached viewing needed in order to become 'teacher as stranger' (Greene 1973) to our own work. This balance helps to guard against 'emotional misunderstanding' (Hargreaves 1999), where the human gap between teacher and taught is hard to bridge in hurry-along conditions. Practitioner research can help to bridge this gap. For example, when the teachers in one of our local primary schools asked children what they didn't like about writing and changed their practices in response to the children's feelings, we were offered a fine example of research being used to enhance the pedagogical emotional understanding of which Hargreaves speaks. When we research our own work, 'we are concerned with the development of a self-critical subjective perspective, not with an aspiration towards an unattainable objectivity' (Stenhouse 1975: 157). Forms of research that deny the inevitability of subjectivity are not well matched to the needs of research-based professionalism, for in the disciplined 'self' of the researcher lies the power that drives the enquiry and determines its usefulness (Dadds 1995) for pupils and students.

So in this subjectivity, we must remember that we are, as researchers, stepping into others' lives – and our actions must make sense to them. In our research ethics we need to move beyond an egocentrism into an empathetic perspective. To this end, children and others with whom we research have a right to understand, and have some control over, our subjective research intentions, however honourable these may be. Different, and possibly conflicting, needs will arise in different contexts (Simons and Usher 2000), so our empathetic moves may require high levels of subjective maturity, insight and judgement.

In addition, subjective research knowledge is enriched in validity when it is shared and critiqued with our research communities. 'If we can say we know, rather than simply I know, we can move towards an inter-subjectively valid knowledge which is beyond the limitations of one knower' (Reason and Rowan 1981: 242).

Moving from subjective to inter-subjective knowledge also blesses us with research processes that become a form of professional conversation. In this, we can learn from, and validate, each others' research at one and the same time. When research can embed itself in learning communities in this conversational way, then it begins to work as it should, as a force for collaborative learning and for the growth of valid practitioner theories. Research, thus, ceases to be reduced to a pitiful target for the research assessment exercise.

Elliott has argued that such 'conversation research communities' (Elliott 1990: 3) are essential if we are to strive for excellence in research. But we need to be free from the pathology of 'dogmatic institutional and political climates' (Elliott 1990: 6) in order to think together with integrity. Climates of exchange that enable growth and that do not abuse or demean are essential. Thoughtful research seminars, institutional research conferences, internal dissemination meetings with colleagues, learners, parents, governors and other stakeholders – these practices can help us to build and sustain our conversational research communities and the quality of our work:

> October 14th, 1998
> A colleague, who I shall name Wanda, pops in to my room, ostensibly to see if I'm getting tidied up from the move. This social communion shifts effortlessly into an energetic exposition by her about action research.
>
> Wanda berates the problematics of traditional research and waxes eloquent about the superior value of self-created knowledge for the understanding of one's practice. Furthermore, she explains, methods' courses that suppose research to be a set of cumulative skills are missing the point. 'Research is not so much skills', she says, emphatically, 'but attitude . . . research is an attitude . . . an approach of mind . . . '
>
> 'Mind you', Wanda adds, as she turns to leave, 'we don't have any time to do any here . . . if they ask me to find any more time to do anything else, I think I'll just resign.'
>
> I note this in my research diary that evening, suspecting that I shall hear more from Wanda. I may learn if I listen.

## Research for critique

If the debate were only about whether or not knowledge was a subjective creation, research would be less vexing than it is. In recent years, however, post-modernism has confirmed what our suspicious epistemic hearts knew all along – that research knowledge, embedded for the most part in language as it is, is slippery, wafer thin and readily self-destructing. Just when we feel we have found certain knowledge, the post-modern phantom bids us to undo it (Stronach and MacLure 1997), examine it from different linguistic angles, disrupt our complacency as we settle on the single, authoritative reading of our research texts. Meaning is, thus, unstable, contingent and questionable.

Post-modernists are quite exhausting friends to have. Yet their irritating theoretical presence saves us from the myth of the single meaning, the single interpretation, the single solution; from the dangers of living unquestioningly within the grand narratives of our day with the attendant spectres of fanaticism and unchallenged, simplistic dogma.

To add to our troubles with myths and single meanings, we also have to battle against public views that have been shaped more by tabloid newspapers (Goodson 1999: 293) than by verifiable, grounded, educational theory. Indeed, some believe that the cultivation of negative public opinion about the state of education, through tabloid newspapers, has been deliberate political strategy to help herald in educational reform. In his inaugural lecture of 1979, Stenhouse warned against the dangers of according the status of 'knowledge' to views of the world shaped in such misconceived ways. He claimed that 'what is represented as authoritative, and established independently of scholarly warrant, cannot be knowledge . . . '. Valid knowledge has its own characteristics, he suggested, in that it 'is questionable, verifiable and differentially secure' (Rudduck and Hopkins 1985: 116). The validity of knowledge, he implied, rests in such scholarly qualities, not in the power it obtains through the status of those who yield it. There are implications for education, here, for if we do not convey this to those we teach then the learners, Stenhouse suggested, will 'take from us in error: the error . . . that faith in authority is an acceptable substitute for grasp of the grounds of knowledge' (Rudduck and Hopkins 1985: 116). The ability to appraise critically the status and validity of knowledge, must, therefore, by implication, be a necessary part of being educated in a civilised democracy.

In an age of centralist certainty about the rightness of political knowledge, politically designed curricular and politically legislated pedagogy, Stenhouse's words, alongside the challenges of post-modernism, are relevant to us. More than ever, our scholarship and research demands of us this pre-disposition to undo and quarrel with the knowledge of received authority, both that of others as well as our own as educators, and to treat knowledge as constantly problematic.

These ideas suggest the need not simply to produce new knowledge, but new critical knowledge, which enable us to conduct an ethical commentary on the practices and consequences of power. There is a need to de-construct the taken-for-granted assumptions of power; 'to stress educational research which acts as a kind of moral witness to the initiatives that are undertaken' (Goodson 1999: 296); to challenge the single story and offer alternative readings. What, for example, were the consequences for children beyond improved test scores, of David Blunkett's decision in 1998 to focus more money on boys' reading attainments in a bid to pressure teachers and pupils to achieve his own political literacy targets before the next election? Did this decision bring benefit or stress to targeted pupils? What were the consequences for pupils who were not in line for booster class funding? What has happened to the children since they received the booster funding and made the transition to secondary school? These are our kinds of questions as professionals whose responsibilities embrace the well-being of students and pupils (Thompson 1997).

Such questions require 'oppositional research', which demands that we enquire against the grain, both of our own realms of power and also that of others. Indeed, according to Bridges (1999), we have, as professional educators, 'a fundamental duty of intellectual citizenship' to engage in 'the production of knowledge with the potential for creating . . . alternative . . . views about the public sphere than those that are officially sanctioned . . . ' (Norris 1992):

> March 9th, 1999
> I head towards the photocopier with a small task for tonight's MA group. Here, to my surprise, is Wanda, copying what looks like, as I try to peer over her shoulder without seeming to . . . yes . . . it is an interview transcript with covering letter. She seems about to deny its existence as I try, nonchalantly, to quiz her about it.
>
> She explains to me, casually, that she thought she'd just try to find out how a few people in the school/college partnership were experiencing one of the latest innovations we've had to adopt with them, in response to government edict. The neat packages of government policy might not appear that neat when you scrutinise their adoption at school and college level, she said.
>
> This explanation is backed by apologia galore about the quality, validity, status of her interviews. They are even denied as anything to do with research. 'Just curiosity,' she explains. 'Not really research at all.'
>
> Our ensuing conversation roams over major issues about the nature of research. As I turn to go, Wanda's voice follows me up the stairs. 'It's just curiosity mind. It's not research.'
>
> I note this in my diary later that evening
>
> The following morning, as I negotiated the motorway junction, the analogy struck me – that a researcher without curiosity is like a comedian without a sense of humour. Wanda has what professional research needs. Curiosity – one of the central driving forces. Research without curiosity is like a joke without a laugh.

Gattegno, claimed that 'there is only one instrument in research in order to find answers . . . and that is to raise questions . . . you only need to open your mind . . . And slowly, you educate yourselves . . . ' (Brown *et al.* 1989: 11–14). Stenhouse went further, defining research as 'systematic self-critical enquiry' (Rudduck and Hopkins 1985: 8), which is 'founded in curiosity and a desire to understand'. For curiosity to develop into research, it must, he claimed, be 'stable, not fleeting' and become 'systematic in the sense of being sustained by a strategy'.

Fertile contemplation is also needed if mature thoughts are to emerge. Yet we speak little of the value of contemplation in these 'hurry along' times of compliance and overload. One could suppose that the systems have been designed to jeopardise contemplative thought, not enrich it. However, researchers need to retreat for a while into some inner sanctum of intellectual creation to cultivate their ideas. For it is in this space that preliminary thought becomes transformed as curiosity and contemplation demonstrate their complementary powers in the creation of credible ideas (e.g. Poincare 1924; Wallas 1926). Curiosity and contemplation are the complementary bookends of a research process that leads to valid knowledge. Without curiosity there would be no question; without contemplation, no response. 'The life of contemplation implies two levels of awareness', wrote Tom Merton (1961) 'first, awareness of the question, and second, awareness of the answer. Though these are two distinct and enormously different levels, yet they are in fact an awareness of the same thing.'

The indispensable power of curiosity must, therefore, be accompanied by motivation and working conditions that allow continuity of questioning and thought. Wanda has this vital curiosity, but does she also have the time, patience and circumstance needed for persistent sequential enquiry? This, I do not yet know.

## Research for improvement

The knowledge that research can offer us is not for its own sake, but to help us to improve educational experiences for learners; to address issues of social and educational injustice in our schools and colleges, for it is our role 'to make a difference in the lives of students regardless of background, and to help produce citizens who can live and work productively in dynamic societies' (Fullan 1993: 18). We also hope that new knowledge can be created that helps us to work for a more humane, caring and self-actualising life for those we educate.

The ethical focus of practitioner research is, thus, on improvement for 'the other' (Noddings 1994). This is a continuous process if we accept the mantle of the professional. 'Research is the constant striving for understanding and improvement', wrote Ken Thomas, 'nothing is cast in stone' (Thomas 1999: 4). However, inasmuch as the focus is, by implication, also on our practices, a secondary spotlight shines on our professional selves. Our practices and our person cannot be separated. To create new knowledge of our practices, we have to disrupt our assumptions through self-critique. 'If I am certain and never ask questions', wrote Ben Cunningham, 'I can't move forward, be transformed' (1999: 253).

Such critical self-knowledge can be painful. Thus, practice-based researchers not only need just curiosity and an ethical sensitivity, but also great courage if they are to take relevant research questions into the heart of their work. There is no research-based professionalism that does not touch on the identity of the researcher, since identity is bound into practice. Psychologically safe communities are needed, therefore, especially for new researchers who render themselves vulnerable in the public arena of research (Dadds 1993):

20th April, 1999

After seven months in this new post, the frustrations of regularly cancelled research meetings with colleagues are becoming hard for me to bear and my sense of relevance is hovering over a void. Research, I have rapidly come to understand, is the last priority in post-1992 institutions, easy to drop off the agenda when other pressures bite hard. But if time were the sole explanation, how is it that some manage to pursue their research, albeit in fits and starts, whilst others do not? I seek Wanda's angle on this, one late afternoon, by the photocopier.

'Seventy percent lack of time; ten percent time management, I would say', is Wanda's hypothesis.

'-yes-?-' Her eyes fix me, looking for some trust. 'The rest is fear', she confessed. 'Fear of what?'

'Fear of failure; of being judged; of feeling that you're not as clever as all those clever people who write fancy things in fancy journals.'

We talk on about the need for creative, innovative forms of research and writing that go well beyond the traditional 'fancy things' for 'fancy journals'. We both become a little inspired. Some optimism is bubbling.

'Mind you', Wanda calls after me as we part, 'if anyone tells me I need to improve my time management, I'll tell them where to get off.'...

As the record of this conversation goes in the diary that evening, I wonder how the academic community has managed to find itself in this state. How can we justify views of research that disenfranchise by creating false hierarchies of knowledge and methodology? What valid and reliable approaches can we foster that are inclusive of Wanda's powers of curiosity and professional commitment, that sustain her sense of self-worth and enhance it through the realisations of writing and practice improvement? What will be the consequences for teacher educators, the teachers they educate and the children who will be influenced, if we cannot legitimate new, appropriate research methodologies? If research is about improvement, how much longer can we tolerate a Research Assessment Exercise that appears to Wanda to put a premium on clever people, researching in more favourable conditions, writing fancy things in fancy journals?

At 2 a.m. I wake from a nightmare in which a menacing phantom figure bearing a close resemblance to our Dean of Research, catches me red-handed stuffing a box full of academic journals (which I have, against my better judgement, systematically ripped to pieces) into the works of the photocopying machine, with the intention of blocking it forever. When I recover my nocturnal bearings, I decide that a weekend away is needed – without my diary.

Constructivism teaches us that we cannot make sense of the world with another's voice or identity: we must employ our own vernacular. There is evidence that we need to capitalise on existing inner strengths, predispositions, preferred cognitive and artistic styles if research is to offer a secure foundation for practice improvement (Dadds and Hart 2001). So we must think about building research communities that legitimate individualised innovative methods (Mellor 1999) in order to develop capability and success. 'One of the biggest . . . constraints on one's development as a researcher', wrote Elliott (1990: 5) 'is the presumption that there is a right method or set of techniques for doing educational research . . . Such a view is a recipe for mediocrity.'

The national agenda for educational research is, now, more overtly an improvement agenda (e.g. Hillage *et al.* 1998) and most of us, I guess, would want to support that, providing there is still tolerance of 'blue skies' research that may lead us into new questions that have not yet crossed our minds. However, where does the person of the practitioner fit into this movement?

The current laudable notion of accumulating the knowledge base on the internet (Reynolds 1999) for improving teaching will not be without major problems if it privileges expert knowledge generated solely from outside practice. Who is going to decide what and whose knowledge counts? There may not be consensus about which knowledge base is the most appropriate nor a single, uncontested view of what constitutes effective teaching or improved standards. And as yet, we have little evidence that the knowledge base of the external researcher is as powerful a force for change as critical self-knowledge. Others' knowledge cannot be 'read off' (Hamilton 1996) and 'read in' unproblematically to professional practices like some supermarket bar code transaction. Judgement, critique, adaptation are needed to build bridges between one person's knowledge and another's improvements. Conversational learning circumstances are needed for these processes to take effect (Hargreaves 1999; Elliott 2000). We are deceived if we believe that outsider knowledge can be downloaded. Only information can be passed on in this way. Knowledge requires more complex transformations of mind and heart.

We must be aware, too, of attempts by those with control over research funding to define 'improvement' narrowly either in terms of imposed training standards, measurable outcomes on national tests or the mind-sets of governments. Education is infinitely broader than these narrow confines. So the quest for educational improvement through research is similarly infinitely broad.

When outside authorities make central decisions about the appropriate knowledge base for practice, we move towards blue-print solutions to improvement. Whilst blue-print knowledge can act as a catalyst for instant change, its life is short-lived if it is not mediated through the practitioner's situational judgement (Dadds 1994). The imposed authority of blue-print knowledge can also displace the value of practitioners' own experience since it privileges the knowledge base of the outside, over that of the inside, expert. Many have suffered dysfunctional crises of confidence because their own knowledge base has been de-valued in the process of educational reform (Nias 1999; Osborn *et al.* 2000). For this reason alone, research that creates good practitioner theories is essential for educational improvement (Elliott 2000; Hart 2000).

We should be celebrating the fact that we have, at last, a government that is serious about putting research on the improvement agenda. Yet there is a worrying absence in the government's education research policy of any reference to the value of practitioner theories in educational improvement. The policy privileges, exclusively, the role of government-sponsored projects in creating legitimate knowledge. It also privileges exclusively the role of government in deciding worthwhile educational improvement (Blunkett 2000). We should be deeply concerned in the midst of our ecstasy:

> September 23rd, 1999.
> 'How are things going with the interviews?' I dare to ask Wanda in passing.

> This apparently innocent question spontaneously sparks a very short fuse and a lethal flea is sharply applied to my left ear.

> What chance is there to attach importance to interviews, she fumed, when the search for a timetable in advance of the students' arrival is proving fruitless; when the weekend ahead promises little but preparation, marking, trouble-shooting, document repair in preparation for yet one more government inspection, yet one more quality assurance scrutiny from the power hierarchy!!!!

> The rest washed over me in my panic to undo the tenor and damage of the past few seconds.

> This, I rapidly conclude, is not the best historical moment to discuss the search for new knowledge about teacher educators' practices. I hurriedly retreat to the safety of my office, glad to have escaped with my life.

> In my diary that evening I indulge (and comfort) myself by trying to imagine different possibilities for Wanda. Just suppose we could turn more of the time and energy that goes into overbureaucratised accountability systems into time for powerful professional questions, deep reflection, transformative contemplation and constructively critical research conversations. How different our workplaces might be as learning organisations. How differently educated our students and pupils might be if their teachers were given genuine opportunities to pursue powerful enquiry in their working lives, rather than being harassed by outside certainties; if they were freer to cultivate inner knowing, to build their practice on the careful foundations of personal theories, not on obedient responses to the unremitting dead hand of outside power. In such a professional world, curiosity would have a central place in professionalism,

professionalism would have educative roots – and Wanda would be avenged – for 'it is in wondering and questioning that learning begins' (Greene 1973: 268).

## Endpiece

So – research as curiosity, as attitude, growth, learning, transformation; as ethical improvement, as critique, conversation, contemplation and creativity. These are possibilities open to us, possibilities that can help to structure a vision for us as research-based professionals.

Yet we work in systems that would burden with bureaucracy, dull with notions of delivery, stifle with centralism and an often-unquestioned authoritarianism, limit with privileged and under-privileged funding.

We have to be prepared to speak out against, and try to change, these adverse conditions, for the minds, hearts and attitudes of teachers and teacher educators have a crucial bearing on the education chain. Hurried, dominated and obedient minds can impact on students. Students can impact on pupils. Pupils can impact on democracy and society.

The key question, it seems to me, in these moves towards research-based professionalism, is not about how external researchers can improve their ways of communicating with user groups (Hillage *et al.* 1998). Rather, it is more important to ask how the conditions of teaching and teacher education can be improved to enable practitioners to become involved themselves in thoughtful pursuit of research that contributes sound critical knowledge to practice improvement. If we cannot tackle this question, then research-based professionalism has little serious means of survival on anything but a limited or technical scale. If there continues to be little time for the careful, systematic pursuit of professional curiosity by those who hold the learning of the next generation in trust, then education as a form of seeking and discovering, may, itself, be undermined.

This issue should be of concern to all who believe that we need research to guard against the excesses of authoritarian knowledge in both the curriculum and the political structures within which we work. Knowledge is political. Research, therefore, political. Professionalism is, therefore, political. We need to understand:

whose questions are legitimated;
for whose research agenda government makes funding available;
whose reports of 'reality' could, and should, make a difference.

Taking curiosity seriously is a risky affair. Questions threaten to de-stabilise the taken-for-granted assumptions of governments and educators alike. In the words of Stenhouse, 'curiosity is as ever dangerous, because it leads to intellectual innovation which brings in its trail a press towards social change. To those who yearn for the support of faith, authority and tradition, research presents a threat of heresy. Yet without the organised pursuit of curiosity we could not sustain our social life' (Rudduck and Hopkins 1985: 10).

## Postscript

May 23rd, 2000

I swear she is masking a slightly satisfied smile as she intercepts me on the way from the photocopier. Would I have time to look at her interview summaries? She has to admit, she explains, that it's amazing what people have said. So much difference. Makes a nonsense of single views of standards. Many new questions raised. Quite fascinating. Extraordinary.

(Here, I note, are a number of my favourite research words – amazing, fascinating, extraordinary). But she doesn't think her writing's up to much, she declares. Anyway, how would she write it up and for whom? Would I look at it and advise? Would a journal be too ambitious or should she settle her sights on the internal Education Research News? Is she good enough?...

I note that my breathing has suddenly become quite shallow as I hold back my suppressed smile – and the desire to punch the air – yes!!!

'Mmm, of course I will,' (mumbled, trying to appear cool, fearing to lose the advantage of this historical moment, as I mentally put Wanda to the top of the list for today).

'Mind you,' her voice trots after me up the stairs – and by now I can read her thoughts.

'I know, it's not really research,' I chant, 'it's only curiosity.'

'Well then,' she retorts, by now knowing my paradoxical thoughts, 'don't go getting too excited. You'll not get me on your list of active researchers that easily.'...

I end my diary that evening by inventing a new professional maxim to guide me through the darker moments:

'A research co-ordinator without a belief in the human spirit of curiosity has (if I can return to the analogy of the comedian) definitely missed the punch-line.'

## References

Bassey, M. (1995) *Creating Education through Research*. Newark: Kirklington Moor.

Bassey, M. (1999) RAE 2001: massacre of the innocents, *Research Intelligence: British Educational Research Newsletter*, No. 69.

Belenky, M.F., Clinchy, B.M., Goldberger, N.R. and Tarule, J.M. (1986) *Women's Ways of Knowing*. New York: Basic Books.

Blunkett, D. (2000) Influence or irrelevance: can social science improve government? *Research Intelligence, British Educational Research Newsletter*, No. 71.

Bridges, D. (1999) Research for sale: moral market or moral maze? *British Educational Research Journal*, 24, pp. 593–608.

Brown, L., Hewitt, D. and Tahta, D. (Eds) (1989) *A Gattegno Anthology*. Derby: Association of Teachers of Mathematics.

Campbell, J. (1999) Recruitment, retention and reward: issues in the modernisation of primary teaching, *Education 3 to 13*, 27(3), pp. 24–31.

Cunningham, B. (1999) How do I come to know my spirituality as I create my own living educational theory? PhD thesis, University of Bath.

Dadds, M. (1993) The feeling of thinking in professional self-study, *Educational Action Research*, 1, pp. 287–304.

Dadds, M. (1994) Becoming someone other: teacher professional development and the management of change through INSET, in G. Southworth (Ed.) *Readings in Primary School Development*. London: Falmer.

Dadds, M. (1995) *Passionate Enquiry and School Development: A Story about Teacher Action Research*. London: Falmer.

Dadds, M. (2001) The Politics of Pedagogy, *Teachers and Teaching*, 7, pp. 43–58.

Dadds, M. and Hart, S. (2001) *Doing Practitioner Research Differently*. London: Routledge-Falmer.

Elliott, J. (1990) Educational research in crisis: performance indicators and the decline in excellence, *British Educational Research Journal*, 16, pp. 3–18.

Elliott, J. (1993) *Reconstructing Teacher Education*. London: Falmer.

Elliott, J. (2000) How do teachers define what counts as credible evidence? Paper presented to British Educational Research Association Annual Conference.

Freire, P. (2000) *Cultural Action for Freedom*. Harvard: Harvard Educational Review.

Fullan, M. (1993) *Change Forces: Probing the Depths of Educational Reform*. London: Falmer.

Goodson, I. (1999) The educational researcher as a public intellectual, *British Educational Research Journal*, 25, pp. 277–298.

Greene, M. (1973) *Teacher as Stranger*. Belmont: Wadsworth.

Hamilton, D. (1996) Peddling feel-good factors, *Forum*, 38(2).

Hargreaves, D. (1999) The knowledge creating school, Paper presented to British Educational Research Association Annual Conference.

Hart, S. (1995) Action-in-reflection, *Educational Action Research*, 3, pp. 211–232.

Hart, S. (2000) *Thinking through Teaching: A Framework for Enhancing Participation and Learning*. London: David Fulton.

Hillage, J., Pearson, R., Anderson A. and Tamkin, P. (1998) *Excellence in Schools*. London: Department for Education and Employment.

Hollingsworth, S. (Ed.) (1997) *International Action Research: A Casebook for Educational Reform*. London: Falmer.

Mellor, N. (1999) From exploring practice to exploring inquiry: a practitioner researcher's experience. PhD thesis, University of Northumbria.

Merton, T. (1961) *New Seeds of Contemplation*. New York: New Directions Books.

Morrison, A. (1998) University research time – what gets in the way? *International Studies in Education Administration*, 26(2), pp. 31–37.

Nias, J. (1999) Changing times, changing identities: grieving for a lost self, in R. Burgess (Ed.) *Educational Research and Evaluation: For Policy and Practice*. Lewes: Falmer.

Noddings, N. (1994) An ethic of care and its implications for instructional arrangements, in L. Stone (Ed.) *The Education Feminist Reader*. New York: Routledge.

Norris, N. (1992) *Evaluation and the Profession of Research: ESRC End of Award Report*. Norwich: Centre for Applied Research in Education.

Ollerton, M. (1997) *Constructions of Equality in a Mathematics Classroom*. MPhil thesis, Open University.

Osborn, M., McNess, E. and Broadfoot, P. (2000) *What Teachers Do: Changing Policy and Practice in Primary Education*. London: Continuum.

Poincare, H. (1924) Mathematical creation, in P.E. Vernon (Ed.) *Creativity*. Harmondsworth: Penguin.

Reason, P. and Rowan, J. (1981) Issues of validity in new paradigm research, in P. Reason and J. Rowan (Eds) *Human Inquiry: A Sourcebook of New Paradigm Research*. Chichester: John Wiley.

Reynolds, D. (1999) The primary schools that we need, Paper presented to the Association for the Study of Primary Education Annual Conference, Liverpool.

Rudduck, J. and Hopkins, D. (1985) *Research as a Basis for Teaching: Readings from the Work of Lawrence Stenhouse*. London: Heinemann.

Simons, H. and Usher, R. (Eds) (2000) *Situated Ethics in Educational Research*. London: Routledge-Falmer.

Stenhouse, L. (1975) *An Introduction to Curriculum Development*. London: Heinemann.

Stronach, I. and MacLure, M. (1997) *Educational Research Undone*. Buckingham: Open University Press.

Thomas, K. (1999) Development planning: reflections and considerations for a dissertation, MA essay, St Martin's College, Lancaster.

Thompson, M. (1997) *Professional Ethics and the Teacher: Towards a General Teaching Council*. Oakhill: Trentham Books.

Wallas, G. (1926) The art of thought, in P. Vernon (Ed.) *Creativity*. Harmondsworth: Penguin.

Winter, R. (1999) *Professional Experience and the Investigative Imagination*. London: Routledge.

Zeichner, K. (1998) The New Scholarship in Teacher Education, Paper presented to the American Educational Research Association, San Diego, April.

Zeichner, K. and Kler, M. (1999) The nature and impact of an Action Research Professional Development Program in one urban school district, Paper presented to the American Educational Research Association, Montreal, April.

# Chapter 4

# What a difference a decade makes

## Reflections on doing 'emancipatory' disability research

*Colin Barnes*

## Introduction

It is now more than a decade since Mike Oliver used the term 'emancipatory' disability research to refer to what for many seemed like a radical new approach to researching disability issues (Oliver 1992). Hitherto, of course, a great deal has been written about this 'new' perspective; some of it positive, some of it less so (e.g. Clough and Barton 1995, 1998; Stone and Priestley 1996; Barnes and Mercer 1997; Oliver 1997, 1999; Moore *et al.* 1998; Truman *et al.* 2000). Whilst most of this literature is on the whole supportive of the principles underpinning the emancipatory research paradigm, it raises several important considerations that need to be addressed when thinking about disability research. And, as a consequence, casts serious doubt as to its desirability, practicality or indeed, effectiveness.

As an advocate of the principles of 'emancipatory' disability research with several years' experience in the field, this, chapter represents a personal reflection on some of the key issues that have arisen from these discussions without addressing directly the work of particular individuals. The emphasis therefore is mainly on the British experience although I would hope that the issues raised have some relevance to people working on disability research in other countries. The chapter is divided into two main sections; the first provides a brief introduction to the notion of emancipatory disability research. The second part focuses on selected key characteristics associated with this perspective. I will argue that the emancipatory research model has made an important contribution to the disability research agenda, and that in certain respects it is no longer that far removed from other more mainstream research strategies.

## Disability or not disability research?

It is important to recognise at the outset that social researchers and sociologists in particular have, in various ways, been researching 'disability'-related issues for much of the last century. The idea of medicine as a mechanism of social control and its implications for doctor–patient interactions, for example, is rooted in the work of the American sociologist Talcott Parsons (1951). Following Parsons a veritable farrago of studies have appeared from a variety of social science perspectives chronicling almost every aspect of disabled people's lives. Important early examples include research on the imposition and meaning of stigma (Goffman 1968; Scambler and Hopkins 1986; Murphy 1987), institutional living (Goffman 1961; Miller and Gwynne 1972; Alaszewski 1986), the role of professionals (Ilich *et al.* 1977) and disability and poverty (Townsend 1979). Furthermore, these have been accompanied by large-scale epidemiological surveys documenting the prevalence of 'disability' within the general population (Harris 1971; Martin *et al.* 1988). Each of these studies has made important contributions to contemporary knowledge of disability and related fields.

Nevertheless, all of these projects and the numerous others that were, and in many cases are still being produced are in one way or another rooted in conventional wisdom; namely, that accredited impairment, whether physical, sensory or intellectual, is the primary cause of 'disability' and therefore the difficulties – economic, political and cultural – encountered by people labelled 'disabled'. Notwithstanding, that some social scientists, particularly those influenced by interactionist and labelling perspectives, such as Thomas Szasz (1961), Thomas Scheff (1966) and Robert Edgerton (1967) had begun to seriously question orthodox explanations for societal responses to 'mental illness' or 'mental retardation–handicap' in the 1960s. However, these insights were not extended to other sections of the disabled population and in particular, people with physical or sensory conditions.

Of course this began to change in the late 1960s and early 1970s with the politicisation of disability by disabled activists throughout the world (Campbell and Oliver 1996; Charlton 1998; Driedger 1989). Of particular importance is the redefinition of 'disability' by Britain's Union of the Physically Impaired Against Segregation (UPIAS) (1976) and the development of the social model of disability. With a small but influential membership of disabled activists UPIAS made the crucial distinction between the biological and the social. Thus 'impairment' denotes a medically defined condition but 'disability is something imposed on top of our impairments by the way we are unnecessarily isolated and excluded from participation in society' (UPIAS 1976: 14). This socio-political interpretation of disability provided the conceptual clarity and language that are the foundations upon which the social model of disability, the theorisation of disability as social oppression, and the emancipatory disability, research paradigm rests.

Employing the insights and terminology of the UPIAS, Mike Oliver (1983: 23) coined the phrase the 'social model of disability' to refer to 'nothing more or less fundamental' than a shift away from an emphasis on individual impairments towards the ways in which physical, cultural and social environments exclude or disadvantage people labelled disabled. Several theories explaining the oppression of disabled people followed (e.g. Priestley 1998) and an alternative approach to doing disability research generally referred to as 'emancipatory disability research' (DHS 1992).

However, it is important to remember at this point that disabled activists have criticised mainstream disability research since at least the 1970s (Hunt 1981; Oliver 1987). Moreover, in the following decade several studies began to appear, mostly produced by disabled researchers, which drew on the experiences of disabled participants to illustrate the extent of the oppression encountered by disabled people and their families in the UK. Examples include, 'Walking into Darkness' (Oliver *et al.* 1988), 'Able Lives' (Morris 1989) and 'Cabbage Syndrome' (Barnes 1990). Significantly, as we shall see later, in 1989 the British Council of Disabled People (BCODP), Britain's national umbrella for organisations controlled and run by disabled people, commissioned a large-scale study of the discrimination encountered by Britain's disabled population in support of their campaign for anti-discrimination legislation (Barnes, 1994).

This was paralleled by a growing disillusionment with conventional social research strategies by researchers working in the 'developing' nations of the majority world, black writers, feminists and educationalists. Out of which emerged a growing literature on 'critical social research' and/or 'action research' that positively allied itself with oppressed groups (e.g. Truman *et al.* 2000). All of which contributed to the thinking behind the emergence of the emancipatory disability research paradigm.

A series of seminars entitled 'Researching Physical Disability' in 1991 funded by the Joseph Rowntree Foundation (JRF) provided a forum for the further development of this new approach. These events brought together disabled and non-disabled researchers working in the disability field along with representatives of various research funding agencies and institutes to reflect on and discuss key issues for disability research. This initiative culminated with a national conference and a special issue of the international journal *Disability, Handicap and Society* (renamed *Disability & Society* in 1993) on researching disability (DHS 1992) which ushered in the concept of emancipatory disability research. Since its inception, however, this approach has stimulated considerable debate within the disability research community both in Britain and the rest of the world (e.g. Rioux and Bach 1994; Stone and Priestley 1996; Barnes and Mercer 1997; Albrecht *et al.* 2001; Brown 2001; Mercer 2002).

In essence, emancipatory disability research is about the empowerment of disabled people through the transformation of the material and social relations of research production. In contrast to traditional investigative approaches, the emancipatory disability research agenda warrants the generation and production of meaningful and accessible knowledge about the various structures – economic, political, cultural and environmental – that created and sustained the multiple deprivations encountered by the overwhelming majority of disabled people and their families. The integrating theme running through social model thinking and emancipatory disability research is its transformative aim: namely, barrier removal and the promotion of disabled people's individual and collective empowerment. From this perspective die role of the researcher is to help facilitate these goals through the research process.

Not too long ago such ideas seemed utopian to say the least. Then, the bulk of disability research was financed by large Government sponsored agencies such as the Department. of Health (DoH), the Medical Research Council (MRC) and the Economic and Social Research Council (ESRC). In many ways these bodies were dominated by traditional medical and academic concerns and conventional assumptions about disability and disability-related research.

Today, the situation is a little different. Although the growing critique of disability research coming from the disabled people's movement was undoubtedly a contributory factor, this transformation is almost certainly also due to other factors. Probably, the most significant is the growing emphasis of market forces within universities and other research institutions (Barnes 1996). Other important considerations include the increased use or misuse of research data, both quantitative and qualitative, by politicians, policy makers and the media, and the consequential and indeed quite understandable widespread disillusionment with anything that passes for social research amongst the general public (Barnes *et al.* 2002).

Furthermore, it is evident that as we delve deeper into the twenty-first century, a large number, if not the majority, of recent and current research projects focusing exclusively on disability and related issues in the UK are funded by charitable agencies and trusts such as the JRF and National Lottery's Community Fund. Both these organisations prioritise user-led initiatives and concerns over those of the academy and professional researchers (www.jrf.org.uk, www.Community-fund.org.uk/research). Additionally, over the last decade or so there have been several pieces of research produced which I believe, implicitly if not explicitly, do adhere, on several levels to an emancipatory research model. Notable early examples include the BCODP research on institutional discrimination against disabled people, cited earlier, Oliver and Zarb's (1992) analysis of personal assistance schemes in Greenwich and subsequent BCODP research projects on direct payments (Barnes 1993; Zarb and Nadash 1994), but more on this later.

Equally important, although the rhetoric has yet to be matched with meaningful outcomes, there is a growing emphasis on user participation, if not control, within the research programmes of the various research councils, the National Health Service (NHS), with the Consumers in NHS Research Support 'Unit, and the newly formed Social Care Institute for Excellence (SCIE) (e.g. www.esrc.ac.uk, www.conres.co.uk, www.scie.org.uk). Whilst these developments might not go as far as some would wish, and certainly their impact has yet to be fully evaluated, they do mark significant moves in the right direction.

However, since its emergence in 1992 several attempts have been made to identify the key characteristics of the emancipatory disability research model (Barnes and Mercer 1997; Stone and Priestley 1996; Mercer 2002). For the purposes of this chapter, these can be summarised as follows: the problem of accountability, the role of the social model of disability, the choice of methods, and empowerment, dissemination and outcomes.

## Some key characteristics of an emancipatory research model

### The problem of accountability

Accountability is a major consideration for all those striving to do emancipatory disability research. Yet this raises a number of important concerns for social researchers that are not easily resolved (e.g. Barnes 1996; Bury 1996; Shakespeare 1996a). Probably the most controversial, relates to the contention that researchers must be accountable to disabled people and their organisations. However, to be accountable to the entire disabled population would be impossible. The issue is particularly problematic because the label 'disabled' can be applied to almost anyone with ascribed impairment or impairments whether physical, sensory or intellectual. Hence, the potential disabled population is vast. It is also the case that for a variety of reasons, structural and interpersonal, many people with ascribed impairments do not consider themselves 'disabled' or members of an oppressed group (Shakespeare 1996b).

But the same can be said of members of other oppressed sections of society such as the working class, women, black people, and lesbians and gay men. John Swain's (1995) account of research in a segregated college offering vocational education for 14–18 year olds with designated 'special educational needs' illustrates the point well. Although most students were from 'working class families and many were from backgrounds of extreme poverty and deprivation' and therefore could be said to experience considerable oppression of different forms,

> Few would have been identified by themselves or others, as disabled people and few would identify themselves as having 'special educational needs'. Nor did they have a political agenda that they wished to articulate.
>
> (Swain 1995: 76–77)

Hitherto, researchers making themselves accountable to organisations controlled and run by disabled people have gone some way in resolving this problem. In my view the standard for accountability was set with the BCODP anti-discrimination project mentioned earlier. After securing funding from JRF and Charity Projects research began in January 1990. The project was coordinated throughout by a research advisory group of five people only one of whom was a non-disabled person. The group met on a bi-monthly basis to comment on and review progress. Moreover, besides collecting relevant data the first five months of 1990 were spent discussing the aims and objectives of the research with key figures representing Britain's disabled people's movement. Data analysis and drafts of chapters were periodically produced and circulated to the advisory group and representatives of disabled people's organisations along with requests for comments and recommendations. These were subsequently discussed at advisory group meetings before amendments were made (Barnes 1994: xi–xix). When the final report was completed a protracted process of dissemination was undertaken: discussed latter. Similar levels of accountability have been achieved by other BCODP research projects including the work on direct payments (Zarb and Nadash 1994) and the more recent study of independent living services controlled and run by disabled people (Barnes *et al.* 2000).

However, whereas a decade ago tile distinction between traditional organisations *for* disabled people run by mainly non-disabled professionals and the more radical organisations *of* disabled people run by disabled people themselves like tile BCODP was quite evident, today it is less clear-cut. Due mainly to the successful politicisation of disability by the latter, many of the former have since adopted the language of rights and amended their constitutions to ensure that their controlling bodies include more disabled than non-disabled people, Whether this development is viewed positively or not is now a highly contentious issue for some disabled activists since it raises serious concerns about the clarity of organisational goals, claims to representativeness and the potential neutralisation of disability politics (Barnes and Mercer 2001; Thomas 2002). The problem can only be resolved by researchers having more than a passing involvement with disability organisations. Through a protracted process of engagement, they can then become familiar with organisational structures, their goals, the membership of their controlling body, and their procedures for accountability to members.

However, such a strategy may pose particular problems for non-disabled researchers, mainly because for some people within the disabled people's movement, social research and particularly that conducted by non-disabled researchers, is still viewed with suspicion. But having a designated impairment does not automatically give someone an affinity with people with similar conditions or disabled people generally nor, indeed, an inclination to do disability research. Emancipatory disability research is not about biology, it is about commitment and researchers putting their knowledge and skills at the disposal of disabled people and their organisations; they do not necessarily have to have an impairment to do this (Barnes 1992). Neither Gerry Zarb nor Pamela Nadash were identified as disabled people when they were conducting research for the BCODP.

Notwithstanding, protracted engagement with disabled people's organisations raises problems for all professional researchers working within a market-led environment where continued employment and future career prospects are all too often determined by an ability to secure lucrative and long-term research contracts. Most of the organisations run and controlled by disabled people are local, hand-to-mouth operations with very limited resources (Morgan *et al.* 2001). In such organisations funding for research is usually accorded a relatively low priority and when it is needed, the demand is usually for small-scale locally based projects that are relatively short term in character. The situation is equally difficult for those working within university settings. Besides the vagaries of the market, they are subject to the demands of a traditionally conservative academic community whose interests are often at odds with those of the disabled people and their organisations. All of this makes meaningful ongoing relations between researchers and disabled people's organisations difficult to maintain (Barnes *et al.* 2002).

## The social model of disability

The social model of disability is a core component of the emancipatory research paradigm. A decade ago adopting an overtly social model perspective represented something of a radical departure from conventional wisdom in discussions of disability and dependency. But this is no longer the case. Indeed, in some respects the social model has become the new orthodoxy. Many of the traditional organisations *for* disabled people now claim allegiance to a social model outlook (Thomas 2002). Social model thinking underpins the work of the British Government initiated Disability Rights Commission (DRC) (www.drc.org.uk). Internationally, social model insights are said to have been incorporated into the newly developed World Health Organisation's (WHO) International Classification of Functioning set to replace its outmoded and discredited predecessor, the WHO International Classification of Impairment, Disability and Handicap (see Bury 2000; Hurst 2000; Pfeiffer 2000; WHO 2002).

All of which has, rightly, prompted considerable debate within and without the disabled people's movement. It is important to remember therefore what the social model of disability actually is, as it seems to mean different things to different people. A model is what social scientists call a 'heuristic device' or an aid to understanding.

> A good model can enable us to see something which we do not understand because in the model it can be seen from different viewpoints ... it is this multi dimensioned replica of reality that can trigger insights that we might not otherwise develop.
>
> (Finkelstein 2002: 13)

Hence, the social model of disability represents nothing more complicated than a focus on the economic, environmental and cultural barriers encountered by people viewed by others as having some form of impairment. These include inaccessible education, information and communication systems, working environments, inadequate disability benefits, discriminatory health and social support services, inaccessible transport, houses and public buildings and amenities, and the devaluing of disabled people through negative images in the media – films, television and newspapers.

Furthermore, the social model of disability does not ignore questions of impairment and/or the importance of medical and therapeutic treatments. Several writers from both sides of the Atlantic have centred on the cultural production of normality/nonmalcy and the consequential interpretations of, and responses to impairment (e.g. Hevey 1992; Abberley 1993; Davis 1995; Thomson 1996). All of which colours our views of self and others. A social model outlook therefore may be used to highlight the interpersonal barriers within the context of personal and family relationships. It also recognises that for many people coming to terms with dire consequences of impairment in a society that consistently and systematically devalues disabled people and disabled lifestyles is often a personal tragedy. But the tragedy is that our society continues to discriminate, exclude and oppress people viewed and labelled as disabled.

This of course raises important questions about the role of experience within the context of emancipatory disability research. Whilst it may be argued that including information about disabled people's experiences in research reports is empowering for some isolated disabled individuals and that the inclusion of participant's narratives is necessary to illustrate the social context in which the research was conducted, it is important to remember that social scientists have been documenting the experiences of powerless peoples, including those who could be defined as disabled, for most of the last century. Moreover, in 1966 the disabled activist Paul Hunt pointed out that much of the writing by people with accredited impairments 'is either sentimental biography, or else preoccupied with the medical and practical details of a particular affliction' (p. ix).

As already mentioned, there is also the problem of selection, and representativeness. Social researchers have yet to devise adequate ways of collectivising experience (Oliver 1997) and experiential research alone has hitherto to yield any meaningful political or social policy outcomes (Finkelstein 2002). It is important therefore that within an emancipatory disability research framework, any discussions of disabled people's experiences, narratives and stories are couched firmly within an environmental and cultural setting that highlights the disabling consequences of a society organised around the needs of a mythical, affluent non-disabled majority.

## Choice of methods

Since its inception, the emancipatory disability research model has generally been associated with qualitative rather than quantitative data collection strategies. This is almost certainly due to the argument that up to now large-scale surveys and detailed quantitative analyses have never captured fully the extent and complexity of the oppression encountered by disabled people. Additionally, these studies are generally favoured by advocates of objectivity and value freedom, and therefore are easily subject to political manipulation (Abberley 1992).

However, there are numerous debates: about the question of objectivity within the social sciences and the sciences generally. The idea that 'scientists' of whatever persuasion, social or otherwise, can interpret data without reference to personal values or interests is one that has been promulgated by philosophers, scientists, and later politicians, since at least the enlightenment. The reality is that *all* information whatever its source and format can be interpreted in a variety of different ways and those charged with the responsibility of interpreting it are influenced by various forces, economic, political and cultural. If anyone is in any doubt about this contention consider the recent 'scientific' debates over the causes of global warming, BSE (bovine spongiform encephalopathy) in cattle, Britain's recent foot and mouth outbreak, and/or the value/dangers of the MMR (measles, mumps and rubella) vaccine for children (Barnes 2001).

In the social sciences, it is frequently argued that all judgements are coloured by personal experience and that all propositions are limited by the meanings, implicit or explicit, in the language used in their formulation. Furthermore, it is also suggested that all theories are produced by and limited to particular social groups, and that all observations are theory laden. Historically, medical and academic interests have dominated disability research. These were generally seen as objective whilst alternate views, such as a social model perspective, were viewed as politically biased and/or subjective. As indicated earlier in many ways this is no longer the case.

Moreover, whilst it may prove uncomfortable for some within the field of disability research, there is much common ground between the emancipatory research paradigm and some contemporary approaches to social research – including positivism and 'post-positivism'. Early positivism is founded on a 'realist ontology', namely, the belief that there is a 'reality out there' that is driven by 'natural' laws. Social 'science' is about discovering the 'true' nature and process of that reality and, in so doing, aims to predict and control it. Contemporary or post-positivism acknowledges that there are differences between the 'natural' and 'social' worlds in that the rules that govern the former are regarded as universal. By way of contrast, social realities are variable across time, place, cultures and context. Advocates also acknowledge that values can enter the research process at any point from the identification of the research problem through the collection and interpretation of data, and to the use of research outcomes. It is also recognised that knowledge generated by social enquiry can also influence future behaviour and attitudes (Guba 1990; Dyson 1998).

Those who adhere to a social model of disability whether traditionalists or rectifiers and regardless of their theoretical leanings – materialist, feminist, or postmodernist – all assert that there is a 'reality' out there, namely, the social oppression of disabled people that is historically, environmentally, culturally and contextually variable, that research is influenced by subjective values and interests, and is politically, and socially influential. The crucial difference between advocates of post-positivism and supporters of an emancipatory research perspective lie in their claims to political neutrality. For the former, although it is acknowledged that they are not always attainable, objectivity and value freedom are the stated goals, for the latter, political commitment and empowerment are the unequivocal aims.

Inevitably, this leads to accusations that politically committed researchers reveal little more than a previous allegiance to a particular version of social reality, and/or that by interpreting everyday life in a particular way they deny the significance of other perspectives, actions and beliefs (Silverman 1998). Although similar criticisms can be made of all social research, it is important to offset such censures. Therefore, researchers must make their standpoint clear at the outset. This means stating clearly their ontological and epistemological positions and ensuring that the choice of research methodology and data collection strategies are logical, rigorous and open to scrutiny and commensurate with the goals of the sponsoring organisation and research participants (Barnes 1992).

Furthermore, all data collection strategies have their strengths and weaknesses. It is not the research methods themselves that are the problem, it is the uses to which they are put. Throughout the modern epoch, politicians and policy makers of all persuasions have used figures and statistics to add weight to their arguments and/or to justify particular actions or policy decisions and initiatives. Since its inception in the 1960s, the disabled people's movement has used similar, tactics to highlight the various deprivations encountered by people with accredited impairments and labelled disabled. The BCODP research on discrimination mentioned earlier, for example, was heavily reliant on Government figures to underline the case for anti-discrimination legislation. Moreover, Zarb and Nadash (1994) utilised both quantitative and qualitative research methods to substantiate the argument for direct payments for disabled people to employ their own personal assistants. Similarly, the National Centre for Independent Living's recent national study of services controlled and run by disabled people employed a similar array of research strategies and procedures (Barnes *et al.* 2000). The BCODP Independent Living Committee commissioned both projects, the former was funded by the JRF and the Community Fund financed the latter.

### Empowerment, dissemination and outcomes

The rationale of the emancipatory disability research paradigm is the production of research that has some meaningful practical outcome for disabled people. After all, emancipation is about empowerment. Yet all research produces data. It could therefore be argued that all research is empowering. The accumulation of data generates knowledge and knowledge is empowering, or so the story goes. However, the new millennium is said to be the information age, but it is also the age of information overload. Too much information can often lead to confusion, uncertainty and apathy, and so be dis-empowering. Although this is a major problem for all sections of society, it is especially so for disabled people such as those from minority ethnic communities, people designated with learning difficulties, deaf people and older disabled people, who are routinely disadvantaged by inadequate and inaccessible education, information and communication systems. Whilst this can generate a general disenchantment with social research, it can also lead to a reliance on those who generate research findings, namely, researchers. It is frequently argued that the principal beneficiaries of social research are the researchers themselves (Hunt 1981; Chambers 1983; Oliver 1999).

Whilst this may be true for some sections of the research community, and I include myself here, I'm not sure that this is the case for the vast majority of social researchers. Due to the insidious but seemingly relentless encroachment of market forces into the organisations that control research production, a career in social research is more often than not characterised by financial and social uncertainty. For most researchers, employment is linked to the length of the research contract.

It is however the case that, historically, many social researchers have undertaken research on sensitive social issues without serious reference to the interests and needs of those being researched, and critics have argued that this is especially evident within the context of disability research (Hunt 1981; Oliver 1992).

But can emancipatory disability research offer anything different? I would argue that it can and has. Partly because of all the reasons already mentioned but also because as Oliver (1997: 20) has pointed out, empowerment is not something that can be given, it is something that people must do for themselves. The salient point here relates to ownership. Within an emancipatory framework, it is organisations controlled and run by disabled people that devise and control the research agenda and, equally important, to whom and how the research findings should be disseminated. Advocates of this perspective recognise that research, outcomes in themselves will not bring about meaningful political and social transformation, but that they must reinforce and help stimulate further the demand for change.

Hence, the main targets for emancipatory disability research are disabled people and their allies. Here again the BCODP research on discrimination provides a useful example. The data from the project were disseminated in various forms and formats. This included presentations by all those involved in the research project at numerous venues and locations throughout the UK and Europe during 1992–93, the production of various articles in journals, magazines and the popular press and an eight-page summary leaflet: the latter was produced in Braille and on tape for people with visual impairments. Two thousand leaflets were produced and distributed free of charge to all BCODP groups and supporters during 1992–93. (Some of the printed material is now available on the Internet via the disability archive UK: www.leeds.ac.uk/disability-studies/archiveuk/index). In this way, the research made an important contribution to the further politicisation of disable people both in the UK, and across Europe.

> The book that BCODP produced in 1991 on disabled people and discrimination in the UK has been the basis for people's thought throughout Europe . . . It is a very important book.
>
> (Hurst 1995: 95)

I would argue that this particular piece of research played a crucial role in getting anti-discrimination legislation on to the statute books in the UK. I would also contend that the production and dissemination of the numerous projects on direct payments and personal assistance schemes generated by disabled people's organisations, only some of which are cited here, provided substance to the argument for the introduction of the 1996 Community Care (Direct Payments) Act. This is not to suggest that these projects by themselves are responsible for these outcomes, they certainly are not, but they did provide some credence to the growing demand for the policy changes put forward by disabled activists and their confederates. And, in so doing, they made an important contribution to the further mobilisation of the disabled people's movement. However, whether the policy outcomes in terms of the changes to the law will live up to disabled people's expectations is another matter. There is now growing concern within the disabled people's movement over the incorporation of disability issues into the mainstream political process and what is seen as the effective neutralisation of the radicalism that once characterised Britain's disabled people's movement (Coalition 2000a,b). But whether such concerns can engender the demand for further research is something that disabled people and their organisations must decide for themselves. It is important to remember here that doing emancipatory disability research cannot and should not be conceived in terms of a unitary project or, indeed, a group of projects, but rather as an ongoing process (Barnes 2001) the organisation and content of which can only be determined by disabled people and their organisations.

## Conclusion

Much has changed over the last ten or so years in the field of disability research. There can be little doubt that the arrival of the social model of disability and the emancipatory research paradigm has had an important impact on agencies and researchers currently engaged in disability research. Where once the disability research agenda was subject almost exclusively to the interests and whims of politicians, policy makers and professional academies, now the situation is somewhat different. Due to a combination of factors including the burgeoning disabled people's movement and the activities of a small but influential group of predominantly disabled writers and researchers, the space has been created within the research establishment for researchers to pursue an implicitly, if not explicitly, emancipatory disability research agenda if they so wish. For the reasons identified here this is not a particularly easy task. For researchers to espouse a specifically partisan approach to researching disability, or any remotely controversial area of enquiry for that matter, carries with it certain risks that must be carefully considered before the adoption of such a position. Nonetheless, the argument presented here suggests that when directly linked to disabled people's ongoing struggle for change, doing emancipatory disability research can have a meaningful impact on their empowerment and the policies that effect their lives. Whether or not there is a future for this approach depends on several factors, not least of which is the future of Britain's disabled people's movement and, of course, the support available to those who choose to adopt and nurture its development within institutions and universities that aspire to conduct disability research.

## References

Abberley, P. (1992) Counting us out: a discussion of the OPCS disability surveys, *Disabitity, Handicap and Society*, 7(2), pp. 139–155.

Abberley, P. (1993) Disabled people and normality, in: J. Swain *et al.* (Eds) *Disabling Barriers – Enabling Environments* (London, Sage/Open University Press).

Alaszewski, A. (1986) *Institutional Care and the Mentally Handicapped: The Mentally Handicap Hospital* (London, Croom Helm).

Albrecht, G. L., Seelman, K. and Bury, M. (2001) Introduction: the shaping of disability studies, in: G. L. Albrecht, K. Seelman and M. Bury (Eds) *Handbook of Disability Studies* (London, Sage).

Barnes, C. (1990) *Cabbage Syndrome: The Social Construction of Dependence* (Lewes, Falmer Press).

Barnes, C. (1992) Qualitative research: valuable or irrelevant, *Disability, Handiap and Society*, 7(2), pp. 115–124.

Barnes, C. (Ed.) (1993) *Making Our Own Choices* (Belper, The British Council of Disabled People). Available on the Disability Archive: www.leeds.ac.uk/disability-studies/archiveuk/index.

Barnes, C. (1994) *Disabled People in Britain and Discrimination: A Case for Anti-discrimination Legislation (Second Impression)* (London, Hurst and Co.).

Barnes, C. (1996) Disability and the myth of the independent researcher, *Disability & Society*, 11(2), pp. 107–110.

Barnes, C. (2001) Emancipatory disability research: project or process? Public lecture for the Strathclyde Centre for Disability Research, *University of Glasgow* (24 October 2001).

Barnes, C. and Mercer, G. (Eds) (1997) *Doing Disability Research* (Leeds, The Disability Press).

Barnes, C. and Mercer, G. (2001) The politics of disability and the struggle for change, in: L. Barton (Ed.) *Disability Politics and the Struggle for Change* (London, David Fulton).

Barnes, C., Merger, G. and Morgan, H. (2000) *Creating Independent Futures, Stage One Report* (Leeds, The Disability Press).

Barnes, C., Oliver, M. and Barton, L. (2002) Disability, the academy and the inclusive society, in: *Disability Studies Today* (Oxford, Polity Press).

Brown, S. C. (2001) Methodological paradigms that shape disability research, in: G. L. Albrecht, K. Seelman and M. Bury (Eds) *Handbook of Disability Studies* (London, Sage).

Bury, M. (1996) Disability and the myth of the independent researcher: a reply, *Disability & Society*, 11(2), pp. 111–113.

Bury, M. (2000) A comment on ICIDH2, *Disability and Society*, 15(7), pp. 1073–1077.

Campbell, J. and Oliver, M. (1996) *Disability Politics: Understanding Our Past, Changing Our Future*, (London, Routledge).

Chambers, R. (1983) *Rural Development: Putting the Last First* (Harlow, Longman).

Charlton, J. I. (1998) *Nothing About Us Without Us: Disability Oppression and Empowerment* (Berkeley, CA, University of California Press).

Clough, P. and Barton, L. (1995) *Making Difficulties* (London, Paul Chapman).

Clough, P. and Barton, L. (1998) *Articulating with Difficulties* (London, Paul Chapman).

Coalition (2000a) Where have all the activists gone: part 1, *Coalition: The Magazine of the Greater Manchester Coalition of Disabled People*, August (Manchester, The Greater Manchester Coalition of Disabled People).

Coalition (2000b) Where have all the activists gone: part 2, *Coalition: The Magazine of the Greater Manchester Coalition of Disabled People*, October (Manchester, The Greater Manchester Coalition of Disabled People).

Davis, L. (1995) *Enforcing Normalcy: Disability Deafness and the Body* (London, Verso).

DHS (1992) Special issue: researching disability, *Disability Handicap and Society*, 7(2).

Driedger, D. (1989) *The Last Civil Rights Movement* (London, Hurst and Co.).

Dyson, A. (1998) Professional intellectuals from powerful groups: wrong from the start, in: P. Clough and L. Barton, *Articulating with Difficulty* (London, Paul Chapman).

Edgerton, R. (1967) *The Cloak of Competence: Stigma in the Lives of the Mentally Retarded* (Berkeley, CA, University of California Press).

Finkelstein, V. (2002) The social model of disability repossessed, in: *Coalition: The Magazine of the Greater Coalition of Disabled People*, February, 10–16.

Goffman, E. (1961) *Asylums* (Harmondsworth, Penguin).

Goffman, E. (1968) *Stigma* (Harmondsworth, Penguin).

Guba, E. G. (1990) The alternative paradigm dialog, in: E. G. Guba (Ed.) *The Paradigm Dialog* (London, Sage).

Harris, A. (1971) *Handicapped and Impaired in Great Britain* (London, HMSO).

Hevey, D. (1992) *The Creatures Time Forgot* (London, Routledge).

Hunt, P. (Ed.) (1966) *Stigma: The Experience of Disability* (London, Geoffrey Chapman).

Hunt, P. (1981) Settling accounts with the parasite people, *Disability Challenge*, 2, pp. 37–50. Available on the Disability Archive: www.leeds.ac.uk/disability-studies/archiveuk/index.

Hurst, R. (1995) International perspectives and solutions, in: G. Zarb (Ed.) *Removing Disabling Barriers* (London, Policy Studies Institute).

Hurst, R. (2000) To revise or not to revise, *Disability & Society*, 15(7), pp. 1083–1087.

Illich, I. *et al.* (1977) *Disabling Professions* (London, Marion Boyars).

Martin, J. *et al.* (1988) *The Prevalence of Disability Among Adults* (London, HMSO).

Mercer, G. (2002) Emancipatory disability research, in: C. Barnes, M. Oliver and L. Barton (Eds) *Disability Studies Today* (Cambridge, Polity).

Miller, E. J. and Gwynne, G. V. (1972) *A Life Apart* (London, Tavistock).

Moore, M., Beasley, S. and Maelzer, J. (1998) *Researching Disability Issues* (Buckingham, Open University Press).

Morgan, H., Barnes, C. and Mercer, G. (2001) *Creating Independent Futures: Stage Two Report* (Leeds, The Disability Press).

Morris, J. (1989) *Able Lives* (London, The Women's Press).

Murphy, R. (1987) *The Body Silent* (London, Phoenix House).

Oliver, M. (1983) *Social Work with Disabled People* (Tavistock, Macmillan).

Oliver, M. (1987) Re-defining disability: some issues for research, *Research, Polity and Planning*, 5, pp. 9–13.

Oliver, M. (1992) Changing the social relations of research production, *Disability, Handicap and Society*, 7(2), pp. 101–114.

Oliver, M. (1997) Emancipatory disability research: realistic goal or impossible dream, in: C. Barnes and G. Mercer (Eds) *Doing Disability Research* (Leeds, The Disability Press).

Oliver, M. (1999) Final accounts with the parasite people, in: M. Corker and S. French (Eds) *Disability Discourse* (Buckingham, Open University Press).

Oliver, M. *et al.* (1988) *Walking Into Darkness: The Experience of Spinal Cord Injury* (Tavistock, Macmillan).

Oliver, M. and Zarb, G. (1992) *Personal Assistance Schemes in Greenwich: An Evaluation* (London, University of Greenwich).

Parsons, T. (1951) *The Social System* (New York, The Free Press).

Pfeiffer, D. (2000) The devils are in the details: the ICIDH2 and the Disability Movement, *Disability & Society*, 15(7), pp. 1079–1082.

Priestley, M. (1998) Constructions and creations: idealism, materialism and disability theory, *Disability & Society*, 5(1), pp. 75–93.

Rioux, M. H. and Bach, M. (1994) *Disability is Not Measles* (Toronto, Ont., Rocher Institute).

Scambler, G. and Hopkins, S. (1986) Being epileptic: coming to terms with stigma, *Sociology of Health and Illness*, 8, pp. 26–43.

Scheff, T. (1966) *Being Mentally Ill: A Sociological Theory* (London, Weidenfield and Nicolson).

Shakespeare, T. (1996a) Rules of engagement: doing disability research, *Disability & Society*, 11(2), pp. 115–119.

Shakespeare, T. (1996b) Disability, identity, difference, in: C. Barnes and G. Merger (Eds) *Exploring the Divide: Illness and Disability* (Leeds, The Disability Press).

Silverman, D. (1998) Research and social theory, in: C. Seale (Ed.) *Researching Society and Culture* (London, Sage).

Stone, E. and Priestley, M. (1996) Parasites, pawns and partners: disability research and the role of non disabled researchers, *British Journal of Sociology*, 47(4), pp. 699–716.

Swain, J. (1995) Constructing participatory research in principle and in practice, in: P. Clough and L. Barton (Eds) *Research and the Construction of Special Educational Needs* (London, Geoffrey Chapman).

Szasz, T. S. (1961) *The Myth of Mental Illness: Foundations of a Theory of Personal Conduct* (New York, Dell).

Thomas, P. (2002) The social model of disability is generally accepted, *Coalition: The Magazine of the Greater Manchester Coalition of Disabled People*, February, pp. 17–21.

Thomson, R. G. (Ed.) (1996) *Freakery: Culture Spectacles of the Extraordinary Body* (New York, New York University Press).

Townsend, P. (1979) *Poverty in the United Kingdom* (Harmondsworth, Penguin).

Truman, C., Mertens, D. M. and Humphries, B. (Eds) (2000) *Research and Inequality* (London, UCL Press).

WHO (2002) *International Classification of Functioning, Disability and Health* (Geneva, World Health Organisation). Available at: www3.who.int/icf/icftemplate.cfm.

UPIAS (1976) *Fundamental Principles of Disability* (London, Union of Physically Impaired Against Segregation). Available on the Disability Archive: www.leeds.ac.uk/disability studies/archiveuk/index.

Zarb, G. and Nadash, P. (1994) *Cashing in on Independence* (Derby, The British Council of Disabled People).

# Part II

# New voices and relationships

# Chapter 5

# Research by children

*Priscilla Alderson*

## Introduction

This chapter draws on a rapidly growing international literature about research by children. There are a few examples from my work with children, but most examples come from the semi-published 'grey literature' of newsletters and reports by voluntary organizations. 'Children' is an awkward word to cover teenagers, but is used to emphasize how young children can also be involved. Three main areas will be discussed: *stages* of the research process at which children can be involved as actors; *levels* of children's participation; and the use of *methods* which can increase children's informed involvement in research, thereby respecting their rights.

For professional researchers to work with child co-researchers poses extra ethical and scientific questions. Can they work together on reasonably equal, informed and unpressured terms? How much should professional researchers intervene to support children or to control the research? How can adults avoid exploiting or manipulating children? Should children be paid? How much must or should their gate keepers – parents or teachers – be involved? And who should have final control over the data and reports?

The idea of seeing the previously 'researched' adult subject as a co-researcher, who helps to produce and analyse data and validate research reports, has long been acknowledged (Bloor 1976; Acker *et al.* 1983), along with the complications for professional researchers who try to work with 'lay' people who have different perspectives and priorities. Arguments proposed by feminist and black researchers for the new insights they can bring when they do research about their own group also apply to children. However, Rhodes (1994) warned about problems of attempting to match black researchers with black subjects. Such efforts risk marginalizing and devaluing the researchers, black people and all their concerns. Other dimensions of inequality between researchers and subjects may be more salient than colour, thus limiting the matching attempts and possibly obscuring important inequalities. Rhodes' view that black researchers should be involved at all stages of research and a general range of topics also applies to children.

Smith (1988: 181–205) did not treat her women subjects as co-researchers, but she consciously showed the advantages and difficulties of taking their 'standpoint' as a mother herself like them. She challenged the 'peculiar eclipsing' of women within men's culture, in order to theorize and shed new light on mothers' 'hidden work' which supports their child's schooling. Unconsciously, Smith also showed how adult-centric research can silence children as powerfully as the male-dominated research, which she criticized, silenced women. For example, mothers' contact with children is conceptualized as 'work', such as 'getting the kids off to school' (Smith 1988: 188), not as friendship, companionship, shared enjoyment or reciprocal support. Children then implicitly appear as dependent receivers of adult child-work, and not as competent contributors. In Smith's account, while mothers and teachers 'work' to 'shape' and 'manage' children, children reactively 'perform' and thereby 'reflect' the quality of mothering or teaching they receive, in a curiously mechanical and non-interactive way. Children's own views, their informed consent, and the effects of the research on them, are not mentioned. Thus, inadvertently, Smith makes a strong case for conducting 'standpoint' research about children and with them, and illustrates how generation can be as vital a dimension for theoretical analysis as gender or ethnicity (Mayall 1994). Smith and other feminists such as Oakley (1981) advocated research *for* and *by* women, and not simply about them. Lay researchers may be adults or children although children are inevitably 'lay'. When they research their own specific sub-groups, they can further develop research methods and theories *with* and *by* seldom-heard groups (Pratt and Loizos 1992; West 1997).

Such research is sometimes justified because it addresses power imbalances in the research relationship. Seven 16 year-olds, who did a short training and then tape-recorded interviews about 'my stay in hospital' with children aged 10 to 12 years, discussed these issues during their follow-up meeting. One interviewer commented:

> The boy I talked to was brain damaged, and he kept jumping around and on and off the bench. But he still kept talking and I think it was a good interview. It didn't matter, because I'm only 16, whereas if I'd been an adult I think I would have had to make him behave more quietly, and I don't think he would have told me so much then.
>
> (Alderson 1995: 108)

Peer research is also justified in terms of efficiency in that it encourages closer intimacy and fuller discussion between researchers and researched, and fuller understanding of the data. There is a danger that researchers will over-identify with interviewees and assume they understand too much, they may take replies for granted and lose their 'enquiring outsider' stance. Yet shared knowledge can be an advantage. Another of the 16-year-old interviewers said:

> I found it a great help that I'd been in hospital. I could think of lots more things to ask her about, and I think I know what she meant, such as when she said there weren't any nurses there at night time. We both knew that there were nurses there, but it felt like you were left all alone, and they don't come when you call them, and Sophia was afraid of waking the other children. I know

that I might mix up some of her answers with my own experience, but I think on the whole it was helpful to know so much about what she was saying.

The young interviewers talked extensively about differences between their own position and those of their interviewees however closely they identified with them, and about finding a balance between encouraging interviewees to talk but not being too intrusively probing. They felt some issues could be raised when the children could partly identify with their young interviewers, as when Deeana aged ten years emphasized during her taped interview:

> They (adults) didn't listen to me, 'cos I was only a child. They don't listen when you're only a child. They should listen to children. . . .
>
> (Alderson 1995: 109)

## Rights and research by children

An explicit and implicit theme within peer research is respect for the researched group and for their own views and abilities. Respect links closely to rights, and conventions about rights offer a principled yet flexible means of justifying and extending respectful practices (Spencer 1998). Rights conventions with quasi-legal status provide formal justification for observing ethical standards in research. Growing awareness of the rights of children, and other 'minority' groups including women, has paved the way for involving children as researchers.

Internationally, children's rights took on a new dimension when so-called *participation* rights were added to traditional rights to *protection* from neglect and abuse and to *provision* of goods and services. Until recently, research about children reflected earlier priorities, by measuring the effects of provision – health or education interventions – in their lives, or exploring children's protection needs as assessed by adults, or by investigating children's gradual development and socialization towards adult competence. However, children's participation rights, enshrined in the UN Convention on the Rights of the Child 1989's 54 Articles, involve moderate versions of adult autonomy rights and concern children taking part more equally, in activities and decisions which affect them. The convention says that state parties should assure

> To the child who is capable of forming his or her own views the right to express those views freely in all matters affecting the child, the views of the child being given due weight in accordance with the age and maturity of the child.
>
> (Article 12)

There is also the right

> To freedom of expression [including] freedom to seek, review and impart information and ideas of all kind . . . through any other media of the child's choice.
>
> (Article 13)

Rights complement yet also conflict with one another.... Children's rights are qualified in being not absolute but conditional, affected by the 'evolving capacities of the child', the 'responsibilities, rights and duties of parents' (Article 5) and the national law. 'The best interests of the child must be the primary consideration' (Articles 1, 21). Rights cannot be exercised in ways which would harm the child or other people. They must 'respect the rights and reputations of others', as well as 'national security and public order, health and morals' (Article 13). The rights are not about selfish individualism but about solidarity, social justice and fair distribution because rights express everyone's equal entitlement, and affirm the worth and dignity of every person. Respect for children's rights promotes 'social progress and better standards of life in larger freedom' (preamble of the convention). Every government except the United States has ratified the convention, undertaking to publicize it 'to adults and children alike', to implement it in law, policy and practice, and to report regularly to the UN on progress in doing so.

Non-Governmental Organizations (NGOs) in accordance with Article 12 are developing research with and by children. Other likely influences on children's greater participation in research include: the aftermath of the English Gillick ruling in 1985 that competent children aged under 16 can give valid consent; new approaches in the sociology of childhood to children as competent social actors, no longer simply subsumed under adult-dominated headings such as the family (Qvortrup et al. 1994; James and Prout 1997) publicity about the youngest children's competencies in many areas of life (Hutchby and Moran Ellis 1998; Alderson 2000). Recent enquiries in England into mismanagement of children's heart treatment and the removal of deceased babies organs re-emphasize the importance of practitioners and researchers requesting informed consent before they intervene. These medico-legal concerns about children's rights to physical and mental integrity are likely to filter into social research in time, although the British Education Research Association (1992) does not even mention children's consent in its ethical guidelines. Respect for children's participation recognizes them as subjects rather than objects of research, who 'speak' in their own right and report valid views and experiences. ('Speaking' may involve sign language and other expressive body language and sounds, such as those made by children with autism and severe learning difficulties (Alderson and Goodey 1998).) To involve children more directly in research can rescue them from silence and exclusion, and from being represented, by default, as passive objects, while respect for their informed and voluntary consent can help to protect them from covert, invasive, exploitative or abusive research.

Researchers' over-complicated or poorly explained terms, topics and methods can misleadingly make children (and adults) appear to be ignorant or incapable. Another obstacle in conducting research with children concerns infantilizing them, perceiving and treating them as immature and inadvertently producing evidence to reinforce notions of their incompetence. This can include 'talking down' to children, using over-simple words and concepts, restricting them into making only superficial responses, and involving only inexperienced children and not those with intense relevant experience who could give much deeper responses. Some young children help adult researchers to set more appropriate levels of talk (Alderson 1993; Solberg 1997) and child researchers may be better able to think of appropriate topics, questions and terms for child interviewees. When children are seen as actors in the social construction and determination of their own lives, the lives of those around them and of their society (James and Prout 1997), they may be more conscious of the importance of respecting the other children who help with their research. The rest of this chapter considers how they can be active researchers.

## Children as researchers

Research is part of everyday life in schools I have visited. Five-year olds made graphs about pets owned by their classmates, 16-year olds tape-recorded interviews with their friends about their parents' divorce or researched local allotments threatened with closure by checking local authority records and observing council meetings. Ten-year olds gathered materials to design a pond for the school. In such examples, learning, the main occupation for everyone at school or college, overlaps with research, but the wealth of research in schools is almost entirely unpublished and so cannot be reviewed in this chapter.

Research in schools tends to be seen as practising rather than worthwhile in its own right, but sometimes it is linked to highly valued activities. In Uganda, through the Child-to-Child Trust which promotes peer education, 600 children at a village primary school became concerned that animals used the main well-pond. They spoke with the village leader who called a meeting where the children presented poems and dramas on their research about the value of clean water. As a result, children and adults worked together on cleaning the well-pond and building fence to keep out the animals, then they celebrated with food and music (International Save the Children Alliance 1995: 236).

A second way in which children are involved in research is in projects designed and conducted by adults. However, besides providing data in their traditional role as research subjects, some children help to plan questions, and collect, analyse or report evidence, or publicize the findings. For example, 'on an accident-prone housing estate, teenagers had little to say about the kinds of events we (the researchers) had thought of as accidents. Nor did they respond well to the notion of safety or safe-keeping. In the end we asked them what our opening question should be. "Ask us about our scars", they replied. So we did, and it resulted in animated and detailed information about a number of accident events' (Roberts *et al.* 1995: 34).

The teenagers' initial responses might have been used to confirm assumptions about their ignorance and incompetence. In contrast, the partnership approach helped to develop new theories and methods for research about accidents and their prevention, and produced conclusions, and further projects with younger children. Children frequently enquire, scrutinize, accept unexpected results, revise their ideas, and assume that their knowledge is incomplete and provisional. Pre-school children ask basic questions about philosophy and method, and by five years have worked out basic understandings which last a lifetime (Tizzard and Hughes 1984;

Gardner 1993; Lipman 1993). Very young children can share in making group decisions and agreeing on priorities (Miller 1997).

The third area is research which is mainly initiated and directed by children and teenagers (Article 12 1999; PEG 1998a,b; West 1997). Methods of involving unschooled adults as researchers, such as through participatory rural appraisal (Pratt and Loizos 1992), are also used effectively with and by children (Johnson *et al.* 1995, 1998).The following sections review the stages, levels and methods through which children are involved as researchers.

## Stages of research when children are involved

Research by children tends to expand the research process through paying great attention to the initial and follow-up stages, as well as to the central stages of collecting, reporting and analysing data. The early stages include selecting and setting up the research team and sample groups, avoiding tokenism, working out team and power relationships and ways of resolving problems as they arise, jointly deciding the agenda, aims, methods and payments in cash or in kind (e.g. Cockburn *et al.* 1997). Follow-up stages include publicity, and efforts to link the findings into policy and practice to change the world, 'We want to show this to the social workers/ planning officers/Department for Education/the United Nations', may be explicit initial aims (West 1997; PEG 1998a; Article 12 1999). The national movement of street children in Brazil, for example, during the late 1980s, influenced the drafting of federal and municipal laws which enshrine children's rights based on research they had conducted (Save the Children 1995). The following examples illustrate work at various stages of research.

The Participation and Education Group (1998a) researched how unhealthy schools can be. The replies to the 14 questions, from 187 young people aged from 5 to 25, vividly combine physical with mental health: 'If you can't do the work you get picked on and called thick. You feel sick and bad.' The lively research report includes graphs and pie charts, poems, quotations and strong recommendations. The Group made dramatic presentations about their research to health professionals and to the Department for Education. They use the equal opportunity methods promoted in assertion training and by rights workers (Treseder 1997) which challenges assumptions that children are inevitably vulnerable. For example, 11-year-old boys wrote the agenda and chaired a meeting of people aged from 8 years upwards, to plan a conference. They stated the rules of listening with respect, and the adults were politely reminded not to interrupt or talk down to children, and everyone had a turn to speak to questions such as: Why are we having this meeting? What did you get out of the meeting? (PEG 1998b).

Bangladeshi young people researched the play and leisure needs of Bangladeshi children in Camden, London, taking account literally of a low-down child's eye view (Howarth 1997). They discovered why so few children used public play facilities and recommended how to make them more safe and attractive. In another project, children aged 3–8 years used cameras and did surveys and interviews about children's views on improving their housing estate. They published an illustrated report, which they discussed with local authority officers who used some of their recommendations, such as putting the playground in the centre of the estate, not on the edge and beyond busy peripheral roads as the adults had planned (Miller 1997).

Young people also help to disseminate research memorably. At the launch at the British Library of a report on pupil democracy in Europe (Davies and Kirkpatrick 2000), school students from Denmark and Sweden described the rights they enjoyed which are less-respected in many British schools. Then Emma and James from Article 12 sternly told the audience to stand up. 'Sit down all of you who are chewing gum', ordered Emma. 'And anyone who has not turned off their mobile phone.' An eminent government adviser sat down. 'And anyone wearing jewellery.' After ten commands almost all the audience was seated. 'If you were at school, you would have a detention and might be told not to attend school next day. But this has nothing to do with education, so why do schools keep doing this?' Emma continued. At the end of their presentation, Emma again ordered everyone to stand and then to sit down if they disagreed with any of her ten statements. These were about making schools more democratic and nearly everyone remained standing, except for the government adviser who sat down at the second statement: 'the convention on the rights of the child should be part of the national curriculum'. Article 12 vividly demonstrated how out of touch government policy on citizenship education was with most people attending the conference.

## Levels of children's involvement

'Child-centred research' is a term that can loosely cover methods, stages or levels of children's involvement (Connolly and Ennew 1996). A crucial element is how adults share or hold back knowledge and control. The different levels of control-sharing and of children's participation have been compared with rungs on a ladder (Arnstein 1969; Hart 1997). The lowest levels are the pretence of shared work: manipulation, decoration and tokenism. The next levels which involve actual participation are children being assigned to tasks but at least also being informed about them; children being consulted and informed; and adults imitating but also sharing decisions with children. The top two levels are projects more fully initiated and directed by children. A single project may work at several levels. The ladder image can help to reveal how far children are or could be participating.

Yet involving them is complicated by inevitable structures in research. Funders seldom fund the important initial stages of contacting young people and sharing initial planning with them. Even after such costly and time-consuming work, the project proposal has the same low chance of being funded as any other research, and during the months before grants are agreed, children and adults may move on to other interests. Despite their new interest in involving 'users', funders usually still require very detailed plans before they make grants, which allows little scope for children to develop ideas through the project.

Levels of participation are affected, for example, by children's capacities to understand theories. Can they understand critical analysis, or the politics of racism? A report of a class of 7-year olds demonstrates that some can (Butler 1998). Their teacher describes how conscious these black children in downtown Chicago became of racial, economic and political oppressions, as they discussed their own experiences intensely in class. When other topics were raised, they would say, 'That's nice, but what does that have to do with peace and power?' 'How you gonna help your Brothers and Sisters by talking about that?' They analysed contradictions between the rhetoric and reality in their lives, the social pressures that restrict individual agency, and how they can work for social justice, power, unity and community change. Their examples suggest that, with help, young children are able to share in the more complex aspects of research like planning and theoretical analysis.

## Methods used by young researchers

Child researchers use a wide range of methods, from selecting topics, questions, samples and observation sites through data collection to analysis and reporting, dissemination and policy discussions (e.g. Ash *et al.* 1997; Article 12 1999; Beresford 1997; Johnson *et al.* 1995, 1998; Kenny and Cockburn 1997; PEG 1998a,b; Save the Children 1996, 1997; Wellard *et al.* 1997). Research reports by young groups range from long typed reports (West 1997) to a simple poster or wall newspaper, a video or photographic exhibition, with reports and drawings by the whole team or from smaller groups (Johnson *et al.* 1995; Howarth 1997) or to work on anti-poverty or anti-racist measures (Centre for Citizenship Studies in Education n.d.; Willow 1997). They may use complex methods, like Emily Rosa, aged 9, who designed an elegant randomized trial of 21 therapeutic touch healers who took part in 280 tests. The healers put their hands through holes in a screen, and Emily spun a coin to determine whether she held her hands just about their left or right hand, to see if the healers felt the energy fields through which they claimed to heal. Accuracy would have to be well above 50 per cent to demonstrate sensitivity, but was under 50 per cent. Experts praised this simple design that casts strong doubt on the healers' claims; previously, complicated expensive trials had compared patients' healing rates after therapeutic touch and orthodox treatments (Rosa 1998).

Young researchers around England used Open College training materials to conduct ambitious projects. School girls investigating children's participation rights decided to interview in six North-East local authorities: the Directors of Education, Social and Leisure Services, the Chief Executives and Council Leaders and some Assistant Chief Constables. They had only one refusal. They piloted interviews with a senior researcher who thought they 'were brilliant' and that he would not have been able to arrange the access, which they achieved (Allan Siddall, personal communication). The girls discussed the merits of qualitative and quantitative methods when analysing their interviews, and considered how their evidence clearly showed that the officers' rhetoric did not fit the reality.

Another example of methods is text analysis. On the Children's Express, the reporters, aged 8–13, conduct penetrating interviews, and the editors are aged 14–18. Most of them come 'from backgrounds which offer little opportunity', and they publish reports in many newspapers and magazines. Twenty-seven of them monitored 400 stories in the national press to find that every article stereotyped children – as victims, cute, evil, exceptionally excelling, corrupted, as accessories to adults or as 'brave little angels'. They held a conference in 1998 *Kids these days* to publicize their research (Neustatter 1998).

Working with a writer-in-residence (myself) six 10–11-year olds worked on a book about their unusual school. They reported and discussed many aspects of the school, surveyed and interviewed pupils and staff, helped to plan the chapter headings and organize the material, and provided much of the text (Cleves 1999). Research reports involving a range of media and methods have been produced, for example, by a group supported by the National Children's Bureau (Tolley *et al.* 1998), and by Article 12 (1999), a group run for and by people aged up to 18 years. They reviewed how well the UN Convention's Article 12, children's rights to express their views, is put into practice across the UK. Their report, to accompany the British government's regular account to the UN Committee on the Rights of the Child, was intended to let the Committee 'know the truth'. It includes 'research tips for young people', with points such as, 'Don't lose the plot. Debate when an adult is needed to help, if so in what areas?' Rather than assess these reports, I have listed a range of examples so that readers may form their own views about them.

### Research and play . . .

A striking aspect of children's research is the combining of work and play. They use 'ice-breaking' sessions to help one another to feel confident and relaxed, more willing to listen and risk sharing ideas, with less fear of being dismissed (Johnson *et al.* 1995; Tresedar 1997). To enjoy *being* together as well as *working* together helps to sustain the enthusiasm of children who are usually volunteers. Play methods can enhance children's research imagination. Talking about 'let's pretend' can involve young children in planning improvements in playgrounds and nurseries (Miller 1997). One well-illustrated pack produced with children shows how to promote genuine participation, negotiation and power sharing through games, with details on promoting equal opportunities and 'chat space methods' (Save the Children and Kirklees 1996). Young children can be good at listening, questioning, challenging, keeping to the point, and helping each other to learn and develop ideas (McNamara and Moreton 1997). Topics and ideas are selected and noted in words or pictures on large sheets and everyone has coloured sticky dots to put beside the most-liked items. It is one of several transparent, fun ways to assess opinions. Very young or unschooled children can contribute detailed data through their songs and dreams, by making models, drawings or maps about their daily mobility and routines (Johnson *et al.* 1995, 1998; Boyden and Ennew 1997) or about their local wild life (Hart 1997: 98). As play is so flexible, and sometimes subversively creative, it enables children to contribute who might otherwise remain silent, hostile or bored during a project.

However, there are risks of play turning into a diversion which interrupts the serious research work which the children might want to do in 'adult' ways. Play can also be confusing if, for example, an adult says to children, 'We're going to have fun and play these games so that you can find out from each other about bullying'. The children might take this introduction seriously and concentrate on the fun and play, and the adults might then conclude that the children are incapable of investigating bullying without informing the children and giving them practical opportunities to show and develop their research skills.

## Research and work

Action research can involve learning from difficulties, planning projects, collecting and applying new knowledge, publicizing the research products (like food and news in the next examples) and testing public responses. During their monthly meetings in New Delhi, the street boys realized that they spent 75 per cent of their money on food. Twelve boys aged 7–17, took an intensive ten day course on cooking, nutrition, cleanliness, looking after customers and book-keeping, and had help with renting a space for a restaurant. They gave free food to some street children and learned Chinese cooking to expand the menu (International Save the Children Alliance 1995: 239). In Sarajevo in 1993, 18 editors aged 10–13-years ran a radio programme, Colourful Wall, with an estimated audience of 80 per cent of all the citizens. They conducted polls of children's views and based their programme planning on the results. Children brought news items to 15 press centres through the city. Many schools were closed at the time, and many children were injured and bereaved. The programme carried education, entertainment and psychological support for them, with counsellors, a personal column section and a daily slot on children's rights. The young disc jockeys were especially popular and, like the New Delhi boys, were keen to evaluate and expand their work. Children are more likely to be involved in practical research as workers, and to be regarded and respected as workers, in countries with high levels of child labour, and in war-torn countries with a shortage of adult workers.

Rights are sometimes criticized as a Western, Anglo-American concept, too individualistic and egotistical to fit, for example, Eastern communities. Yet Bangladeshi street children suggest that the people who are most conscious of rights to justice, to respect for the child's worth and dignity, to speak and to be heard are those whose rights are least respected (Khan 1997). Eleven researchers aged 10–15 years interviewed 51 street children aged 7–15 years and, being illiterate, they narrated all they could remember to adults transcribers. The young researchers were staying in a shelter and training to be tailors, carpenters and rickshaw repairers; previously they had been rag pickers, sex workers and house servants. They planned the research methods and questions, data analysis and recommendations, and they listened to and checked every word of the four research reports.

After much discussion the young researchers identified 11 issues they thought most important after comparing and synthesizing many issues from their interview data. It is striking that only two issues are about material resources – food and education. Their main concerns are for their human rights and the main problems they want to stop are as listed here:

(1) torture by police;
(2) torture by muscle men (also theft, and being forced to deal drugs, sex work);
(3) misbehaviour of adults (name calling, never using child's own name, chasing children away);
(4) dislike present job;
(5) cannot get job without a guardian;
(6) marriage problems of girls (even slum girls can get husband, even street boys would not marry bad dirty street girls);
(7) uncertain future (older girls cannot stay on street but no where else to go);
(8) poor income, cheated by adult traders, dirty rotten food;
(9) street girls are hated as they are involved in bad things (adults force children to do bad things then punish and blame even innocent ones);
(10) cannot protest against injustice without relatives' help; and
(11) no education (though they want part-time vocational training rather than schooling).

It is rare for intended beneficiaries of international aid programmes to be asked for their views, still rarer for them to present research reports of their peers' views. The Bangladeshi children's answers challenge global aid programmes by their requests for minimal help to make realistic improvements in their daily lives. They also show how adults may not know children's best interests without consulting them. Sometimes, as this research shows, adults themselves are the worst problems for children, as well as being part of the potential solution. Individually and on the largest international scale, this small study illustrates the importance of listening respectfully to young people's views when planning services intended to help them.

## Discussion

I set out to write a chapter on ethics and rights in research *about* children, which kept turning into a chapter on research by children. This chapter simply explores key issues in a new area, a prelude to more systematic and extensive evaluations and does not attempt to provide firm answers to the questions in the introduction, but rather to include them in this early mapping. A brief initial review reveals impressive skill, knowledge and dedication among young researchers, but to avoid presenting too glowing an account, this chapter ends with a few points about the problems and advantages of research by children.

Researchers of all ages and experience tend to produce pristine reports which gloss over the numerous inevitable difficulties during the research process, such as matching funding to costs, gaining access, maintaining records, managing teamwork, meeting deadlines and many other complications. Added to these, for young and lay adult researchers, are their inexperienced and usually unpaid status (Pratt and Loizos 1992), so that they themselves, their research subjects, and their professional colleagues may doubt that they are adequate to the task. Yet these latter types of difficulties appear to arise through social expectations rather than through any integral inadequacies in young researchers, indeed, their projects reported so far challenge traditional under-estimations. The importance of training and supporting young researchers and helping them to achieve high standards is stressed by one reviewer (Kirby 1999) who recommends careful training (Worrall 2000). However, almost all the useful points would apply to novice researchers of any age.

How much professional researchers should intervene to support them or to control the research, and how they can avoid exploiting or manipulating children, as in the participation ladders mentioned earlier, will depend on informed negotiation within each team, with generous time allowed for frank discussions. Adults are concerned about how much to encourage young researchers to analyse their interviewees' responses critically, and to distinguish between rhetoric and reality. An advantage in formally funded NGO projects is that they tend to involve disadvantaged young researchers with practical experience of the services they are investigating. Payment is especially controversial, with uncertainty about how much time children can be expected to give to research beyond the work they may already do at school, at home or outside the home, or begging, whether they should be paid in cash or in kind, and how to meet extra expenses for young researchers, their adult escorts and their assistants if they are disabled. Many professional research teams dispute ownership over data and publication rights; it is helpful to agree these early during a project, ensuring that the young people are properly informed before they decide. Working with child researchers does not simply resolve problems of power, exploitation or coercion. Methods need to be planned, tested, evaluated and developed with them, to turn problems into opportunities for children and adults to increase their skill and knowledge.

To summarize the advantages the growing literature on children as researchers suggests that children are an under-estimated, under-used resource. Just as research about women has become far more insightful because women are involved as researchers, the scope of research about children could be expanded by involving children as researchers in many methods, levels and stages of the process. Children are the primary source of knowledge about their own views and experiences. They can be a means of access to other children, including those who may be protected from access by strange adults, such as Muslim girls (Johnson *et al.* 1995). The novelty and immediacy of children's research reports can attract greater publicity and interest in using the findings than much adult research does. Doing research helps children (perhaps disadvantaged ones especially) to gain more skills, confidence and possibly determination to overcome their disadvantages than adult researchers working on their behalf could give them. Adult researchers note their surprise at child researchers' competence, and describe plans to do more complicated work with children as well as to work with younger children in future. Adult researchers frequently emphasize the value of listening to children, a point that is made more effectively when children can express themselves through doing the relevant research.

As more children's research is published, the dangers of ignoring their views (Cooter 1992) and the benefits of working with them become more obvious. Funding bodies increasingly expect researchers to work closely with user groups. This has potential disadvantages when powerful commercial or professional bodies prevent researchers from being adventurous, independent and critical. Working with young researchers to consult children, as the largest 'user group' of research affecting them, can help to redress inter-generation imbalances of power, open up new directions for research, respect their rights, and draw on children's unique perspectives to inform social policy and practice.

## References

Acker, J., Bary, K. and Essenveld, J. (1983) Objectivity and truth: problems in doing feminist research. *Women's Studies International Forum* **6**: 423–465.

Alderson, P. (1993) *Children's Consent to Surgery* (Buckingham: Open University Press).

Alderson, P. (1995) *Listening to Children: Ethics and Social Research* (Barkingside: Barnardo's).

Alderson, P. (2000) *Young Children's Rights: Exploring Beliefs, Attitudes, Principles and Practice* (London: Save the children/Jessica Kingsley), 151.

Alderson, P. and Goodey, C. (1998) *Enabling Education: Experiences in Special and Ordinary Schools* (London: Tufnell Press).

Alderson, P. and Goodwin, M. (1993) Contradictions within concepts of children's competence. *International Journal of Children's Rights* **1**: 303–312.

Arnstein, S. (1969) Eight rungs on the ladder of citizen participation. *Journal of the American Institute of Planners* **35**: 216–224. Adapted by R. Hart (1992) *Children's Participation: From Tokenism to Citizenship* (UNICEF, Innocent essays).

Article 12 (1999) *Respect: A Report into how well Article 12 of the UN Convention on the Rights of the Child is put into practice across the UK* (Nottingham: Article 12).

Ash, A., Bellew, J., Davies, M., Newman, T. and Richardson, L. (1997) Everybody in? The experience of disabled students in further education. *Disability and Society* **12:** 605–621.

British Education Research Association (1992) *Ethical Guidelines for Educational Research* (Slough: British Education Research Association).

Beresford, B. (1997) *Personal Accounts: involving Disabled Children in Research* (York: Social Policy Research Unit).

Bloor, M. (1976) Bishop Berkeley and the adenotonsillectomy enigma. *Sociology* **10**: 43–51.

Boyden, J. and Ennew, J. (1997) *Children in Focus; A Manual for Participatory Research with Children* (Stockholm: Radda Barnen).

Butler, M. (1998) Negotiating place, in S. Steinberg, J. Kincheloe (eds) *Students as Researchers* (London: Falmer), pp. 94–112.

Centre for Citizenship Studies in Education (no date) *Citizenship Education*, no. 31 (Leicester: Centre for Citizenship Studies in Education).

Cleves School (ed.) P. Alderson (1999) *Learning and Inclusion: the Cleves School Experience* (London: David Fulton).

Cockburn, T., Kenny, S. and Webb, M. (1997) *Moss Side Youth Audit: Phase 2, Indicative Findings in Employment and Training* (Manchester: Manchester City Council and Manchester Metropolitan University).

Connolly, M. and Ennew, J. (eds) (1996) Children out of place: special issue on working and street children. *Childhood* **3**: 2.

Cooter, R. (1992) *In the Name of the Child* (London: Routledge).

Davies, L. and Kirkpatrick, G. (2000) *A Review of Pupil Democracy in Europe* (London: Children's Rights Alliance).

Gardner, H. (1993) *The Unschooled Mind* (New York: Fontana).

Hart, R. (1997) *Children's Participation* (London: Earthscan/UNICEF).

Howarth, R. (1997) *If We Don't Play Now, When Can We?* (London: Hopscotch Asian Women's Centre).

Hutchby, I., Moran Ellis, J. (eds) (1998) *Children and Social Competence: Arenas of Action* (London: Falmer).

International Save the Children Alliance (1995) *UN Convention on the Rights of the Child Training Kit* (London: Save the Children).

James, A. and Prout, A. (eds) (1997) *Constructing and Reconstructing Childhood* (London: Falmer).

Johnson, V., Hill, J. and Ivan-Smith, E. (1995) *Listening to Smaller Voices: Children in an Environment of Change* (Chard: Action Aid).

Johnson, V., Ivan-Smith, E., Gordon, G., Pridmore, P. and Scott, P. (1998) *Stepping Forward: Children and Young People's Participation in the Development Process* (London: Intermediate Technology).

Kenny, S. and Cockburn, T. (1997) *The Moss Side Youth Audit: Final Report* (Manchester: City Council and Metropolitan University).

Khan, S. (1997) *A Street Children's Research* (Dhaka: Save the Children UK and Chinnamul Shishu Kishore Sangstha).

Kirby, P. (1999) *Involving Young Researchers* (York: Joseph Rowntree Publications).

Lipman, M. (ed.) (1993) *Thinking Children and Education* (Dubuque Iowa: Kendall/Hunt), 152.

Mayall, B. (1994) *Children's Childhoods Observed and Experienced* (London: Falmer).

McNamara, S. and Moreton, G. (1997) *Understanding Differentiation: A Teachers Guide* (London: David Felton).

Miller, J. (1997) *Never Too Young* (London: National Early Years Network. Save the Children).

Neustatter, A. (1998) Kids – what the papers say. *The Guardian*, 8.4.98.

Oakley, A. (1981) Interviewing women: a contradiction in terms?, in H. Roberts (ed.) *Doing Feminist Research* (London: Routledge), pp. 30–61.

PEG – Participation Education Group (1998a) *Schools can Seriously Damage your Health: How Children Think School Affects and Deals with their Health* (Gateshead: PEG).

PEG – Participation Education Group (1998b) *PEG Newsletter, Celebration Issue* (Gateshead: PEG).

Pratt, B. and Loizos, P. (1992) *Choosing Research Methods: Data Collection for Development Workers* (Oxford: Oxfam).

Qvortrup, J. *et al.* (1994) *Childhood Matters: Social Theory, Practice and Politics* (Aldershot: Avebury).

Rhodes, P. (1994) Race of interviewer effects: a brief comment. *Sociology* **28**: 547–558.

Roberts, H., Smith, S. and Bryce, C. (1995) *Children at Risk? Safety as a Social Value* (Buckingham: Open University Press).

Rosa, E. (1998) Race of interviewer effects. *Journal of the American Medical Association* **279:** 1005–1010.

Save the Children (1995) *Towards a Children's Agenda* (London: Save the Children).

Save the Children, Kirklees Metropolitan Council (1996) *The Children's Participation Pack: A Practical Guide for Play Workers* (London: Save the Children).

Save the Children (1997) *Learning from Experience: Participatory Approaches in Save the Children*, November (London: Save the Children).

Smith, D. (1988) *The Everyday World as Problematic* (Milton Keynes: Open University Press).

Solberg, A. (1997) Negotiating childhood, in A. James and A. Prout (eds) *Constructing and Reconstructing Childhood* (London: Falmer).

Spencer, S. (1998) *The Implications of the Human Rights Act for Education*. Keynote address to the fifth international summer school of the Education in Human Rights Network, Birmingham.

Tizzard, B. and Hughes, M. (1984) *Young Children Learning* (Glasgow: Fontana).

Tolley, E., Girma, M., Stanton-Wharmby, A., Spate, A. and Milburn, J. (1998) *Young Opinions, Great Ideas* (London: National Children's Bureau).

Treseder, P. (1997) *Empowering Children and Young People: A Training Manual for Promoting Involvement in Decision-Making*. London: Save the Children and Children's Rights Office.

Wellard, S., Tearse, M. and West, A. (1997) *All Together Now: Community Participation for Children and Young People* (London: Save the Children).

West, A. (1997) Learning about leaving care through research by young care leavers. *Learning from Experience: Participatory Approaches in Save the Children* (London: Save the Children).

Willow, C. (1997) *Hear! Hear! Promoting Children's and Young People's Democratic Participation in Local Government* (London: Local Government Information Unit).

Worrall, S. (2000) *Young People as Researchers: A Learning Resource Pack* (London: Save the Children).

# Chapter 6

# The ethical and methodological complexities of doing research with 'vulnerable' young people

## Gill Valentine, Ruth Butler and Tracey Skelton

Recent studies of children and young people have drawn attention to the fact that youth is not a homogeneous group (Cohen 1997). Indeed, there is increasing evidence that some groups of young people find the period of transition from childhood to adulthood particularly difficult and as such are at risk of failing at school, of becoming estranged from their families and of experiencing homelessness, unemployment and social isolation (Coles 1997). The term 'vulnerable youth' (Coles 1997: 81) has been coined to describe those who have a greater likelihood of becoming socially excluded in these ways. In this chapter we focus on some of the methodological and ethical issues involved in working with one particular 'vulnerable' group: lesbians and gay young people.

These young people are 'vulnerable' because lesbian and gay sexualities are largely stigmatised identities. In most Western countries anti-discrimination legislation does not cover sexual minorities, lesbian and gay relationships have only limited recognition before the law and homophobia is still commonplace (Valentine 1993, 1996a). As a result children who begin to experience same-sex desire or to identify as lesbian and gay (research suggests that young people tend to become aware of their sexual orientation between the ages of 10 and 16) can feel very confused and isolated. It is common for them to internalise negative representations of homosexuality and as a consequence to be too ashamed or fearful of rejection to 'come out' to friends and family members (Hunter *et al.* 1998). This in turn can make them vulnerable to low self-esteem, depression and self-hatred. Numerous studies suggest that lesbian and gay youth are at high risk of making suicide attempts (McBee and Rogers 1997; Savin-Williams 1998). For example, in a study of members of lesbian, gay and bisexual youth groups in the USA and Canada, Proctor and Groze (1994) found that over 40 per cent had attempted suicide at least once, while a further 26 per cent had seriously contemplated it. While many young people who 'come out' have positive experiences, it is also commonplace for children to be rejected by their families and to face bullying and victimisation from their peers (Nardi and Bolton 1998; Valentine *et al.* 2000).

Given the specific ways in which lesbian and gay young people are marginalised, there is obviously a need for research to explore how such processes can be resisted and how appropriate support can be provided for them. Commonly, academics carrying out research with young people are able to contact them and to work with them either at school or in the 'family' home (Valentine 1999). Yet, the very nature of lesbian and gay young people's vulnerability means that both of these environments are potentially difficult spaces in which to access and work with this group. Here we use examples from our own research project with young lesbian and gay men aged 16–24 from two towns. One town in the Midlands and one in the north of England are used to examine in detail the specific methodological and ethical issues that arise in the locations of the school and home when sexuality is the topic under investigation.

## The school

In 1988 the UK's Conservative government passed a Local Government Act which included a section dealing with the question of homosexuality in schools. Section 28 stated that a local authority shall not: (1) intentionally promote homosexuality or publish material with the intention of promoting homosexuality; or (2) promote the teaching in any maintained school of the acceptability of homosexuality as a pretended family relationship. In the debates which surrounded the introduction of this law the moral right constructed heterosexuality as 'natural' but also paradoxically as precarious in that their support for this legislation implied a recognition that teenagers' sexuality is not biologically fixed, but rather is emergent and as such subject to influence. In the eyes of the moral right, information about homosexuality might corrupt children's 'innocence' and incite them to engage in 'inappropriate' sexual activity. As such they argued that the emphasis on school sex education should be firmly on heterosexual monogamy and the biological facts of reproduction (Gordon et al. 2000; Thorogood 2000). Indeed, sex education guidelines which are being developed by the current Labour government in conjunction with churches are expected to stress the importance of marriage and family life (Department for Education and Employment 2000).

Although a prosecution has never been brought under Section 28 of the Local Government Act 1988, nonetheless it remained on the statute books in England and Wales until November 2003 (it was repealed in Scotland in 2000) and has had a profound impact on teachers. In a study of 307 schools commissioned by Stonewall and the Terrence Higgins Trust, Douglas et al. (1997) found that 82 per cent were aware of homophobic bullying within the institution. However, while 99 per cent of the schools had an anti-bullying policy in place, only 6 per cent had a specific anti-homophobic bullying policy. In the following quotations, Bob (now aged 20) describes his experiences of bullying and his teachers' reluctance to address the way he was treated by his peers:

> it [homophobic bullying] started up in year 10 and it put me right off my studies, I used to really enjoy school up until I got into secondary school, I used to, I used to love it but then I got to secondary school and I hated it,

I just wanted it to be over, I just thought, I just can't do this, I was glad the day I walked out, I know I got really, really, poor grades. They did, they'd hear it, they, they'd sort of half heartedly tell the students off, but they didn't mean it, deep down they weren't bothered, either way, it was like oh stop being homophobic but they wouldn't take the, they'd say oh stop saying that about that person or whatever, but they wouldn't say stop being homophobic, they'd just say oh you shouldn't say that about people, so they, they weren't really bothered. I think there was one or two teachers that knew about homophobia but again they were scared, I think they were scared of saying anything.

The explanation for such failures to acknowledge or respond to homophobia is found in Epstein's (2000) research. This suggests that both heterosexual and lesbian and gay teachers were unsure about the parameters of Section 28, and that as a result of their uncertainty and confusion they feel inhibited about discussing homosexuality within the classroom, or responding to cases of homophobia lest they break the law. Given the legal history of Section 28, it is not surprising that headteachers are fearful of entertaining research about homosexuality within their schools.

Even it if were possible to get beyond cautious gatekeepers it is unlikely that lesbian and gay young people would be willing to come forward and participate in such research. Children have to negotiate their individuality within the context of intense pressure to conform with their peers (James 1993). While the location of children within narratives of identity predicated on 'innocence' (Valentine 1996b) tends to 'nurture an apparent desexualisation of schools as institutions' (Epstein and Johnson 1998: 217), numerous studies have demonstrated that the school is an environment saturated with heterosexuality (Mac an Ghaill 1994; Holland *et al.* 1998; Holloway *et al.* 2000; Hyams 2000; Valentine 2000).

Sex and sexuality are important in a whole repertoire of student–student and even student–teacher interactions, including name calling, flirting, harassment, homophobic abuse, playground conversation, graffiti, dress codes and so on (Haywood and Mac an Ghaill 1995). Lesbian and gay pupils commonly experience harassment and social exclusion at the hands of their peers (Epstein and Johnson 1998; Khayatt 1994; Epstein 1994). Abusive terms such as 'poof' are also levelled at those children who are not gay, but who do not fit in with hegemonic understandings of masculinity and femininity for other reasons (Haywood and Mac an Ghaill 1995; Holloway *et al.* 2000). Indeed, children also use similar accusations of homosexuality in a derogatory way to harass teachers (Lahelma *et al.* 2000). Consequently, in the face of the overwhelming heterosexuality of young people's peer group cultures and the stigmatisation of lesbian and gay sexualities, to ask young people to identify themselves as gay in school-based research would be tantamount to putting them at risk of bullying and social exclusion.

## The 'family' home

Several studies have highlighted the crucial importance of parents, relatives and friends in supporting and sustaining young people through the transition from dependent childhood to independent adulthood (Jones 1995; Coles 1997). Yet, for lesbian and gay youth the overwhelming, and taken for granted, heterosexuality of the family home can be experienced as oppressive and alienating (Johnston and Valentine 1995; Elwood 2000). As Nardi and Bolton (1998: 141) explain, 'frequently, gay youths are rejected and abused by parents, siblings and other kin because of their homosexuality. Thus, where other minority youth generally do not face problems with racism and religious intolerance within their own families, for gays and lesbians often abuse begins at home.'

A fear of such a reaction prevents many lesbians and gay young people from disclosing their sexuality to their families even though they may be 'out' to other people in their lives. Peter describes the risks he has to weigh up:

> My mother would be fine, but she would tell my Dad. My Dad is okay sometimes, other times he sounds off, in the recent debate about gays in the military he said that all gays should be destroyed. He wasn't serious, but it still hurt. I need to work out if he hates gays more than he loves me.

Such secrecy raises a number of issues in relation to the ability of lesbians and gay young people who are legally minors (under 18 years of age) to consent to participating in research without their parents' knowledge and agreement. Legal minors are normally regarded as the responsibility of their parents or guardians. The implication is that they do not have the competence to understand and make a decision in their own best interests. If such an approach were to be adopted in relation to participation in academic research, a young person could only give their assent or agreement to take part in a study. Consent for their participation would have to be obtained from their parents or guardians (Tymchuck 1992). As such it would be impossible to gain permission for many lesbian and gay young people to take part in research about their sexuality because this would necessitate them 'coming out' to their families.

However, in the 1980s a UK court case about a child's ability to consent in relation to their own medical treatment established a legal definition of a child's competence to consent. This states that a competent child is one who 'achieves sufficient understanding and intelligence to enable him or her to understand fully what is proposed' and that the competent child has 'sufficient discretion to enable him or her to make a wise choice in his or her interests' (Morrow and Richards 1996: 95). Although this ruling has not been tested in the courts specifically in relation to a young person's right to consent to participate in social research, it does provide a justification for not involving parent(s) and guardians where to do so would harm the interests of the young person concerned.

The need to conceal the content of interviews from family and friends also creates methodological problems in relation to where to conduct the research. While the home is usually reified as a private space, in practice it is a space where young people are under the constant surveillance of other family members (although children do also oppose or subvert the way adults circumscribe their lives). Indeed, children have fewer rights to the same degree of privacy as adults (Allan and Crow 1989). As such the dangers of attempting to conduct a 'private' interview in most familial homes where space is at a premium and other household members may be tempted to eavesdrop are self evident. Instead, community spaces (such as women's centres, health centres and youth drop-in spaces) and venues within the lesbian and gay scene can prove effective substitutes for the home, offering safe and private environments for sensitive conversations. E-mail also emerged for us as an important way of contacting and working with some lesbian and gay young people. The cloak of anonymity provided by the disembodied nature of on-line forms of communication can provide closeted young people with the self-confidence and security necessary to overcome their fears about talking about their sexuality. Hinkinson-Hodnett (1999) argues that young men in particular can find it easier to deal with their emerging sexuality through a computer screen rather than by talking face-to-face.

Indeed, young gay men had, until recently, particularly good reason to be fearful about discussing their sexuality because the legal age at which a gay man could consent to sex was 21. As a result young men under this age engaging in consensual sex were breaking the law. In December 2000 the UK government finally reduced the age of consent for gay men to 16, in line with the heterosexual age of consent. Where our informants told us about 'illegal' sexual relationships during their interviews we necessarily sought to protect their confidentiality. For this reason we have taken great care to anonymise all the material arising from the project. This includes not only the extracts from interviews and information which are used in publications but also the notes and interview transcripts which are stored on file. We are also aware of the need to tailor the way we disseminate our findings to individual participants in order to avoid unwittingly breaching their confidentiality, for example, by not sending our findings to familial homes where they may be read by household members who are not aware of the informants' sexuality.

## Conclusion

In discussing methodological and ethical codes for working with children there is a danger that young people can become homogenised as a social category. In this chapter, we have tried to draw attention to the way that common methodological and ethical dilemmas, for example, in relation to accessing potential interviewees or gaining consent, can become more complex and significant when the research involves work with a 'vulnerable' group of young people. Here we have outlined some of the specific issues that arise in the locations of the school and home when homosexuality is the topic under investigation. Research with lesbians and gay young people is particularly sensitive because of the specific laws which frame (or until recently framed) homosexuality and because of the way that children are popularly constructed as asexual or innocent. While we do not wish to be prescriptive about how the problems outlined in this chapter should be addressed, our research does demonstrate the fundamental importance of finding safe and private spaces in which to carry out research with young people and the crucial significance of making every effort to protect the anonymity and confidentiality of those who agree to participate in such studies.

## References

Allan, Graham and Crow, Graham (eds) (1989) *Home and Family: Creating the Domestic Sphere*, Basingstoke: Macmillan.

Cohen, Phil (1997) *Rethinking the Youth Question*, London: Macmillan.

Coles, Bob (1997) Vulnerable youth and processes of social exclusion: a theoretical framework, a review of recent research and suggestions for a future research agenda, in: Bynner, John, Chisholm, Lynne and Furlong, Andy (eds) *Youth, Citizenship and Social Change in a European Context*, Aldershot: Ashgate, 69–88.

Department for Education and Employment (2000) Revision of DfEE circular 5/94, 7 February, London: Department for Education and Employment.

Douglas, Nicci, Warwick, Ian, Kemp, Sophie and Whitty, Geoff (1997) *Playing it Safe: Responses of Secondary School Teachers to Lesbian, Gay and Bisexual Pupils, Bullying, HIV and AIDS Education and Section 28*, London: Institute of Education, University of London.

Elwood, Sarah (2000) Lesbian living spaces: multiple meanings of home, *Journal of Lesbian Studies*, 4, 11–27.

Epstein, Debbie (1994) 'Real boys don't work': boys' 'underacheivement', masculinities and the harassment of sissies, in: Epstein, Debbie, Elwood, Jannette, Hey, Valerie and Maw, Janet (eds) *Failing Boys? Issues in Gender and Achievement*, Buckingham: Open University Press, 96–108.

Epstein, Debbie (2000) Sexualities and education: catch 28, *Sexualities*, 3, 387–394.

Epstein, Debbie and Johnson, Richard (1998) *Schooling Sexualities*, Buckingham: Open University Press.

Gordon, Tuula, Holland, Janet and Lahelma, Elina (2000) Moving bodies/still bodies: embodiment and agency in schools, in: McKie, Linda and Watson, Nick (eds) *Organising Bodies*, London: Macmillan, 81–101.

Haywood, Chris and Mac an Ghaill, Mairtin (1995) The sexual politics of the curriculum: contesting values, *International Studies in Sociology of Education*, 5, 221–236.

Hinkinson-Hodnett, A. (1999) *The Pink Paper*, 12 March.

Holland, Janet, Ramazanoglu, Caroline, Sharpe, Sue and Thomson, Rachel (1998) *The Male in the Head: Young People, Heterosexuality and Power*, London: Tufnell Press.

Holloway, Sarah, Valentine, Gill and Bingham, Nick (2000) Institutionalising technologies: masculinities, femininities and the heterosexual economy of the IT classroom, *Environment and Planning A*, 32, 617–633.

Hunter, Ski, Shannon, Coleen, Know, Jo and Martin, James (1998) *Lesbian, Gay and Bisexual Youths and Adults*, London: Sage

Hyams, Melissa (2000) 'Pay attention in class ... [and] don't get pregnant': a discourse of academic success amongst adolescent Latinas, *Environment and Planning A*, 32, 635–654.

James, Allison (1993) *Childhood Identities*, Edinburgh: Edinburgh University Press.

Johnston, Lynda and Valentine, Gill (1995) Wherever I lay my girlfriend that's my home: the performance and surveillance of lesbian identities in domestic environments, in: Bell, D. and Valentine, G. (eds) *Mapping Desire: Geographies of Sexualities*, London, Routledge, 99–113.

Jones, Gill (1995) *Leaving Home*, Buckingham: Open University Press.

Khayatt, D. (1994) Surviving school as a lesbian student, *Gender & Education*, 6, 47–61.

Lahelma, Elina, Palmu, Tarja and Gordon, Tuula (2000) Intersecting power relations in teachers' experiences of being sexualised or harassed by students, *Sexualities*, 3, 448–463.

Mac an Ghaill, Mairtin (1994) *The Making of Men. Masculinities, Sexualities and Schooling*, Buckingham: Open University Press.

McBee, S.M. and Rogers, J.R. (1997) Identifying risk factors for gay and lesbian suicidal behaviour: implications for mental counsellors, *Journal of Mental Health Counselling*, 19, 143–155.

Morrow, V. and Richards, M. (1996) *Transitions to Adulthood:a Family Matter?*, York: Joseph Rowntree Foundation.

Nardi, Peter and Bolton, R. (1998) Gay bashing: violence and aggression against gay men and lesbians, in: Nardi, Peter and Schneider, B. (eds) *Social Perspectives in Lesbian and Gay Studies*, London: Routledge, 133–141.

Proctor, C.D. and Groze, V.K. (1994) Risk factors for suicide among gay, lesbian and bisexual youths, *Social Work*, 39, 504–513.

Savin-Williams, R. (1998) *'And then I Became Gay': Young Men's Stories*, London: Routledge.

Thorogood, Nicci (2000) Sex education as disciplinary technique: policy and practice in England and Wales, *Sexualities*, 3, 425–438.

Tymchuck, A.J. (1992) Assent processes, in: Stanley, B. and Sieber, J. E. (eds) *Social Research on Children and Adolescents: Ethical Issues*, London, Sage, 46–54.

Valentine, Gill (1993) (Hetero)sexing space: lesbian perceptions and experiences of everyday spaces, Environment and Planning D: Society and Space, 11, 395–413.

Valentine, Gill (1996a) An equal place to work? Anti-lesbian discrimination and sexual citizenship in the European Union, in: Garcia Ramon, Maria Dolores and Monk, Jan (eds) *Women of the European Union: the Politics of Work and Daily Life*, London: Routledge.

Valentine, Gill (1996b) Angels and devils: moral landscapes of childhood, *Environment and Planning D: Society and Space*, 14, 581–599.

Valentine, Gill (1999) Being seen and heard? The ethical complexities of working with children and young people at home and at school, *Ethics, Place and Environment*, 2, 141–155.

Valentine, Gill (2000) Exploring children and young people's narratives of identity, *Geoforum*, 31, 257–267.

Valentine, Gill, Butler, Ruth and Skelton, Tracey (2000) Negotiating difference: lesbian and gay transitions to adulthood, paper available from the authors.

# Chapter 7

# Children with special needs, teachers with special needs

*Ros Frost*

---

> I feel overwhelmed, detached, dizzy, they're coming at me, I wish they would go away, I'm past my point, I can not stay in here any longer, I want to get out ... (*I stay*). . . . I need to get our. . . . I must stay. . . . (*I stay*) . . . I must get out . . . nothing is as important as getting out of here ... RIGHT NOW. I get to the staff room as a colleague takes my class over. I cry ... I sit ... I think . . . .
>
> *How am I ever going to get back in that classroom again?*
>
> (My own classroom. Thursday 30 November 1995, 2.30 p.m.)

This study is a reflection on my attempts to answer this question and is of an exploratory, problem-solving nature. I am taking you on the same journey that I made between September 1995 and February 1996. I want you to travel with me and see what I saw as I met the issues that faced me. It has not been my intention to look in depth at all issues I have encountered along the way. When new signposts have appeared I have had to consider the merit of continuing further on a particular track or, using the compass of my reasoning, keep travelling over unknown land with my sights set on returning to work. It would have made me very unhappy had I not been able to do so.

I will outline the layout and furnishings of the train we will be riding, introduce your fellow passengers and myself, your guide. Before doing this, however, I will take some time to explain the rationale behind the research methods I have used to aid my exploration.

It became clear to me from the outset that this study would be of an exploratory nature, that I would be like Spradley's explorer 'trying to map an uncharted wildness'. Spradley (in Hitchcock and Hughes 1989) likens the positivistic researcher to a petroleum engineer who already knows what he is looking for, how to look for it and what to expect. I knew that it would be unlikely to be this way for me. Faced with an inability to cope, in a situation that I would normally have been able to cope in, sent urgent messengers out from my brain, scouting for the reasons why this had happened. In order to sort through each layer of my experience in the classroom, and out of it, I considered that I would need a more interpretative approach, one that allowed me to set my general direction, begin gathering information, but change direction and tools as and when appropriate; to be rigorous yet flexible. I found Cochran-Smith and Lytle's (1993) description of purposeful teacher research helpful in this matter, finding rigour in their theoretical underpinning yet flexibility in their methods, particularly as they drew on sources I as a teacher was familiar with and knew to be helpful in my everyday teaching 'research', for example, the use of personal reflective journals. They define teacher research as 'systematic, international inquiry by teachers about their own school and classroom work' reflecting their desire to make sense of their experiences. Berthoff (in Cochran-Smith and Lytle 1993) states that teacher research need not involve new information but rather interpret the information one already has. She calls this 'REsearching'.

In keeping with Berthoff's thinking, then, this is in a part a 'REsearch' study about revisiting the old to inform the new. Yet it is also a systematic and intentional inquiry into fresh questions generated from the combination of old information in a new context.

I will be 'revisiting' two areas in particular: the conclusions that I formed from my first three years of teaching; and the effects of teacher/school communication on myself as a pupil at secondary school. I have used the personal documentation of a termly evaluation from my second year of teaching and an annual school report to aid my thinking.

I have also used classroom observation as a method for gaining further insights into my own practice and children's behaviour. By direct observation of one pupil in his familiar environment I wanted to find out more about what the pupil was doing and how this related to everyday classroom factors. Before setting off, here is your itinerary.

## Your itinerary for the journey

After an introductory talk by your guide about your travel arrangements, fellow passengers and destination, you will be calling at all stops along the way including:

1   Harried hill                                          (Not for the faint-hearted)
   *A new academic year and new challenges. An introduction to the pressures faced and stress experienced.*
2   Mount development                                     (A scenic viewpoint)
   *The vantage point received from gaining insights into the current Special Educational Needs debate. The light it shed on my own experience of school and the management of the children in my class.*
3   Finder's sharers                                      (A voyage of discovery)
   *Further exploration into behavior management. Surprising findings from a classroom observation of one pupil.*
4   Crisis point                                          (A lemming's paradise!)
   *The smouldering fire of stress becomes consuming.*

*The lethal cocktail of pupil's disruptive behaviour and too many hours worked for too long.*

5    The path of approach                                    (The final destination)
*From Initial Teacher Training through recent educational charge. A proposal for return.*

So, welcome aboard!

You are asked to observe the health and safety regulation of the train and to be aware of any *FLASHBACKS* encountered. Please consult the guard when you see one as these electrical occurrences have the potential to delay or advance the train's journey.

REFRESHMENTS will be served prior to arrival at some stops. They will be served by the guard from a personal selection of thoughts.

The train you are on is educational. The School Express has over 500 passengers, 10 per cent of whom are staff. The pupils range in age from four to eleven.

The guide has been a passenger on this School Express for the past three and a half years. Before this she was a passenger on the Initial Teacher Training Intercity for four years, specialising in the teaching of seven- to eleven-year-old passengers and of art, and before that she spent the previous thirteen years as a keen 'guard and passenger observer' on the same Local Education Authority's Network service from the ages of five to eighteen. Your guide joined the School Express just after the train's National Curriculum time-tables has changed for the second time, and a year and a half prior to a further National Curriculum re-timetabling. The carriage this study is based in has adequate space, water and toilet facilities. Resources are satisfactory to deliver the school's aims effectively.

Within the carriage there are thirteen children working towards National Curriculum level one and fourteen towards level two in English and maths. Thirteen children receive extra language learning support; of these, nine are also on the Local Education Authority's Stages of Assessment with specific programmes for supporting a variety of needs is speech, hearing, learning and behaviour. The majority of family housing is privately owned, and four pupils receive free school dinners. There are also other health considerations such as asthma, eczema and toileting needs to be taken into account. The guide receives four and a half hours' classroom/welfare support and two hours' learning support a week, with two hours' support from parent helpers with reading each week. One-third of the class are girls, and all of the pupils have English as their first language. This does not fully explain the diversity within this carriage, but it may help to set a context for understanding the purpose of this study.

The journey begins.

## Harried hill

I had started the new academic year with a change of age groups, from teaching Year 2 and 3 to Year 1, to which I was looking forward. In the nine months prior to this new term I had also experienced some personally taxing situations outside work, which had left me feeling emotionally drained but not exhausted. These involved an intimate bereavement, the break-up of a relationship, concern over a serious family illness, and domestic problems. I had also been in the process of buying a house. However it was the beginning of year, and I looked forward to embarking on new challenges and leaving time to heal the upsets of the last few months. I was not far into the new term before my initial enthusiasm became strained, as I realised that I had more a challenge on my hands than I had anticipated.

Although it was early in the new academic year, the behaviour of two boys, Eddy and Todd, in the class was already starting to cause me concern. The following summary is taken from notes I kept about their behaviour between September and November. The following were displayed by one or both most days:

- attention-seeking noises at inappropriate times
- not sitting still
- talking when others were talking
- bad language
- hurting other children
- taking others' property
- damaging others' work and school property
- refusal to work
- refusal to co-operate/enter classroom
- sometimes rude and dangerous behaviour to classroom helpers
- out of classroom problems, such as bullying before and after school, at break and lunchtimes.

It became increasingly difficult to maintain a calm working atmosphere within the carriage and direct my energies to teaching. How should I deal with this old but new situation?

FLASHBACK   I had experienced similar behaviour with one of the children's relatives in my first year on the Express. I knew that I would still have to meet the same standards of teaching and learning, even with continual disruption to my practice. Could I cope with this for another year, with the knowledge at the time that there would be no extra classroom support, and of all that it had meant last time in terms of personal strain and disrupted teaching? How could I use my concerns to prevent what I feared from happening, rather than allowing them to act as a self-fulfilling prophecy so early on in the year?

I could feel the pressures begin to mount around and within me. At first I perceived these as challenges, but as the weeks went on I became increasingly worn out from dealing with the unpredictable behaviour of the two children, as well as that of a small handful of others in competition with them. I knew from previous reading on stress that a fair amount of pressure, seen in a positive way, helps improve performance (Dunham 1992: 95). But I recognised in myself the symptoms of excessive pressure. Appley (cited in Dunham 1992: 94) proposes that individuals pass through stress thresholds when attempting to cope with pressures, starting with early warning signs such as anxiety and irritability, and moving on to loss of concentration, psychosomatic symptoms such as skin irritations, exhaustion and eventually burnout.

Dunham in his book *Stress in Teaching* says of the fine line between pressure and stress:

> The extent to which work demands made upon a teacher result in stress depends on a number of factors including pressures from sources external to teaching, personality and previous experience of similar demands.
>
> (Dunham 1992: 2)

I had certainly experienced similar demands before, which had left less than favourable expectations for the current year. There had been, and was still continuing, a considerable amount of pressure on me outside work. Dunham defines stress as:

> A process of behavioural, emotional, mental and physical reactions caused by prolonged, increasing or new pressures which are significantly greater than coping resources.
>
> (Dunham 1992: 3)

Normally I would have coped with these pressures by putting more time and energy into my work. However the physical, emotional and mental demands of managing difficult behaviour now, while needing to maintain thorough planning, assessment and record keeping, had totally depleted these resources. I listed all the areas from which I felt under pressure, and identified from these three elements which concerned me most: difficult behaviour in the carriage, workload, and the meeting of contractual obligations. These were important departure points for me on my journey which needed to be addressed. The next three sections are devoted to their consideration. In retrospect it is easy to see how pressures in these areas built up to such a pitch, yet at the time I was so busy reacting that I was unable to step back and gain a clear perspective on them.

After discussion with the Special Educational Needs Co-ordinator, Todd and Eddy were placed on Stages 2 and 3 respectively of the Local Education Authority's Stages of Assessment, with individual programmes drawn up to support behaviour development. Through the advice of visiting behaviour specialist I was able to recognise patterns in Eddy's behaviour. What struck me was that in drawing up programmes to manage Eddy's behaviour, there were considerable implications for my own practice. For example, when he became aggressive upon entering class, was his frustration in part owing to inappropriate classroom organization on my part?

Although the Special Educational Needs Co-ordinator and I were planning for desired changes to Eddy's behaviour, I questioned where the safeguard was for the child against unhelpful teacher behaviour, within the Staged Assessment procedure. I could see that, if I wanted them to be, all the behaviour problems in the class could be attributed to problems in the children, and they could have programmes to sort them out. Yet I had seen that the teacher and school had very real responsibilities in this. Such sharing of responsibility for change, to meet the special needs of children, became even more apparent over the following months.

REFRESHMENT   It appears that not only the pupil but the teacher and the school need to be prepared to change to meet the special needs of pupils.


## Mount development

The following quote is from one which particularly echoed my thinking:

> Special educational needs are needs that arise within the educational system rather than the individual, and indicate a need for the system to change further in order to accommodate the individual differences.
>
> (Dyson 1990: 59)

Dyson draws this conclusion making reference to the 'individual change' model of change in Special Needs education, influenced by the Warnock Report (DfE 1978) and the 1981 Education Act, where it is the pupils who are expected to change their behaviour regardless of their environment. Warnock's proposal talks of an alternative 'system-level change', where an environment which is not favourable to the child should consider changing itself instead to accommodate the pupil more effectively.

FLASHBACK   I remembered a similar conflict myself from secondary school. Achievements that I had made appeared to be given less formal recognition when they were in areas that I perceived were valued less highly by the school at the time.

During our first week on the Masters' course we were invited by a tutor to think back, and reflect on, a learning difficulty that we had experienced at school.

I did not think that I had had a particular learning difficulty at school, except that my time at secondary school had left me with a very negative view of my abilities, further confirmed by my exam results. Although these events had taken place years before, their effects remained with me. I could not believe that I was this same person now beginning a higher degree. This might have been hilarious if there had not been a down side to it as well, the handicapping of myself through insecurity about my own ability. Purkey describes the results of continual affronts to our self-esteem:

> Even the most insensitive parent or teacher can usually recognise and take into account a crippling physical handicap. Negative self-esteem however is often overlooked because we fail to take the time and effort it requires to be sensitive to how children see themselves and their abilities.
>
> (Purkey 1970: 37)

I knew I had caused some disruption at school, but equally knew, from my position now as a primary teacher, that there was more to it than purely blaming the teacher or the child. I did not want to pass on the same handicap that I still experienced but now was in a position to prevent. I was concerned to help Eddy, not hinder him.

FLASHBACK   Could my teaching and communication leave Eddy with same negative impressions of himself as a learner that I had felt at school?

Dyson again contributes that

> Even event in a pupil's life may have some bearing on his or her capacity to learn. When 'normal' individuals show an inability to learn in school, yet are perfectly capable of learning in other situations, *one should be driven to consider what aspects of the society are creating negative attitudes to schools and whether changes are necessary in the schools themselves.*
>
> (Dyson 1990: 55, italics added)

It is with such an exploration, through observation in the carriage, that the following section is concerned.

REFRESHMENT   A full and thorough consideration of the child and his or her life experience as a whole should be taken into account when planning learning programmes.

## Finder shares

As already noted, it was Eddy's behaviour that caused me the most concern. I wanted to see exactly what he was doing in the carriage and not make ill-informed judgements based on inadequate evidence. I decided that I would observe him at work.

I asked the pupils to think about a special person that they would like to come to their house, and then to draw and colour a picture showing this guest and the kind of preparations they would make in order for this special visit. I did not tell the class that I would be observing Eddy, yet I was glad that he gave me an indication he knew I was watching him. As I looked for patterns within my written record I became aware of looking at Eddy's actions and considering different ways of interpreting them; first with the insight of seeing the full picture from my position in the class observing, and second to ask myself, 'How else might I have interpreted his behaviour when under greater stress myself, and what actions might I have taken?'

FLASHBACK   I was much more relaxed as I observed Eddy. In fact the absence of a 'stressed' teacher trying to 'control' him all the time probably did his behaviour the world of good! I was prepared to see the lighter side of things rather than feeling, 'I must be on top of Eddy's behaviour always', and that, 'If he misbehaves it is my lack of classroom control and I am therefore a failing teacher', regardless of the other twenty-six children behaving 'well', who could also be said to be the 'product' of my classroom management.

I have summarized in Table 7.1 the main points I drew out from the observation of Eddy, my initial interpretations of them and an alternative interpretation.

To me this observation illustrates how one action can have so many interpretations held in the hand of the teacher. I consider this serves to reinforce the importance of open-ended exploration before making conclusions about reasons for behaviour and setting the wheels in motion for dealing with 'deviance' or 'disruption'. Martin (1988: 501) suggests the use of a broad evaluative framework

*Table 7.1* Alternative interpretations of Eddy's behaviour

| Time | Action | Relaxed interpretation | Stressed interpretation |
|------|--------|------------------------|-------------------------|
| 9.32 | Talks when working | Helpful automatic self-expression | Disturbing concentration of others |
|      | Joking | Values friends and humour | Lack of concentration |
| 9.35 | Visits friend's table | Needs to relate to others | Disturbing concentration of others |
|      | Asks politely for something | I may have missed this good behaviour from across the room | |
|      | Sharpening pencil | I forgot to organise the helpers | Work avoidance tactic |
|      | 'Wooden Willy' action | E's humour; he's happy | Inappropriate behaviour |
|      | Tells friend colour of eyes | Helping his friend | Lack of concentration |
| 9.41 | Propels rubber using ruler with description of mechanical catapult | Understanding of technology | Throwing rubber – disruption |
|      | 'B' for balloon | Initial sound practice | Disturbing concentration of others |
|      | Birds have stripes | Knowledge of natural world | Disturbing concentration of others |
| 9.45 | Discusses friend's eyes and choice of pencil | Accuracy and attention to detail | Disturbing concentration of others |
| 9.46 | Stands up and colours at table | Comfortable working position | Disturbing concentration of others |
| 9.50 | Describes picture | Expression about relationships | Disturbing concentration of others |

for assessing children, as an alternative to the 'expert'-led, jargon-riddled and straightjacketed formats that she found unhelpful. We should consider seriously:

> The child's stance in the world, the child's emotional tenor and disposition, the child's mode of relationship to other children and to adults, the child's activities and interests, the child's involvement in formal learning, the child's greatest strengths and areas of greatest vulnerabilities.
>
> (Carini, in Martin 1988: 496)

REFRESHMENT  Should we build a similar sensitivity to the one Martin suggests towards our staff as well as pupils? Teachers who feel they are 'failing' need as much support as the children who feel they are failing. It would make an interesting study to explore the similarities and differences with which pupils and staff facing difficulties are managed, especially regarding the use of the concept of 'failure'. Hence the title for my study: Children with special needs – teachers with special needs.

In the following section, I will be considering the nature of the 'special needs' in my own experience as a teacher on this journey.

## Crisis point

At this point there may appear little to suggest that there was about to occur the 'crisis point' which prompted this study. The observation of Eddy shows the everyday antics encountered in the classroom. It is when we look at the personal events outlined briefly in the introduction, and the concerns regarding the children's behaviour listed in 'Harried Hill', that it is possible to see how the tinder of frayed nerves from a demanding summer could so easily be ignited by the sparks of daily conflicts within the carriage. I could have dealt with each of these demands separately, yet coming one after the other, and drawing on depleted reserves, they became increasingly difficult. I have highlighted in italics, in the opening statement, the conflict I felt between my own need and my professional duties. I had faced this hurdle of overwhelming pressure before, but this time I was not able to round up my strength and carry on. I was exhausted. I could see my targets but had no way of meeting them. When I pulled back the throttle, nothing came out. I was just too tired. My health was suffering. I had lost my appetite, was unable to sleep or relax and was prone to tears, anxiety and panic attacks. I suffered skin complaints and could not remember things, make decisions easily or keep things in perspective.

In returning to the question, 'How am I ever going to get back in that classroom again?', I began to consider what was preventing me from doing so. Obviously something was stopping me. I asked myself, could I go back tomorrow? My answer was 'no', because nothing would have changed. The pressures would still be the same. I began to look at which of those pressures could be changed, and what I could do about changing them. I have already considered the difficult behaviour of some pupils within the class. The Special Educational Needs Co-ordinator and I appeared to have exhausted our strategies within the carriage, and it was to be a while before *Curriculum Organisation and Classroom Practice in Primary Schools* echoed my thoughts or gave rise to them is hard to say.

> With the introduction of the National Curriculum and the School Development Plan initiative, there has been a recognition that teachers must plan together to ensure consistency and progression across classes and year groups and that formally structured short and long term plans are essential to effective classroom teaching.
>
> (Alexander *et al.* 1992: 20)

I had also been trying to find my own philosophy for effective teaching practice while ducking the pendulum of change that was swinging again in educational ideology. I was very much aware, from my Initial Teacher Training period, of the polarisation between 'progressive' and 'formal' methods. At times I found myself lacking in confidence when faced with situations that required more formal teaching skills than I was used to. Alexander *et al.* also noted, giving regard to recent research into children's learning, that 'recent studies . . . place proper emphasis, on the teacher as teacher rather than "facilitator" ' (Alexander *et al.* 1992: 18). Again this was largely contrary to the messages that I had received during my training. It has taken me a long time to shake off the shackles of prejudice regarding certain teaching methods, such as whole class teaching, and develop my confidence in a wider range of skills. It became clear to me that effective links between Initial Teacher Training, Newly Qualified Teacher induction and continuing in-service provision, for the continuing development of teaching skills, are of great importance for confident and effective teaching. The management on the School Express also demonstrated their commitment to this by funding my higher degree.

I realised that through these first three years I had not only been experiencing the stress of meeting requirements with inadequate skills in some areas, for example, when more 'formal' methods would have delivered a teaching point more effectively, but had also been depriving myself of the chance to develop these skills through fear of doing 'the wrong thing'. One of the blessings of 'falling apart' as I did was that many unnecessary burdens were shown to be just that: unnecessary. I could not expect to do everything, and I became more able to put things in perspective.

December had passed, January was coming to an end and I was about to return to work. I was no longer exhausted. Something else had happened in me on my journey. I had shed the weighty luggage of the many unrealistic expectations that I had of myself and the children, and gained a new confidence in my teaching ability through my research. I was pleased to become acquainted with new insights into children's learning, especially in the work of Vygotsky and his theory of 'a zone of proximal development'; which 'refers to the gap that exists for children between what they can do alone and what they can do with help from someone more knowledgeable or skilled than themselves' (Vygotsky in Bourne 1994: 24). This helped dramatically to increase my confidence as a teacher and confirm my reason for being in the carriage. I was not just a facilitator who drew out what children already knew, but someone who had skills and knowledge to help them develop. If this was the case, though, how could I hope to provide adequate quality interaction to aid development in twenty-seven pupils by myself? I could see that I would have to plan well but lower my expectations of myself. I found this hard, knowing that the greater the input I could give in the early years, the greater the benefits would be as the pupils matured. Fortunately, though, during my absence a teaching assistant for Eddy and Todd had been allocated for five mornings per week, thus providing the opportunity for much more of this desired interaction and support.

So the train has pulled up at its next destination. I have left much baggage behind but I have also gained some. Through reflecting on the educational experience of the children I teach, and myself as learner and teacher, this study has enabled me to deepen my understanding and develop my classroom practice. It has also helped me to locate my personal experience within the insights of others and to draw strength from this, to use this time as a period of growth. Regardless of the varied educational terrain travelled, it is this element of reflection on personal circumstance and practice, informed by the wisdom of others and supported by rest, that has enabled me to put events into perspective and return to the classroom.

## References

Alexander, R., Rose, J. and Woodhead, C. (1992) *Curriculum Organisation and Classroom Practice in Primary Schools*, London: DES.

Bourne, J. (1994) 'A question of ability' in Bourne, J. (ed.), *Thinking Through Primary Practice*, London: Routledge.

Cochran-Smith, M. and Lytle, S.L. (1993) *Inside Outside: Teacher Research and Knowledge*, New York: Teachers College Press.

Department for Education (DfE) (1978) *Report of the Committee of Enquiry into the Education of Handicappd Children and Young People*, London: HMSO.

Dunham, J. (1992) *Stress in Teaching*, London: Routledge.

Dyson, A. (1990) 'Special Educational Needs and the concept of change', *Oxford Review of Education* 16(1): 55–66.

Hitchcock, G. and Hughes, D. (1989) *Research and the Teacher: A Qualitative Introduction to School-based Research*, London: Routledge.

Martin, A. (1988) 'Teachers and teaching: screening, early intervention and remediation – obscuring children's potential', *Harvard Educational Review* 58(4): 488–501.

Purkey, W.W. (1970) *Self-Concept and School Achievement*, Englewood Cliffs, NJ: Prentice Hall.

# Chapter 8

# 'Do you get some funny looks when you tell people what you do?'

## Muddling through some angsts and ethics of (being a male) researching with children

*John Horton*

### Introduction: why write about ethics (again)?

| | |
|---|---|
| *Miss H:*<br>(*Year 5 teacher*) | You say this is the first time you've done . . . anything like this? |
| *JH:* | Yes, yes it is. |
| *Miss H:* | Well you've got a real knack for getting children to talk, you know . . . I could just tell as soon as you started talking to them, you know, I thought 'he's good at talking with kids' . . . You're a natural at it. |
| *Miss H:* | . . . Do you get some funny looks when you tell people what you do? |
| *JH:* | Erm yes I probably do. |

This chapter is an attempt – and a plea – to *get real* about the ethics of practising social science '*with* children rather than *on* or *for* children' (Matthews *et al.* 1998: 312, emphasis in original). I am writing it because, when thinking, reading, writing and talking through the ethicality of (my) research amongst geographies of childhood, I am troubled by the following question.

> I have been called 'a natural at talking with kids'. I am 'police cleared' to conduct research with children. I have completed workshops on 'Child protection', 'Ethics of teaching and learning' and 'Implementing codes of practice'. My research conduct has always been well within the legal–ethical strictures of the Children Act 1989, the United Nations Convention on the Rights of the Child 1989 and the Human Rights Act 2000, as well as codes of practice prescribed by the Medical Research Council (1991), the British Sociological Society (1993), the Market Research Society (2000) and the National Children's Bureau (2000). I am confident that my past and proposed qualitative research with children is 'ethical' by all of the criteria laid down by

Matthews *et al.* (1998) and Valentine (1999). Why then, when all of these seductive ethical certainties (see White 1998) are subtracted, do I still feel a vague, nagging, indescribable sense of unease when recalling research I have done with children?

What remains after this subtraction? Approaching this question, I have extracted four empirical moments from my research with children when – looking back, reading the interview transcripts and discussing them with fellow researchers – my unease is heightened. There and then, these moments seemed 'off the point', 'a waste of time and tape' or just 'bad data'. Re-presented here and now, they over-run my ability fully to understand them (Strathern 1999), but suggest some causes of my unease. Individually and collectively, then, they gesture towards how research ethics might be made 'more alive, more real and more immediate' (Truzzi 1968: 1).

## Moment 1: 3.30 p.m., 5 July 1997

> Mr P (Year 4 teacher): I love [the kids] to bits, I just love teaching really . . . [But] it is difficult sometimes. I mean if you ever go to an interview for a teaching job . . . the first thing you get asked is 'why do you want to work with children?' They don't actually say '*you're a man*' but you just know that's why they're so quick to ask it. And that hurts . . . but its understandable. I mean you think 'what if I *was* dangerous?' . . . It's a bloody awful thing to say, but once you're in . . . what the hell could they do to stop you?

When I tell people about the research I am doing, I *do* usually get 'funny looks'; invariably these are followed by a barrage of morbidly curious or sarcastic questions: 'What if a child tells you they're being abused?'; 'What if you get accused of being abusive?'; 'What if you're a paedophile?'; 'How do we know you're not?'; 'How do *you* know you're not?; and so on. I know exactly what Mr P meant: 'they don't actually say '*you're a man*', but . . . '. This is a bitter pill to swallow but, like many other researchers currently interested in children's geographies, I cannot escape my resemblance to the following statistics:

> Many child abusers are highly respected members of the community. Many consciously or unconsciously choose career paths that will bring them regularly in contact with children, often working diligently to build an exemplary record of competence in their activities . . . Approximately 19 out of 20 identified sexual abusers are male, less than half are married. The national average age is 24.
>
> (Lenett and Crane 1996: 9)

Why do I feel so out of my depth when confronting this resemblance? Is it because reminders of the threat I supposedly pose are so irreconcilable with my happy memories of research with children? Or is it because this sort of threat was so absent from my own happy, probably pretty sheltered childhood? Or is it the realisation of just how flimsy and utterly inappropriate the literatures and idealistic pretensions of my academic training *feel* next to the unpleasant realities of child death, child abuse, paedophilia, 'paediatricians' mistaken for 'paedophiles' and so on. Or is it the helplessness of finding that 'the literature' has a blind spot to these issues (see Widdowfield 2000)? Or is it because of my inability to convincingly answer Mr P's latter question (*'what the hell could they do?'*)? After all, on reflection, I am simply amazed at the ease with which – lacking any uniform or, for that matter, any particularly rigorous proof of my identity, status or 'police clearance' – I have gained close, sometimes unattended, access to primary school children. I have found this a troubling position to have to think, practise and write my way through (McDowell 1992; Rose 1997). I am left with a vague feeling that research with children is something I *want* to be doing, something I'm *good* at doing, but not necessarily something I *ought* to be doing (after Thrift 2000a). For, while I do not think that I constitute a 'threat', the precedent set by my (ease of) access to children is potentially risky. For all my ethical safeguards and angsts, I am left feeling socially irresponsible for contributing to that precedent and opportunistically profiting from it, almost wishing that it had been made much harder for me (and people like me) to research. This unease is compounded when I reflect on research situations that could have 'gone either way' were I inclined to be a 'threat'.

## Moment 2: 10.30 a.m., 12 July 1997

*Dave (8):*   You're alright you!
*JH:*   Aw ta!
*Dave:*   Will you come over the park and play football after school mate?
*JH:*   Sorry, I can't, I don't think that'd be a good idea.
*Dave:*   Aw why not? Go on . . . It'll be really cool!

Was I patronising, paranoid, guilty of treating 'Dave' with 'kid gloves' in refusing to go 'over the park'? Or was I right to protect myself? After all, what *was* I afraid of? Reflecting on this moment, my unease is with precisely this ambivalence, with what *might* have happened, and with the frequency with which I have found myself in and of similarly ambiguous research settings and situations. I contend that such risky ambiguity is an inevitable consequence of (my) research with children being ethically and practically 'underdetermined', through an absence of directly relevant legislation, training, codes of practice and systems of regulation or accountability (and few literatures addressing these absences, although see Riches (1991) and Daniels and Jenkins (2000)). This is worryingly resonant with concerns of the Hunt Report into multiple abuse in nursery classes: . . .

> a key issue is that not all adults who have access to children at school are teachers. This is not, of course, to say that classroom helpers, students, playground supervisors, volunteer parent, meals staff [and, I would add, researchers], etc.

pose a greater threat than anyone else, but vetting procedures will operate more formally for teachers than for others.

(Newcastle upon Tyne City Council 1994: 14,

text in parentheses added)

On reflection, I have coped with resulting uncertainty over what to do with myself, and institutional confusion over whose responsibility I might be, by occupying positions in between and within institutional boundaries whilst researching, at once a potentially persuasive 'grown up' (with access to the staff room, conversations with teachers and cups of coffee between lessons, etc., approaching children with the blessing of other adults in positions of authority over them, and able – unwittingly or otherwise – to enrol or become enrolled in practices of peer group pressure) and a 'mate' who might go 'over the park' behind the teacher's back. This was no pre-planned strategy; *it just happened*.

## Moment 3: 10.00 a.m., 30 June 1997

*Mark (7):*    Postman Pat, Postman Pat, Postman Pat is a blackie . . .
            [*Group laughs.*]
*JH:*        Aw, that's not very nice is it?
*Mark:*      Blackies stink.
            [*Group laughs.*]
*Paul (7):*    Yeah, when they get on the bus, they smell the whole thing out.
            [*Group laughs.*]

Should I have challenged Mark's comments? Or should I have sat back, pragmatically accepting them as particularly insightful 'data' (or even laughed along, to encourage such insights)? Moments like this – which again *just happened*, in spite of rigorous ethical preparation – prompt a different sort of unease, through the reminder that children's geographies are often *horrible* to 'adult' sensibilities. My 'friendship group' interview transcripts are full of references to 'blackies', 'pakis', 'wogs', 'puffs', 'benders', 'gaylords' and 'spackers', words which – here and now – I find it hard to type, let alone say out loud. It would be impossible to write a 'real' account of my experiences in primary schools without using some of these words, or writing about children mercilessly bullying 'hearing impaired' and 'special needs' classmates, kicking a hedgehog to death in the playground or stabbing a baby blackbird with a compass. Nonetheless, I have difficulty reconciling to the fact that all of the above were important, intractable parts of the sorts of geographies I was investigating, with the fact that I would walk out if anyone sang 'Postman Pat is a blackie' in a social situation. Although operating in a far less emotionally charged context, I know the 'welter of emotions' and 'conflict' Rowles (1978: 179) describes in his account of research in hospices for the elderly:

> . . . sitting by his bed my mind would be a welter of emotions. Sometimes I experienced anger. 'Damn it, you can't die now. I haven't finished my

research.' Immediately I would be overtaken by feelings of self-revulsion. Did our friendship mean only this? Thus I would engage in a conflict between my human sensibilities and my scholarly purpose.

My unease is not so much that I *did not* plan for such conflicts, but more that they are 'not regular, repetitive, monotonous and predictable in a way that would allow them to be represented as rule guided . . . they cannot be exhausted by any "ethical code"' (Bauman 1993: 11), nor prepared for in any neat, complete, planful sense.

## Moment 4: 2.30 p.m., 11 July 1997

*Kerry (6):*   I've drawn a picture for you.
*JH:*            Aw ta!
*Kerry:*        It's not for your work, it's a present . . . It'll be rubbish next week when you're not here.
*JH:*            Aw!

My concern that no amount of 'ethical' reading or preparation can completely prescribe or alter what I might feel or do once *there* is amplified by moments such as this, where there was a different sort of conflict between my 'gut reaction' and societal responsibility. When researching with children I have always guarded against becoming *too* close, of being imagined as some kind of ideal round-the-clock buddy of a father figure, but I know exactly what Furlong and Maynard (1998: 111) mean: . . .

> it's easy to fall into the trap – react to something they've done . . . 'my pencil's gone', 'he's taken my book'. Sometimes I want to cuddle them, run after them in the playground, or play with them, just play . . . but I can't do that. I find that difficult.

I have found it similarly difficult to know what to do with myself when children volunteer to forgo breaktime to participate in research, ask me if they can chat with me about football or pop music, go out of their way to carry and tidy up stationery for me or cry on my departure when research ends. I remember these moments fondly precisely because of their unexpectedness and spontaneity, but this quality – the way they *just happened* in spite of my rigorous 'ethical' preparation – also makes me feel that I ought to sweep them under the carpet in case anyone might construe them as sinister. This contradiction troubles me, not least because of current trajectories of disciplinary enthusiasm towards 'the small scale, the local and the mundane . . . to break with the abstractions and pro-establishment complicities of . . . grand theory and empiricist research methods' (Crook 1998: 523), and towards the methodological or conceptual elision of distinctions between 'adulthood' and 'childhood' (Moore 1992; Wilson *et al.* 1999), suggest that future research might be characterised by more, rather than less, bodily and relational closeness between children and (potentially threatening) adults. These research futures urgently demand rigorously developed and *real* ethical futures.

## Conclusion: 'getting real' about ethics

> ...the cultural turn is caught up in its own pretensions. Written into its very fabric is a sense that it is both avant garde – ahead of the game – and, by extension, on the very margins of society...even though much of the cultural turn still consists of intellectual habits that might not have appeared out of place at the end of the last century, or before.
>
> (Thrift 2000b: 2)

Thrift's description of the 'cultural turn' – of which the present enthusiasm for research *with* children's geographies is a constituent and consequence (Philo 1992, 1997; Matthews *et al.* 2000) – 'turning bad' evokes a troubling caricature of researchers leaping before looking, bungling head first on to ethical *terrae incognitae* in their gung-ho enthusiasm to follow the latest disciplinary 'turn', without first stepping back to think through its ethical consequences or preconditions. This chapter's contribution to this step back has been to demand (or, more precisely, to articulate a demand for) a more 'real' ethics with which to attack the unease remaining even after 'seductive ethical certainties' are subtracted. I mean this in two senses. First, there is an urgent need to address aspects of research with children which have, for whatever reason, been hitherto *underrepresented*, or *unrepresented*. This means confronting head on the unpleasant nitty gritty of 'child protection' literatures and practices, sharing experiences within and between research communities and developing a rigorous micro-ethical sensibility to rival that prescribed for teachers, scout and youth leaders and the like. Second, there is an equally urgent need to address the possibility that many causes of *real* ethical unease – gut reactions, angsts, 'funny looks', 'what ifs', in fact practically everything that bothers me about the moments re-presented in this chapter – are unprescribable and unpredictable there and then, and *unrepresentable* here and now. This is an unsettling realisation. It demands much work to establish and practise 'relational, as opposed to individual, understandings of ethical agency and to recognise the significance of embodied, as against abstract, capacities in shaping ethical competence and considerability' (Whatmore 1997: 37). It also demands a more modest 'immature' ethical sensibility (Lee 1998), one that does not confidently claim to know it all – or be prepared for it all – before the event. In conclusion, then, I agree with Moore (1992: 129): . . .

> if we are going to 'do' work with children we have to use the child within, yet at the same time retain our professional knowledge and judgement. We have to be comfortable with ourselves as we are.

# References

Bauman, Zygmunt (1993) *Postmodern Ethics*, Oxford: Blackwell.

British Sociological Society (1993) *Statement of Ethical Practice* (archived at http://www.britsoc.org.uk/ethgu2.htm).

Crook, S. (1998) Minotaurs and other monsters: 'everyday life' in recent social theory, *Sociology*, 32, 523–540.

Daniels, D. and Jenkins, P. (2000) *Therapy with Children: Children's Rights, Confidentiality and the Law*, London: Sage.

Furlong, J. and Maynard, T. (1998) *Mentoring Student Teachers: The Growth of Professional Knowledge*, London: Routledge.

Lee, Nick (1998) Towards an immature sociology, *Sociological Review*, 46, 459–482.

Lenett, R. and Crane, B. (1996) *Its OK to Say No! A Parent/Child Manual for the Protection of Children*, Wellingborough: Thorson.

Market Research Society (2000) *Guidelines for Research among Children and Young People* (archived at http://mrs.org.uk/code.htm).

Matthews, Hugh, Limb, Melanie and Taylor, Mark (1998) The geography of childhood: some ethical and methodological considerations for project and dissertation work, *Journal of Geography in Higher Education*, 22, 311–324.

Matthews, Hugh, Taylor, Mark, Sherwood, Kenneth, Tucker, Faith and Limb, Melanie (2000) Growing up in the countryside: children and the rural idyll, *Journal of Rural Studies*, 16, 141–153.

McDowell, Linda (1992) Doing gender: feminism, feminists and research methods on human geography, *Transactions of the Institute of British Geographers*, 17, 399–416.

Medical Research Council (1991) *The Ethical Conduct of Research on Children* (archived at http://www.mrc.ac.uk/ethics b.html).

Moore, J. (1992) *The ABC of Child Protection*, Aldershot: Arena.

National Children's Bureau (2000) *Guidelines for Research with Children* (archived at http://www.ncb.org.uk/resguide.htm).

Newcastle upon Tyne City Council (1994) *Independent Enquiry into Multiple Abuse in Nursery Classes (the Hunt Report)*, Newcastle upon Tyne: Newcastle upon Tyne City Council.

Philo, Chris (1992) Neglected rural geographies: a review, *Journal of Rural Studies*, 8, 193–207.

Philo, C. (1997) War and peace in the social geography of children, paper delivered at meeting of the Economic and Social Research Council 'Children 5–16' programme, University of Keele, 17 March.

Riches, P. (1991) The Children Act: an overview, *Children and Society*, 5, 3–10.

Rose, Gillian (1997) Situating knowledges: positionality, reflexivities and other tactics, *Progress in Human Geography*, 21, 305–320.

Rowles, Graham (1978) Reflections on experiential fieldwork, in: Ley, D. and Samuels, M.S. (eds) *Humanistic Geography*, London: Croom Helm, 173–193.

Strathern, Marilyn (1999) *Property, Substance and Effect*, London: Athlone Press.

Thrift, Nigel (2000a) Afterwords, *Environment and Planning D: Society and Space*, 18, 213–255.

Thrift, Nigel (2000b) Introduction: dead or alive?, in: Cook, Ian, Crouch, David, Naylor, Simon and Ryan, James (eds) *Cultural Turns/Geographical Turns: Perspectives on Cultural Geography*, London: Prentice Hall, 1–6.

Truzzi, M. (1968) *Sociology and Everyday Life*, London: Prentice Hall.

Valentine, Gill (1999) Being seen and heard? The ethical complexities of working with children and young people at home and at school, *Ethics, Place and Environment*, 2, 141–155.

Whatmore, Sarah (1997) Dissecting the autonomous self: hybrid cartographies for a relational ethics, *Environment and Planning D: Society and Space*, 15, 37–53.

White, Susan (1998) Interdiscursivity and child welfare: the ascent and durability of psycho-legalism, *Sociological Review*, 46, 265–292.

Widdowfield, Rebekah (2000) The place of emotions in academic research, *Area*, 32, 199–208.

Wilson, K., Kendrick, P. and Ryan, V. (1999) *Play Therapy: A Non-directive Approach*, London: Bailliere Tindall.

# Chapter 9

# 'This won't take long...'

## Interviewing, ethics and diversity

*Carol Vincent and Simon Warren*

## Introduction

This chapter draws on data collected for a qualitative project which studied the role of parent groups and organizations in relation to the mainstream education system. It considers the factors affecting the development of our relationships with diverse respondents and the implications of these varied relations for the research process. Before turning to these issues, however, we offer some background to the project. We refer to the various parent groups by the collective label of Parent Centred Organizations (PCOs). Such organizations are of interest to researchers because they often have a mediating function. That is, they intervene in interactions between individual parents and educational institutions. They may do this by offering parents information, support and, in some cases, advice and advocacy, relating to educational issues. PCOs provide a channel through which parents can become involved in, and try to influence, processes of teaching and learning; a channel that is separate from their relationships with their own children's schools. We were particularly interested in the extent to which such groups and organizations disseminated notions of an 'appropriate' parental role in relations to schools.

Discourses surrounding parenthood and responsibility, and the related notions of a 'good' parent, have a long history. The attributes required of a parent have altered over time, in accordance with socio-political and economic imperatives (Brown 1990). We wished to consider dominant discourses of parenting with specific reference to children's schooling. Currently, for instance, home – school agreements, which enshrine an individual school's version of 'appropriate' parenting, are mandatory for UK schools. In most cases, it appears that the role considered suitable for parents is one which is supportive of the professionals and also subordinate to them (Vincent and Tomlinson 1997).

The research therefore explores the extent to which PCOs disseminate attitudes, values and beliefs about the 'appropriate' role for parents in relation to the education system and – the second part of the equation – parents' responses and reactions to this. We collected data through the study of four very different parents' groups, their variety being indicative of the ways in which parents in the UK can become involved in educational issues, other than, or in addition to, their relationship with their own child's individual school. The four were:

- an advice centre offering parents information and support with regard to special educational needs provision;
- a parent education group offering parents an accredited practical skills course which involved the students in making educational materials suitable for early years children;
- a pressure group, campaigning for enhanced educational funding;
- a self-help support group of African-Caribbean women who met to discuss various educational issues.

As the first two groups – the advice centre and the parent education group – were run by professionals for parents, a major theme for analysis was professional – parent–client relationships. We identified a Gramscian framework as providing a useful starting point for our overall analysis, and we have written about this in detail elsewhere (Vincent 1997). For the purposes of this chapter, we want to consider just one idea, that of 'structures of feeling', which is derived from Gramsci's work, and which we felt usefully applied to a study of professional – client relationships. We examined the role that the PCOs' professional staff played in relation to the dissemination of ideas around 'appropriate' parenting. One of the focal points of Gramscian theory is the role of 'intellectuals', which he described as that of 'deputies' to the dominant group (1971: 12). Gramsci argued that in the course of their work, those we would now call professionals, such as doctors, priests and teachers, disseminated hegemonic beliefs in order to win the 'active consent' of subaltern social groups. Our research asked whether this role was applicable to this particular group of welfare professionals, and if so, how was it enacted? Renate Holub (1992) argues that professionals disseminate ideas and values through a shared '*structure of feeling*', a concept she derives from Gramsci's notion of '*esprit de corps*'. The term '*structure of feeling*' describes the series of assumptions, ideas, and values that structure communication between members of a 'community'. It was used in this sense by Raymond Williams, in an attempt to describe an area of activity where the individual and the collective, the public and the private meet. Fazal Rizvi describes Williams's understanding of the term:

> Williams uses the term 'structure of feeling' to describe 'the most delicate and least tangible part of our activity' (Williams 1977: 64). It is the structure of feeling that makes intimate communication between people in a community possible because it contains the taken-for-granted assumptions and the key ideas that gives a community its qualitative coherence.
>
> (Rizvi 1993: 150)

A 'structure of feeling' is a distillation of many elements, feelings and assumptions: the elements of place, of history, of economics, feelings of belonging, exclusion or 'ownership', and assumptions of values and beliefs that translate into 'mental maps', attitudes, and actions (Taylor *et al.* 1996). The term has pluralist connotations as there are many different communities with varying 'structures of feeling' arising from diverse experiences, assumptions, and exclusions. Briefly, Holub argues that professionals working in a particular location have *partial* access to that 'community's' 'structure of feeling', and can utilize that access to propose and propound values that support the status quo (Holub 1992). However, Gramsci also argued that the relationship between professional and nonprofessional may succeed in opening up spaces in which dominant understandings can be disrupted, thereby producing political counter-hegemony (Showstack Sassoon 1980; Femia 1981).

In this chapter, however, our aims are slightly different. We are not focusing on the access that the case study professionals had to the 'structures of feeling' of their clients. Instead we wish to analyse and evaluate *our* access to the different 'structures of feeling' inhabited by the various respondents involved in the project. We seek to do this by problematizing the relationships between respondents and ourselves. We consider a number of issues – negotiating access, securing informed consent, the debates around symmetry and asymmetry between researcher and respondent, the processes of interviewing, data analysis and dissemination – and comment on the formation and development of our relationships with respondents. We seek, in particular, to tease out the differences and similarities of age, race, social class, language, and gender, and to suggest how these disjunctions and connections affected the process of data collection and analysis. Finally, we conclude with a brief consideration of the implications of our arguments for future research design and conduct.

## Problematizing researcher–respondent relationships

### An attempt at reflexivity

This chapter constitutes an attempt to look reflexively at our conduct of the PCO project, concentrating in particular on the relationships we established with respondents. Reflexivity is now a fairly established part of qualitative research, particularly that informed by postpositivist, critical ethnographic or feminist stances. As Kelly *et al.* (1994: 46) comment:

> Feminists have been stern critics of 'hygienic research'; the censoring out of the mess, confusion and complexity of doing research, so that accounts bear little or no relation to the real [*sic*] events. But many accounts are full of silences too.

We agree strongly with their last statement. All attempts at reflexivity should be recognized as highly partial. 'Confessional' research is to some degree, and despite appearances to the contrary, 'a selective reconstruction of the research process'

(Troyna 1994: 7; see also Paechter 1996). In this case, we remain the arbiter of what we disclose, and what we do not, of how such disclosures are framed and presented for public consumption. In this context, our voices as researchers remain dominant, even when it is the research respondents who are speaking.

The formation and development of relationships between respondents and ourselves were influenced, as is always the case, by myriad factors, including gender, ethnicity, and differential backgrounds, occupations, and perceived status. The next sections attempt to elucidate some of these connections and discrepancies and point to their potential effects on the data gathered.

## Access: informed consent?

In two of our case studies (the advice centre and the parent education group) access was initially negotiated via the professionals working with the parents. This immediately raises questions about who has the power of refusal. The professionals concerned were White, middle class and involved in education, as we are. The manager of the advice centre was previously known to one of us revealing shared social networks. Therefore we shared certain aspects of the 'structures of feeling' of this group. Obviously each interview at the advice centre, whether with parent or worker, was negotiated with every individual concerned, but by this point the 'negotiations' were rather more perfunctory.

This also applied in the parent education group. After the course tutor had expressed interest in the project, one of us (CV) went to visit the group to talk with the women students about the project. Nobody demurred. But it may have appeared to them that to do so would have meant positioning themselves in opposition both to Christine, the course tutor, and perhaps to their peers. Our experience of the actual interviews leads us to emphasize a slightly different point. None of the women students showed any reluctance to talk, or to answer questions, and most were extremely forthcoming and expansive in their answers. Being asked about one's own views and opinions, having a sympathetic listener as one recounts part of one's life story, is often quite seductive, and we think for most of the women the experience was an enjoyable one. We also kept personal questions about their own home circumstances to a minimum, relying on the information which was volunteered, and concentrating most of the questions on their perceptions of the course, and the effect it had had on them and their children.

However, we felt, as we did on occasion with other groups of respondents in this study, that neither the research itself nor our explanations had much meaning for the women. In saying that, we are not suggesting that they did not understand the words or concepts we used, but rather that the idea of conducting such a research project simply seemed a rather bizarre thing to be doing. One of the difficulties of the research design and conceptualization was that of making it seem coherent to participants. The case studies appeared so disparate that it was quite difficult to justify the threads and linkages between them without resorting to the developing conceptual framework. However, we found it consistently difficult to express that in language shorn of its academic references. This contrasted with earlier research one of us had done on parent–teacher relationships in primary schools (Vincent 1996a), which had an immediate and accessible rationale from the perspective of respondents. Parent–teacher interactions were a part of the experience of all the respondents, whereas a research focus on diverse parents' groups and organizations seemed by contrast hazier and less concrete.

Although over the course of the time spent with the group we tried out various ways of explaining the study, and what we were hoping to achieve, none of them seemed completely satisfactory. However, we worried less about this as the research progressed and we got to know the women better. Finally, we came to the conclusion that the research and ourselves were just not particularly important in these women's lives (see also Phoenix 1994). At best, we offered a period of undivided interest in and attention to what they had to say (which several said they enjoyed). At worst, we asked a series of questions of which they did not really see the point but that were at least not overly intrusive. However, we remain doubtful as to whether we could claim that we had fulfilled the basic ethical principle of obtaining informed consent.

## Symmetry and asymmetry

When we contacted the tutor of the parent education group to discuss researching the students' experiences of the course, she commented that she felt it would be more appropriate for Carol to conduct the research, rather than Simon. Carol's femaleness was seen as having less disruptive potential than Simon's maleness, and she would be, by virtue of her gender, in a better position to build a rapport with the women who attended the group. Implicit in such a view of course is the idea that researcher–respondent symmetry is crucial for 'good' qualitative research. Anne Oakley's (1981) seminal paper argued that women researchers and respondents are capable of building a close rapport based on their shared experiences of being female within a patriarchal society (see also Finch 1984). A similar argument has been applied to race-related research, with the additional critique that the focus of White researchers on Black people themselves has too often resulted in Black individuals and groups being defined as problematic, rather than critically analysing oppressive institutional power structures (Bourne 1980; Lawrence 1982). In the light of these criticisms, gender and ethnic matching appears to offer the possibility of nonexploitative, nonhierarchical researcher–respondent relationships. However, the link between the (justifiable) criticisms and the 'solution' owes something to a sleight of hand. Gender and ethnicity matching are rooted in a 'realist epistemology, the central tenet of which is that there is a unitary truth about respondents and their lives which interviewers need to obtain', (Phoenix 1994: 66). Such an approach has been challenged of course (e.g. Stanley and Wise 1993), on the grounds that it overlooks all the other possible aspects, contradictions and disruptions – pertaining to class, age, occupation, race, gender and so on – which influence not only the individual identities of both researcher and respondent, but also their relationship with each other. A good example of this is provided by

Mehreen Mirza's (1998) account of her relationships with women of South Asian origin. Despite the matching between herself and her interviewees on the grounds of gender and ethnicity, Mirza notes that placing did not always occur. Placing, she explains, refers to the way in which we use personal attributes and characteristics to place one another within wider social structures. However, Mirza's occupation, her wearing of non-traditional dress, her lack of familial links to the communities which she was researching, the fact that she lived apart from her own family, all contributed to the difficulties her respondents, many of whom were from more conservative communities, had in placing her. Instead she sometimes found herself consigned to a role as 'other' rather than the 'same' (see also Connolly 1996; see Farhana Sheikh's *The Red Box* (1991) for a fictionalized account of some of these issues).

As Mirza points out (1998: 92), identities are 'multi-layered', 'based on a host of structures', and continually open to '(re)negotiation and (re)invention'. Therefore an attempt to explain an individual's subjectivity in terms of one subject position is unlikely to capture that complexity. Close researcher–respondent relationships may develop despite a lack of obvious symmetry. Mac an Ghaill (1988) presents an example of this in his research presented in *Young, Gifted and Black*. In a later paper, he discusses the close relationships that developed between himself (a White teacher) and his young, Black respondents. As one of them, Judith, explains

> You can't show what it's like for a black woman in this society and of course we should carry out our own studies, but you can't reduce everything to race. We all had black teachers, but we felt close to you. It all depends on things like your political position. Like I would agree more with your interpretation of our lives at school and college than a black conservative view, or a black man's view that was sexist. Of course, I'm biased because we contributed so much to the study. You took serious the way that we saw things, you listened.
>
> (quoted in Mac an Ghaill 1991: 113)

Nor is it self-evident that a close identification between researcher and respondent is necessarily a 'good thing'. It may mean that the one of the pair will assume what is known and understood between them, which may be counter-productive for the researcher's attempt to understand the respondent's subjectivity. Mirza (1998) notes that there were advantages for her research, if not herself personally, of not being easily placed as it allowed her to become a 'stranger within' (Collins 1990) and often prompted her respondents to explain their perspectives, reasoning, and understandings to her in detail, assuming that she would be unfamiliar with what we have termed their 'structures of feeling'.

## Disjunctions and connections

As our research project involved professionals and clients from four very different parent organizations located in London and the Midlands, it involved an extremely heterogeneous group of respondents. This resulted in a different pattern of symmetries and asymmetries between ourselves and respondents. Of course, group differences and similarities are not the only things to affect the development of researcher–respondent relationships: individual temperament and personal differences clearly have a role to play, cross-cutting group symmetries and asymmetries. However, the complex intersection of race, class, gender, and professional background between ourselves and the different groups of respondents throws some light on the way in which research relationships are constructed and the constraints and opportunities thereby afforded.

For reasons of space, we shall concentrate on the two case-study groups run by professionals for parents as they provide examples of diverse relationships. [. . .]

With regard to the parent education group, we have already noted that shared gender was perceived as a basis for establishing mutual placing with the student respondents. However, through the course of the fieldwork, I (CV) became aware of the asymmetry between myself and respondents. My position within a university, the way I spoke, the fact that I was from outside the local area, my ethnicity in the case of the Bangladeshi women students, all set me apart from the group. These disjunctions were sharpened by the fact that my position within the group was clearly different from that of the students. Sometimes, the course tutor referred to me when in doubt over particular things – spellings perhaps, or bits of 'general' knowledge. We also had acquaintances in common whom she would occasionally mention. On one occasion, Christine invited me to a session of the All-Party Parliamentary Group on Parenting (a group of Members of Parliament and members of the House of Lords interested in issues around parenting) to give a 'research input' to its members. This meeting necessitated Christine missing a session with the parent education group, and she explained this to the women, saying, 'Carol and I are going to an important meeting at the Houses of Parliament'. I had happily agreed to attend seeing it as a small way of being able to thank Christine for her support of the research. I had not, however, realized that this positioning within an apparently 'elite' group would serve to (re)emphasize my 'otherness' to the women students. As a result of these disjunctions, I felt keenly that my participation in the practical course activities was a clear piece of play-acting. Unlike the students, who had to fulfil course requirements, I had no need to learn how to make flowers from wool, or do 'magic water' experiments. As a result of all this, I felt I was positioned as the other 'adult' in a classroom situation, with the course tutor as teacher and the students as pupils.

My perceptions of the distance between myself and the women in the group arose, therefore, partly as a result of the different structural locations that we inhabited, which were reflected in my positioning within the group. These could have been ameliorated, perhaps, with a different research design, one that allowed us to spend longer periods of time with the group over the course of the year. This would been of considerable help in allowing us to become more integrated into the group. However, time constraints made this impossible. Our project consisted of four case studies, and as we were only funded for a year, the pressure to complete the fieldwork was intense. This could be seen as a flaw in the research design and we are willing to accept it as such. However, we question whether funding could have been obtained for a project with a much narrower focus.

My relationships with many of the group members underwent a qualitative shift due to one particular event. Having not seen the group over the summer I went back in the autumn with the news that I was pregnant. Although the women, without exception, had been extremely friendly towards me, and ready to chat informally during the sessions or in the tea-break, I had noticed that they rarely asked me questions about myself. This changed when I became pregnant, and the growing baby and the experience of pregnancy proved to be popular topics of conversation. On consideration, this shift is unsurprising. The teacher–taught relationship was neatly reversed. This was my first pregnancy, and at that time I knew relatively little about pregnancy and birth. The majority of the women had two, three, and in several cases four or five children. Motherhood was a crucial aspect of their identity and one I was preparing to share.

The parents' advice centre produced the most heterogeneous range of respondents. The professionals and clients were male and female, of various ethnicities, social classes, and ages. During the periods of time we spent at the centre, we felt we had developed good relationships with the workers, and with some of the parent clients. However, we felt we failed to do this in relation to particular parents. Many of the centre's clients were working-class Bangladeshi parents from the well-established local Bangladeshi community. We negotiated permission to visit some of these parents through the intervention of the Bangladeshi workers at the centre. We then visited those parents at home with an interpreter, a woman of Bangladeshi origin who lived locally, dressed in Bangladeshi style (as did all our respondents), was not connected to the centre or the LEA and was fluent in Sylheti (the relevant Bangladeshi dialect) and English. Our interpreter was not trained, but she had all the advantages just listed, and indeed she seemed an excellent interpreter. However, even with her help, we very often left a house feeling that we had not succeeded in placing or being placed by our respondents. Actually, that is not quite right, they *did* place us, but not in a way we wished to be placed. For our respondents, we think, we were another set of White middle-class professionals turning up on their doorstep to ask them about their children's difficulties (although we were actually interested in their experiences of the advice centre). For some, especially those whose children had physical as well as learning difficulties, we were the latest in a very long line of professionals asking them to tell us their story. It is perhaps unsurprising that the differences between us as researchers and other educational and social service professionals, differences that seemed so acute to us, seemed so blurred to them. Although they answered our questions, and gave us information, we felt we had failed to make connections with these parents, in other words, to access their structures of feeling.

This has implications for the data collected. The risk is that the absences and silences of these Bangladeshi parents are understood in a way which reflects negatively upon them as parents rather than upon us as researchers. This danger was brought home to us in a separate evaluation of the advice centre, conducted by others but concurrently with our research, which drew upon the data in our interim report to suggest that Bangladeshi parents were more likely to be 'passive and dependent' in their relationships with the advice centre workers, a conclusion our own report had not reached. On reflection, we feel that had we been able to carry out repeat interviews our relationships with all the respondents would have benefited. Repeat interviewing would have allowed a closer relationship to have developed which may have made the respondents feel more comfortable with us personally, as well as more involved in the research, able perhaps to ask us about the study, question our agendas, findings, and interpretations. However, as we noted earlier, the exigencies of obtaining funding for research do encourage a 'hit and run' climate as shorter, apparently more cost-effective studies proliferate.

## Interviewing

We find the ideas of 'translation' and 'interpretation' useful here – both in a literal sense, and also as a metaphor for the researcher–respondent interaction during the interview, and especially for the processes of data analysis which the researcher undertakes (see later text).

The attention focused on the 'postmodern moment' has meant that the assumptions inherent in the interview process have been problematized further still. The literary turn, what Norman Denzin (1994) has labelled the 'crisis of representation and the crisis of legitimacy', has raised fundamental questions about the stability of language. As James Scheurich notes,

> The language out of which questions [and responses – CV and SW] are constructed is not bounded or stable; it is persistently slippery, unstable, and ambiguous from person to person, from situation to situation, from time to time.
>
> (1997: 62)

He continues (1997: 73) by employing a phrase of Foucault's, that 'an indeterminate ambiguity, a 'wild profusion' lies at the heart of the interview interaction'. He argues that researchers cannot therefore claim to simply *present* their respondents' views. Instead, they are involved in a process of carefully and systematically *creating* ordered packets of meaning from a swirl of indeterminacy.

This process is made even more explicit when an interpreter is present for the interview, adding another voice to the interaction. The resulting texts then contain the views and ideas of the respondent as understood by the interpreter. In our experience, interpreters vary in the extent to which they seek to translate not only the words (slippery as these are) but also the meanings and perceptions that inform the words. Whilst this can alert White monolingual researchers, such as ourselves, to nuances, the impact of which they may have overlooked, it clearly adds another interpretive layer to the process, influenced by the interpreter's own social positioning.

Scheurich also questions another aspect of the symmetry/asymmetry issue: the idea that there is an asymmetry of power in the interview interaction in favour of the researcher, but that the researcher can and should try to rectify this by 'empowering' respondents (empowerment being a notably slippery and we suggest a somewhat grandiose claim, see, for example, Troyna 1994; Fielding 1996; Vincent 1996b). There are a number of points to be made here. Certainly, the concern is an important one. A researcher with a fixed list of questions, visiting a respondent once and then 'disappearing' with the data (i.e. a part of the respondent's 'world-view') cannot be said to have engaged in an egalitarian relationship, or made the respondent feel that she/he could actively contribute to the shaping of the research process. However, as Scheurich argues, it is a mistake to assume that respondents are always the 'powerless' ones during the interview interaction. Indeed, when an interpreter is involved, the researcher's (apparent) control of the interview is often explicitly ceded to the interpreter as he/she is the one who is actively engaged in constructing a direct relationship with the respondent. A different example is offered by Sarah Neal (1995) who documents a situation – herself as a young, female PhD student, trying to elicit the views of male, middle-aged vice-chancellors on the equal opportunities policies within their universities – which reverses assumptions about the power balance during an interview. Nor is this 'resistance' to the researcher and his/her questions confined to situations whereby the respondent can call on structural and institutional sources of power.

> Interviewees do not simply go along with the researcher's program, even if it is structured rather than open. I find that interviewees carve out spaces of their own; that they can often control some or part of the interview; that they push against or resist my goals, my intentions, my questions, my meanings. Many times I have asked a question that the respondent has turned into a different question that she or he wants to answer. While sometimes this may be the effect of misunderstanding, at other times, it is the interviewee asserting his or her own control over the interview. In other words interviewees are not passive subjects; they are active participants in the interaction.
>
> (Scheurich 1997: 71)

We saw examples of this process as we sifted through the interview transcripts. It is harder, however, to give illustrations in the short quote form that is acceptable and possible in papers such as this one. The examples do not lend themselves to easy extraction, being firmly embedded in the text of the interview; particular themes, questions, misunderstandings surface and then disappear during the course of the conversation. However, we have attempted to give an example by presenting this extract from an early interview in the project's history, a discussion with a key activist in the campaigning group. Our reading of the interview suggests to us that he is not wholly comfortable with the language of social class, and, perhaps picking this up, our questions lack clarity.

SW:          When you say parents, are they men, women, what kind of jobs?

Respondent:  I would say 60–70%, no possibly 75% are women, it may even be higher. They are mainly in white-collar jobs, but there are quite a few in the local group who are in blue-collar jobs. In Midshire City, there are quite a few more that are teachers or involved in the Health Service.
             [conversation moves on to discuss the role played by parents who are also teachers]

CV:          You mentioned the middle classes, and also you were talking earlier about Middle England . . .

R:           They're not necessarily the same thing.

CV:          Right. One of the things we're particularly interested in is the range of parents [the group] reaches. Does it reach out to different groups in terms of social class, to the inner cities for instance?
             [group membership had a rural/suburban majority]

R:           Yes, very much so.

CV:          How does it manage that, because most groups find that quite hard?

R:           I think at the top we've got some very, very committed people who are not concerned about class, or class bias. We've got people that have come up through the system, and have seen the devastation caused by elitism in education [elaborates on this point] . . . We've got local groups in what you would call the Shire counties, we're getting new groups in Sussex, in Kent, the Tory heartlands . . . [he talks about the large class sizes to be found in schools in these places, we try and reintroduce social class]

CV:          What research there is on voluntary groups and the people who get involved with them does suggest that people who do get involved tend to have a middle-class lifestyle. Would you say that was true of [the campaigning group]?

R:           No, I think it crosses all barriers and I think that's been its success. I mean I think we've been lucky that we had this [group's logo] at an early stage [goes onto talk about logo]
             . . . We go into schools all over the country, I've been into, I don't know how many schools, and spoken to a dozen parents in, you know, some fairly low, fairly deprived areas, so I think the beauty is, and I think you're right, the beauty is that we attract across the social divide . . .

We had, of course, made no such suggestion.

This extract also provides an example of Scheurich's concept of 'chaos/freedom'. Having emphasized respondent resistance to the researcher's agenda, he insists that the dominance–resistance binary lacks sufficient explanatory power. He adds a third space, which he calls 'chaos/freedom':

> [This] is everything that occurs that is neither dominance nor resistance, every-thing that escapes this binary is chaos (because it is not encapsulated by the binary) and represents openness or freedom for the interviewee.... There is more to living, working and interviewing than can be circumscribed by the dominance–resistance binary.... For instance the researcher may perform for the interviewee for reasons that have nothing to do with the dominance of the goal of the research. The researcher may use the interview experience to satisfy his/her relational or emotional needs. The same is true of the interviewee.... Many aspects of the interview interaction simply exceed either the dominance of the researcher... and the resistance of the interviewee to that dominance.
>
> (1997: 72–73)

## Data analysis

Another related set of issues surrounds the process of data analysis. It is at this point that the researcher's power is unrivalled by respondents (Limerick *et al.* 1996: 457). As Coffey argues (1996: 72), 'crafting authoritative texts is not an innocent' objective process of representation, rather it is a highly subjective process of creation, as we forge 'our story of their story' (Limerick *et al.* 1996: 450).

The problems bound up in this understanding of data analysis are legion. We will concentrate on two here: the process of thinking and writing about the data, and the process of dissemination. [...] It is as crucial to theorize the process of data collection as to theorize about the data itself:

> Contrast what the researcher brings to the written representation with what I argue is the radical, indeterminate ambiguity or openness that lies at the heart of the interview interaction itself, at the lived intersection of language, meaning, and communication. The researcher then fills this indeterminate openness with her or his interpretative baggage; imposes names, categories, constructions, conceptual schemes, theories upon the unknowable; and believes that the indeterminate is now located, constructed, known. Order has been created. The restless appropriative spirit of the researcher is (temporarily) at peace.
>
> (Scheurich 1997: 74)

Ribbens and Edwards (1998a) approach this crucial issue of presentation of data from a slightly different angle. For them the dilemma is how to present marginalized cultures understandings, and ways of living within Western public and academic discourses. They argue that the juxtaposition of 'authentic' respondents' voices with academic writing can make those voices appear naive and simple. Beverley Skeggs

(1994) reaches similar conclusions in relation to her own research:

> I became aware of how, when interspersing the young women's spoken com-
> ments into my academic writing, they were made to sound authentic and
> simple . . . . Ethnography requires the researcher/writer to adopt stylistic tech-
> niques usually associated with literature. It relies upon particular narrative and
> constructive methods. It defines topics, shifts from one locale to another, jux-
> taposes other perspectives and thus decides which context, and at what level
> and from whose perspective the reader will see. It uses the label of authentic
> voice to give weight to the shifts.
>
> (1994: 86)

Presenting respondents' voices involves a process of 'translation', but much can
get lost or corrupted in that process. Kay Standing (1998) considers this issue and
concludes:

> The dilemmas we face as feminists writing the voices of the less powerful are
> those of translation and compromise. How much of the women's voices and
> experiences do we lose by translating them into more academic language? Yet
> if we do not translate . . . their words, how do we stop reproducing dominant
> cultural constructions of poor and working class women? It is the dilemma of
> trying to challenge not reproduce hierarchies of power and knowledge; the
> dilemma of not losing the 'authenticity', emotion and vibrancy of women's
> voices, whilst not positioning them as 'Other'; and distancing ourselves from
> the political challenge of feminist research in the so called 'objective' language
> of academia.
>
> (1998: 201)

[. . .]

The parallels between 'writing up' (a term that suggests a straightforward recording of reality) ethnography and writing fiction have often been noted (e.g. Van
Maanen 1995). Amanda Coffey (1996) gives an example of this in relation to her
study of graduate trainees in a large accountancy firm. When she returned to the
field after a period away, she became aware that her portrayal of her respondents
was slightly nuanced to emphasize the points she was making. Her 'roles as observer
and selective filter, note-taker, reader and author' (1996: 66) had served to accentu-
ate particular individual characteristics and minimize others. Patti Lather and Chris
Smithies (1997) address this issue in their book on women living with HIV/AIDS.
They make a deliberate effort to interrupt their authorial authority by interweav-
ing interview texts, sections engaging with the history, poetry, and sociology of
HIV/AIDS, and comments from the researchers on the research process. This mul-
tilayered textual fabric serves to disrupt expectations of a conventional narrative
structure told through the expert authority of the researcher (Lather 1997).

### Dissemination

As Coffey notes (1996: 61), the negotiation of 'space, voice and authority in the research enterprize and its productions' can be highly problematic. Once access is agreed, however, it is likely that different interpretations of 'reality' between respondents and researcher will not come to light until some feedback is provided.

This proved a critical point for Coffey when the multinational accountancy firm objected strongly to parts of her account. She comments that the institutional power of a large multinational firm which could potentially be used against her and against the graduate trainees allowed the firm to question the authenticity of her text and in doing so question her authorial authority. However, other groups of respondents do not have recourse to such power, and in these cases it is possible for the researcher's voice to remain dominant, in the way in which we described earlier, even in apparently confessional accounts.

This became clear to us during a debate with a key respondent over a draft paper concerning the parent education group. The paper sought to juxtapose our initial reading of the parent education course with the more positive interpretation of the students, and asked questions about the meaning of this apparent contradiction. We felt that this tentativeness, this attempt to 'deal in paradoxes and resist theoretical closure' (Ball 1997: 268) was a strength. However, we had overlooked the power which accrued to us, as authors, through the process of fashioning an account. This was strongly brought home to us when we sent a draft of the paper to the group's tutor, Christine. The tentativeness, the openness to other readings, the nuances of academic writing was, to her, a chimera. Instead she read our account as sweeping and insensitive, the theorizing as alienating and abstract. Her anger and feelings of betrayal were evident. We spent a long time talking to Christine, to each other, and to other colleagues to try and understand how this situation had arisen. [. . .]

Colleen Larson (1997) recommends engaging in 'deliberative dialogue' to allow the negotiation of meanings between the researcher and the respondent. Indeed we accept that we should have spent more time discussing the developing analysis and its theoretical underpinnings with the group *as a whole* (for the students' reactions and responses were still missing). This form of dissemination and negotiation is an ethical practice much praised but – despite some notable exceptions especially amongst feminist researchers (e.g. Lather and Smithies 1997) – more infrequently practiced by social science researchers. Christine made some important comments which we incorporated into the published version of the paper. However, despite our attempt at collaboration, we acknowledge that the power of the account, the way in which the written word generates implications of authority and 'correctness', still rested with us as authors.

## Conclusion

In this chapter we have reflected on the processes of forming and developing relationships with a heterogeneous range of respondents. Those processes raised a number of ethical dilemmas concerning negotiating access, the incomplete nature of apparently informed consent, interviewing, data analysis, and dissemination. We have tried to indicate the differences and similarities of age, race, social class, language, profession, gender, and motherhood between ourselves and the respondents, and to identify the impact of these disjunctions and connections on the research process. We do not have space in this chapter to foreground in its entirety, what Scheurich (1997) calls our 'interpretive baggage', the intellectual and personal values, histories and beliefs with which we approached the research, but this too is clearly important if the reader is to be offered as much information as possible to allow him/her to engage with our conclusions (although it is important to remain alert to the dangers of excessive 'navel-gazing'!).

Such a process of reflection can be defended only if this undertaking to examine the ways in which our actions and beliefs shape the research process informs future work. With this in mind, we derive two main, and fairly simple, conclusions. The first is the desirability of a research design that allows for repeat interviews, if we are aiming to develop egalitarian and nonexploitative relationships with key respondents. 'Hit and run' research allows the respondents very little space in which to try and access the research process, let alone try and influence it. The second conclusion is that we need to acknowledge the processes of interpretation in which we engage during analysis. As we are involved in creating meaning, maintaining contact with respondents is a vital strategy (although by no means an unproblematic one) for ensuring that we include their views and understandings of our attempts to present and translate their words into a public academic arena. It has become almost commonplace amongst qualitative researchers to acknowledge that 'we need to recognize ambiguity, to be open about the dilemmas we face and the choices we make, and to think through the implications of these choices for the knowledge we produce' (Ribbens and Edwards 1998b: 205). Putting these values into operation, however, as a central part of our research design and conduct remains easier said than done.

## References

Ball, S. (1997). Policy sociology and critical social research. *British Journal of Sociology of Education*, 23(3), 257–274.

Bourne, J. (1980). Cheerleaders and ombudsmen: the sociology of race relations in Britain. *Race and Class*, 21, 331–335.

Brown, P. (1990). The 'Third Wave': education and the ideology of parentocracy. *British Journal of Sociology of Education*, 11(1), 65–85.

Coffey, A. (1996). The power of accounts: authority and authorship in ethnography. *Qualitative Studies In Education*, 9(1), 61–74.

Collins, P. (1990). *Black Feminist Thought*. London: Unwin Hyman.

Connolly, P. (1996). Doing what comes naturally? Standpoint epistemology, critical social research and the politics of identity. In E. Stina Lyon and J. Busfield (Eds), *Methodological Imaginations*. Basingstoke: Macmillan.

Denzin, N. (1994). Evaluating qualitative research in the poststructural moment: the lessons James Joyce teaches us. *Qualitiative Studies in Education*, 7(4), 295–308.

Femia, J. (1981). *Gramsci's Political Thought*. Oxford: Clarendon Press.

Fielding, M. (1996). Empowerment: emancipation or enervation? *Journal of Education Policy*, 11, 399–417.

Finch, J. (1984). It's great to have someone to talk to: the ethics and politics of interviewing women. In C. Bell and H. Roberts (Eds), *Social Researching: Politics, Problems and Practice*. London: RKP.

Gramsci, A. (1971). *Selections from the Prison Notebooks*. (Q. Hoare and G. Nowell Smith, Eds. and Trans.). New York: International Publishers.

Holub, R. (1992). *Antonio Gramsci: Beyond Marxism and Postmodernism*. London: Routledge.

Kelly, L., Burton, S. and Reagan, L. (1994). Researching women's lives or studying women's oppression? Reflections on what constitutes feminist research. In M. Maynard and J. Purvis (Eds), *Researching Women's Lives from a Feminist Perspective*. London: Taylor and Francis.

Larson, C. (1997). Re-presenting the subject: problems in personal narrative inquiry. *Qualitative Studies in Education*, 10(4), 455–469.

Lather, P. (1997). Drawing the line at angels: working the ruins of feminist ethnography. *Qualitative Studies in Education*, 10(3), 285–304.

Lather, P. and Smithies, C. (1997). *Troubling Angels: Women Living with HIV/AIDS*. Columbus, OH: Greyden Press.

Lawrence, E. (1982). In the abundance of water the fool is thirsty: sociology and black 'pathology'. In *CCCS, The Empire Strikes Back*. London: Hutchinson.

Limerick, B., Burgess-Limerick, T. and Grace, M. (1996). The politics of interviewing: power relations and accepting the gift. *Qualitative Studies in Education*, 9(4), 449–460.

Mac an Ghaill, M. (1988). *Young, Gifted and Black*. Milton Keynes: Open University Press.

Mac an Ghaill, M. (1991). 'Young, gifted and black': methodological reflections of a teacher/researcher. In G. Walford (Ed.), *Doing Educational Research*. London: Routledge.

Mirza, M. (1998). 'Same voices, same lives?': revisiting black feminist standpoint epistemology. In P. Connolly and B. Troyna (Eds), *Researching Racism in Education*. Buckingham: Open University Press.

Neal, S. (1995). Researching powerful people from a feminist and anti-racist perspective: a note on gender, collusion and marginality. *British Educational Research Journal*, 21(4), 517–531.

Oakley, A. (1981). Interviewing women: a contradiction in terms? In H. Roberts (Ed.), *Doing Feminist Research*. London: RKP.

Paechter, C. (1996). Power, knowledge and the confessional in qualitative research. *Discourse*, 17(1), 75–83.

Phoenix, A. (1994). Practicing feminist research: the intersection of gender and 'race' in the research process. In M. Maynard and J. Purvis (Eds), *Researching Women's Lives from a Feminist Perspective*. London: Taylor and Francis.

Ribbens, J. and Edwards, R. (1998a). Epilogue. In J. Ribbens and R. Edwards (Eds), *Feminist Dilemmas in Qualitative Research*. London: Sage.

Ribbens, J. and Edwards, R. (1998b). Living on the edge. In J. Ribbens and R. Edwards (Eds), *Feminist Dilemmas in Qualitative Research*. London: Sage.

Rizvi, F. (1993). Williams on democracy and the governance of education. In D. Dworkin and L. Roman (Eds), *Views beyond the Border Country*. London: Routledge.

Scheurich, J. (1997). *Research Method in the Postmodern*. London: Falmer Press.

Sheikh, F. (1991). *The Red Box*. London: Women's Press.

Showstack Sassoon, A. (1980). *Gramsci's Politics*. London: Croom Helm.

Skeggs, B. (1994). Situating the production of feminist ethnography. In M. Maynard and J. Purvis (Eds), *Researching Women's Lives from a Feminist Perspective*. London: Taylor and Francis.

Standing, K. (1998). Writing the voices of the less powerful. In J. Ribbens and R. Edwards (Eds), *Feminist Dilemmas in Qualitative Research*. London: Sage.

Stanley, L. and Wise, S. (1993). *Breaking out Again: Feminist Epistemology and Ontology*. London: Routledge.

Taylor, I., Evans, K. and Fraser, P. (1996). *A Tale of Two Cities*. London: Routledge.

Troyna, B. (1994). Blind faith? Empowerment and educational research. *International Studies in the Sociology of Education*, 4(1), 3–24.

Van Maanen, J. (Ed.) (1995). *Representation in Ethnography*. London: Sage.

Vincent, C. (1996a). *Parents and Teachers: Power and Participation*. London: Falmer Press.

Vincent, C. (1996b). Parent empowerment? Collective action and inaction in education. *Oxford Review of Education*, 22(4), 465–482.

Vincent, C. (1997). Community and collectivism: the role of parents' organizations in the education system. *British Journal of Sociology of Education*, 18(2), 271–283.

Vincent, C. and Tomlinson, S. (1997). Home school relationships: the 'swarming of disciplinary mechanisms'? *British Educational Research Journal*, 23(3), 361–377.

Williams, R. (1977). *Marxism and Literature*. Oxford: Oxford University Press.

# Chapter 10

# 'Parents as partners' in research and evaluation

## Methodological and ethical issues and solutions

*Sheila Wolfendale*

## Introduction

The area of home–school links and parental involvement has been designated and legitimate within education for a number of years, and research and project initiatives have spanned curriculum, school organisation, community perspectives, special educational needs provision and other facets of school life. Certain themes thread consistently through some of these initiatives. For example, parental involvement to raise children's educational achievement; factors that promote parents as effective 'tutors' of their own children; and ways in which empowered parents contribute as equal partners within the educational process.

Over the past 30 years there has been considerable research and development into facets of home–school and 'parents as partners', but they are sometimes prompted by ideology and rarely predicated on neutral, value-free premises. Sometimes research findings can, in turn, influence the adoption of social policies and legitimate ideological commitments (Tizard 1990). There is a circularity in the process evident in, for example, a government commitment to increasing parental rights and involvement in education which may have stemmed as much from an ideological stance as from research evidence.

This chapter sets out to investigate a seldom-explored facet within research into parents and home–school, namely, parents' status within research, and will look at some research paradigms that have been used. A number of inherent methodological and ethical issues will be identified and several fundamental aspects will be examined, such as whether

- research into aspects of parental involvement and parent partnership is consistent with 'partnership with parents' principles, that is, are parents treated more as subjects or objects of research than as partners in an investigatory process?
- researchers are more interested in the research process and outcomes than in the effects of studies upon parents themselves;
- researchers (be they academic or practitioner researchers) apply ethical principles and guidelines when carrying out studies with, or on, parents and their children.

The question will be posed, 'how problematic is this observed phenomenon within research into this area?', and finally, suggestions will be made as to how researchers could proceed in future, within an ethical and equitable framework, which does not compromise research integrity and is grounded in equal status between all participants.

## A brief review of research methods

Research into the inexhaustible aspects of the interface between parents and professionals, and the working relationship between school and home, has taken many forms. Some studies have been seminal and highly influential, even if small-scale, such as the Haringay 'experiment' into parental involvement in reading (Hewison 1985) or in Belfield (Hannon *et al.* 1985); others have been larger scale, funded projects, such as the Kirklees Paired Reading Project (Topping 1996a) which have likewise had an impact upon practice elsewhere. These and others within the area of parental involvement in reading and, later, family literacy (Wolfendale and Topping 1996), have been characterised by the use of classic hypothesis-testing, pre- and post-testing exercises, with quantitative as well as qualitative outcomes.

In the realm of hypothesis-testing research linked to practice, have been the initiatives with which this author has been associated over the years. For example, (i) 'Guidelines for writing a parental profile', as part of statutory assessment, now subsumed into *The Code of Practice for the Identification and Assessment of Special Educational Needs* (DfE 1994) and (ii) the parent completed early years developmental profile, *All about Me* (Wolfendale 1998).

There have been many surveys of parents' involvement in their children's education:

- of their opinions of various aspects of parenting, Ferri and Smith (1996);
- of their views on the Ofsted inspection process, Research and Information on State Education (RISE) (1995); Tabberer (1995);
- of their attitudes towards caring for a severely disabled child, Beresford (1995);
- of the challenges faced by families of children with learning disabilities, MENCAP (1997).

There are also practice-orientated projects, in which the notion of research is subsumed into 'development' work, epitomised by, for example, the two-year Royal Society of Arts initiative exploring the feasibility of teachers, parents and pupils working together in a range of schools and circumstances (Bastiani 1995). Other research is concerned with the evaluation of parental involvement initiatives, such as

- Wolfendale and Cook (1997), into the effectiveness of the SEN Parent Partnership Schemes;

- Wolfendale (1996a), on the effects of a parental involvement programme which was part of an inner city *City Challenge* initiative;
- White (1997), a national review into the take-up and enduring effectiveness of Portage, the early years/SEN teaching programme wherein parents are the teachers and are supported by practitioners;
- Bastiani (1997), a review of the SHARE parental involvement, primary school-based programme.

This chapter illustrates the varied ways in which research has been carried out in the parental involvement domain. The taxonomy outlined here (hypothesis-testing; survey; practice-orientated evaluation research) covers a wide range.

Research to date, in these various spheres, has tended to reflect a benign, liberal, facilitating ideology that seeks to promote or advance parents-as-citizens/consumers' interests, rights and participation in the delivery of public services for and on behalf of their children. As stated earlier, outcomes from some research endeavours lead directly to government policies and action (namely, family literacy and numeracy, parenting programmes, parent partnership in SEN, Portage, parental profiles, home–school agreements), and were endorsed by the previous, as well, as the present Government. Parental involvement is amongst key indicators for an effectively functioning school looked for by Ofsted inspectors.

This cited research, as well as a plethora of other initiatives, has utilised well-known research paradigms, within quantitative and/or qualitative research traditions. My contention is that we have been guilty of having given scant regard to the methodological and ethical factors and limitations inherent in parent-focused studies, especially when so many of the projects have been predicated upon partnership with parents principles, namely those of rights/entitlement, equality, reciprocity, and empowerment (Wolfendale 1992).

It must be stressed that the critique that follows applies in a general way to parental involvement studies. There is no intention, even obliquely, to be destructive towards past research endeavours. Rather the intention is to learn from the hard-won insights and methods of previous work, in order to inform future directions of research and development work with parents and, particularly, to evolve towards an ethical, principled approach to such research.

## Methodological limitations into researching parental involvement

All sorts of human and reality factors compound the neat blueprint of a research design and, in the realm of parental involvement studies, can often render the findings suspect, or, at least, less reliable. The myriad of contributing variables affecting children's educational performance makes it difficult, methodologically, to identify parents' engagement with their children's education as a significant influencing factor, if we only use educational achievement scores as a criterion measure. We can probably 'partial out' direct parental input as a contributing factor, but should be wary of making greater claims. In Wolfendale (1996b) a way of conceptualising the parental contribution to children's education was to posit the notion of the 'value added' components of parental involvement as an educational intervention area (pp. 33–34), which is offered as a way of singling out what it is that parents contribute without having to rely solely on often spurious or misleading statistics.

Hannon (1996) likewise queries reliance upon test scores as the sole outcome criteria of home–school literacy initiatives, and lists a range of methodological shortcomings. In the same realm, Topping (1996b) reviews a range of studies, and draws attention to a number of research features, such as the maintenance of gains, generalisability, robustness of assessment instruments, and the 'political, social and economic circumstances in which programmes operate' (p. 161).

These points refer mainly to hypothesis-testing and intervention studies. Research in the attitude survey and evaluation domains can, without rigorous design and control, fall prey to any one or more of a number of hazards spelled out in any textbook on methodology. For example, research asking parents their views on past experiences of child-rearing or their relationship with schools is susceptible to the difficulty of verifying information given retrospectively. Human memory can be selective or faulty, with reconstructions of past events 'contaminated' by recency factors. Asking parents for their contemporaneous views, whilst ostensibly more reliable, still makes researchers prey to being given selective, partial, filtered information. There is also the possibility of a researcher not being in tune with parents' belief-systems and lifestyles, and misconstruing responses.

Another methodological limitation in survey and attitude work is the issue of representativeness. Statistical considerations concerned with numbers, range, 'type' or category of parents operate in this realm as well as in evaluation research, as was found during the recent DfEE-funded evaluation study into Parent Partnership Schemes (Wolfendale and Cook 1997). Focus groups of parents in 25 local educa-tion authorities (LEAs) were a key part of the study, and local professionals within SEN identified and approached parents, to attend a focus group meeting. Thus already self-selection, bias and probably unrepresentativeness were methodological factors. These limitations were offset by building into the design:

- LEA representativeness, that is, 25 case study LEAs from a range of geographical and social settings;
- a sufficient number of focus groups and parents to obtain some reliable indices, ranging from 'prevalent/common' to 'less common/infrequent' views;
- the avoidance of an over-reliance on the data, which was regarded as illuminative, illustrative and significant of trends, but not definitive.

## Ethical considerations when researching parental involvement

The ethical dimensions to research in this area of parental involvement and home–school have not really been directly addressed to date, certainly not with regard to parent partnership principles. An increasing number of organisations and institutions have come to recognise that research in the social sciences has not traditionally operated equal opportunities policies and practices. Many have now developed ethical guidelines for conducting research, which confer some rights and entitlements upon the participants, and it seems opportune to look at these in relation to researching parental involvement.

One of the predominant ethical issues in research is the status of people approached to be the target of research studies. The British Psychological Society (BPS 1993) has recently adopted a policy change, that is, the people on and with whom research is undertaken, that is, the focus of research scrutiny are no longer to be called 'subjects', or even 'objects'. The word 'participants' is seen as a less loaded and a more benign term and denotes a shift in thinking amongst researchers, from regarding people in research and experiments as manipulable, research fodder, to perceiving them as *partners* in an enterprise. The reciprocal aspect is that researchers are, after all, heavily dependent upon the willing participation of the subjects' approached. Banister *et al.* (1994) summarises the change of attitude:

> The very use of terms such as 'participants' (or 'co-researchers', depending on the precise methodology adopted) rather than 'subjects' emphasizes the realisation of the imbalanced power relationships inherent in much research and attempts to address and remedy such problems.
>
> (p. 175)

Another salient issue is that of 'informed consent', integral to sanctioned research within the Health Service, but which has had variable application within educational research. Only three out of seven contemporary textbooks on research methodology consulted by this author listed 'informed consent' in their subject indexes. Banister *et al.* (1994) provide some guidance on how to operate within an 'informed consent' model, to ensure

- full and frank disclosures to potential or confirmed participants about the purpose and outcomes of the research;
- evidence of participants' understanding of the purposes and outcomes of the research, and of their part in it;
- minimisation of participants' anxieties;
- guarantees on confidentiality and anonymity, and a promise to terminate the research if participants become too uncomfortable to continue, or are unwilling to maintain their commitment.

These 'solutions' will be returned to.

There are other ethical aspects to the traditional researcher–researchee relationship, which could now be seen to be invidious and certainly not expressive of a relationship based on equality, or parity of esteem. One is the categorisation of survey respondents into, for example, social class or other categories without respondents being aware

(a) that a categorisation mapping is a fundamental part of the study;
(b) of the category, for example, social class to which they have been assigned.

Clearly there is a schism between, on the one hand, a need for social science and social policy researchers to operate classification systems when investigating social phenomena, and on the other, a need for transparency, honesty and account-ability towards respondents who are being asked to divulge personal information. Another ethical issue resulting from the researcher–researchee relationship is the power imbalance, wherein the researcher may have privileged access to *more* infor-mation about the research context and purposes than the participant. The *researchee* in the traditional relationship has had no power or influence over the outcomes of the research or the purposes to which it has been put and, as Banister *et al.* (1994) point out, at worst the power imbalance can lead to the participant's exploitation.

During the data collection process, other ethical issues arise with regard to those studies which utilise face-to-face, 1:1 interviewing. In addition to the above-mentioned factors, others are concerned with ensuring the ease and comfort of the interviewees, the courtesy with which they are treated, and adequate time for them to complete their responses. Richardson and colleagues (1996) identify 'interviewer responsibility' and broaden their discussion of these issues by includ-ing interviewer as well as interviewee feelings during the sensitive period of the interview meeting. For these writers, a central issue is trust which is and should be reciprocal, and they offer helpful guidelines for the ethical conduct of interviews.

The final ethical consideration to be included in the discussion is that of 'the ethics of intrusion', wherein the advent of a researcher into the personal or private domain of the participant is bound to influence the research process and the researcher–researchee relationship, which is also a methodological factor. The invasion of personal privacy by researchers can epitomise, at worst, the power imbalance; at best, with the willing engagement of the researchees into the process, the researcher becomes a 'participant researcher' (well documented in methodology textbooks, especially on qualitative research).

Vetere and Gale (1987) devote a chapter to 'Ethical issues in the study of family life', in which they raise crucial and fundamental dilemmas concerning access, informed consent, permission, confidentiality, and the role of the researcher as 'an instigator of change' by his or her presence within the family. These authors were research psychologists who 'lived' with a family for the best part of a year as semi-participant researchers and they state that the reasons for so little first-hand research into family life are obvious. Family life is for all of us a sacred domain, with even relatives and friends entering the family nucleus by invitation only. Likewise, researchers and professionals, such as teachers, health visitors, social workers, educational and clinical psychologists, can only 'intrude' into the family by invitation and it follows that there should be clear ground rules, mutually accepted, for the conduct of the research.

Gilgun *et al.* (1992) are also amongst the few authors who have addressed ethical issues within the domain of family research. They raise the various considerations that have already been identified in this section, and another, namely, the ethical, moral dilemma for the researcher and the emotional dilemma for the researchee when the latter makes an unanticipated and perhaps unintentional personal disclosure. This potentially serious side-effect of the research needs anticipating within the research design and its ethical framework.

## Have parents and families been partners in research?

At the beginning of this chapter, a number of speculative questions were posed, amongst which was how problematic is this area. Problem-areas have been identified with methodological limitations and ethical considerations, and especially problematic in the view of this author is that the conduct of much research into parents and home–school has not been consistent with principles of partnership with parents. Even those surveys and attitude studies may not have treated the respondents as equals within the process. Hannon (1996) laudably argues for the inclusion of stakeholders' views (typically parents and teachers) into intervention studies, such as home–school literacy, but does not go on to propose that such inclusion should be within an equality model.

A catalogue of omission would include that parent-participants have

- in some studies been excluded from fully knowing the purposes and outcomes of the research;
- not been in receipt of written ethical guidelines;
- not had the opportunity to contribute their experience and perspectives to the conduct and outcomes of the research.

Wolfendale (1992) considers whether such a model (including the definitions of the four key elements: rights/entitlement; equality; reciprocity; and empowerment) can be applied to co-operative research wherein parents are partners:

1  *Rights/entitlement.*  'the concept of rights can act as a springboard for ensuring not only that parents know their rights but that they can guarantee that these rights will have expression' (p. 3). This would mean that they would have the right and entitlement to be in possession of as much information about the proposed research as possible; they would know of informed consent; they would have the right to withdraw from participation without harassment.

2  *Equality.*  '. . . equal status between parents and professionals (researchers). . . each bringing different but equivalent experience and expertise to that joint enterprise' (p. 3). This 'parity of esteem' would ensure that parents were treated

as vital and equal contributors to the research process, bringing an invaluable dimension of experience and perspectives which could inform the research design, enrich the outcomes and, possibly, the effects of the research.

3    *Reciprocity.* 'reciprocal involvement rests on the premise that each person involved is contributing and sharing information, expertise and ultimately the responsibility for actions and decisions. Thus all are accountable' (p. 3). The ultimate responsibility for the research (design, conduct, etc.) must rest with the researchers; it would not be proper to saddle parent-participants with disproportionate and irrelevant responsibilities. However, parents would know and be assured that they are valued for their contribution (Richardson 1996).

4    *Empowerment.* 'empowerment usually refers to the means as well as the ends of realising and expressing wants, needs and rights and of ensuring that the parental voice is heard and has influence' (p. 3). In the co-operative research model, parents are not regarded as passive 'subjects', accepting what is thrust upon them by way of research design or research instruments; they have an inbuilt right to express their views, and constructively influence the process. Such an egalitarian stance might, of course, even influence decisions on what phenomena should be under research scrutiny.

## Towards an equitable model of co-operative research

One 'solution' to the unequal relationship between researchers and parent-participants in applying a partnership model to co-operative research in the home–school domain was proposed earlier. But this section takes the proposition further, in suggesting that in order for such an approach to work, written codification of the principles and practices is needed. A written 'Code of Conduct' would be a visible manifestation of good intent on all sides, setting out core values as well as best practice. The cardinal principle is expressed within the British Psychological Society's *Code of Conduct* (1993):

> The essential principle is that the investigation should be considered from the standpoint of all participants; foreseeable threats to their psychological well-being, health, values or dignity should be eliminated.
>
> (p. 33)

The elements set out here are focused on ethical considerations and less upon the methodological limitations identified earlier. A vital corollary of proceeding towards co-operative research is that these methodological constraints are anticipated, dealt with, combated, minimised in all the ways offered in textbooks on methodology. Parent-participants, as partners in research enterprises, could themselves contribute to discussions on how these constraints could be minimised, particularly if, as a canon of co-operative research, the researchers are honest at the outset about the factors of sample size, representativeness and memory effects.

A Code of Conduct, resting upon partnership in research, is a step beyond the pro-forma used by many academic institutions. For example, the University of East London Ethics Committee has devised a model form of consent, the headings of which require the researcher to: spell out the aims and objectives of the proposed research in lay language; explain the contribution required from the participant; describe the process; provide reassurance about confidentiality and anonymity; and offer a disclaimer in these words:

> ... you are not obliged to take part in this study and are free to withdraw at any time ... should you choose to withdraw from the programme, you may do so without disadvantage to yourself and without any obligation to give a reason.

The speculative Code of Conduct proposed is offered to readers for discussion and trial. It is not a finished product and, after use, would be developed and amended and could, over time, become an accepted part of the methodology of co-operative research with parent-participants across all domains. The elements in the Code are culled, not only from the partnership model outlined earlier, but from the ethical guidelines for conducting research contained in several of the textbooks on methodology already cited in this chapter.

## A Code of Conduct for co-operative research

### Section 1: Statement of values and principles and purpose of the Code

This section would set out core values and principles along the lines of the partnership model outlined earlier, the main elements of which are rights and entitlement, equality, reciprocity and empowerment.

### Section 2: Responsibilities and commitment by the researcher(s)

This section would include elements such as

- open and honest descriptions of the aims and objectives of the proposed research;
- the provision to participants of verbal and written information about the proposed research, including a showing of the research instruments;
- clear statements about the nature of the involvement of the participants and the estimated time scale;
- sensitive, respectful handling of participants;
- guarantees (e.g. confidentiality, anonymity);
- provision of conducive surroundings in order to put participants at ease (depending, of course, on the kind of study);

- a promise to provide information regarding the research outcomes and possible uses to which the findings could be put (debriefing);
- build into the research design, opportunities for participants to contribute ideas at various stages;
- ensure full understanding on the part of the participant before the consent form is signed;
- if payment is offered, be clear about the amount and terms;
- offer a clear disclaimer;
- propose the formation of a research committee, with parent-participant representatives.

### Section 3: Entitlement and the rights of participants

Elements could include the right to

- receive written information about the proposed research, including the research instruments, the written request to contribute, and the estimated time scale;
- be treated sensitively and with respect;
- ensure that the research is carried out in conducive surroundings, where appropriate;
- comment upon and contribute to the research process;
- receive information about, and contribute to, the research findings;
- help to shape the research agenda (depending upon the nature of the proposed research);
- clarify how the participant might gain by contributing;
- withdraw from the research, without citing a reason.

### Section 4: Responsibilities and commitment by the participant

Elements could include that

- participants demonstrate that they understand the nature of the proposed research, and the contribution required (including time commitment);
- by giving their informed consent (i.e. signing the consent form), they agree to keep appointments and to co-operate along the agreed lines.

## Concluding comments

Research into the area of parental involvement and home–school has a venerable and respectable pedigree, wherein a range of methodologies have been explored and developed. This chapter has argued a case for adopting a partnership model for co-operative research in this area and has attempted to combine it with a set of ethical guidelines. On the basis of overwhelming evidence and signs of continued commitment, on the part of national and local government and schools, to parental engagement with their children's education, including special needs, we can predict that research and development studies will continue into

- parental involvement in the curriculum;
- parental contributions towards the 'effective school';
- the part that parents might play in the new Education Action Zones and the Early Years Partnerships;
- parents' possible support of moves towards inclusive education for children with special needs;
- home–school agreements (contained within the 1998 Education Act);
- whether parents can make a valued contribution towards baseline (on entry to school) assessment.

All these and other related contemporary areas will doubtless become part of research agenda. It therefore seems appropriate to apply partnership principles to research on this topic.

## References

Banister, P., Burman, E., Parker, I., Taylor, M. and Tindall, C. (1994) *Qualitative Methods in Psychology: A Research Guide*. Buckingham: Open University Press.

Bastiani, J. (1995) *Taking a Few Risks*. London: Royal Society of Arts.

Bastiani, J. (1997) *Evaluation of the SHARE Pilot Programme*. Coventry: Community Education Development Centre.

Beresford, B. (1995) *Expert Opinions* (a national survey of parents caring for a severely disabled child). Bristol: The Policy Press, University of Bristol.

British Psychological Society (1993) 'Ethical principles for conducting research with human participants', *The Psychologist*, 6 (1), 33–35.

Department for Education (1994) *The Code of Practice for the Identification and Assessment of Special Educational Needs*. London: DfE.

Ferri, E. and Smith, K. (1996) *Parenting in the 1990s*. London: Family Policy Studies Centre.

Gilgun, J., Daly, K. and Handel, G. (eds) (1992) *Qualitative Methods in Family Research*. London: Sage Publications.

Hannon, P. (1996) *Literacy, Home and School: Research and Practice in Teaching Literacy with Parents*. London: Falmer Press.

Hannon, R., Jackson, A. and Page, B. (1985) 'Implementation and take up of a project to involve parents in the teaching of reading', in K. Topping and S. Wolfendale (eds) *Parental Involvement in Children's Reading*. Beckenham: Croom Helm.

Hewison, J. (1985) 'Parental involvement and reading attainment: implications of research in Dagenham and Haringey', in K. Topping and S. Wolfendale (eds) *Parental Involvement in Children's Reading*. Beckenham: Croom Helm.

MENCAP (1997) *Left in the Dark*. London: MENCAP.

Research and Information on State Education (RISE) (1995) *The Ofsted's Experience: The Parents' Eye-view*. London: The Research and Information on State Education Trust.

Richardson, J. (ed.) (1996) *Handbook of Qualitative Research Methods in Psychology and the Social Sciences*. Leicester: British Psychological Society Books.

Tabberer, R. (1995) *Parents' Perceptions of Ofsted's Work* (a report by NFER for Ofsted). Slough: NFER.

Tizard, B. (1990) 'Research and policy: is there a link?', *The Psychologist*. October. 435–440.

Topping, K. (1996a) 'Tutoring systems for family literacy', in S. Wolfendale and K. Topping (eds) *Family Involvement in Literacy: Effective Partnerships in Education*. London: Cassell.

Topping, K. (1996b) 'The effectiveness of family literacy', in S. Wolfendale and K. Topping (eds) *Family Involvement in Literacy: Effective Partnerships in Education*. London: Cassell.

Vetere, A. and Gale, A. (1987) *Ecological Studies of Family Life*. Chichester: John Wiley and Sons.

White, M. (1997) 'A review of the influence and effects of Portage', in S. Wolfendale (ed.) (1997) *Working with Parents of SEN Children after the Code of Practice*. London: David Fulton.

Wolfendale, S. (1992) *Empowering Parents and Teachers: Working for Children*. London: Cassell.

Wolfendale, S. (1996a) 'The contribution of parents to children's achievement in school: policy and practice in the London Borough of Newharn', in J. Bastiani and S. Wolfendale (eds) *Home–School Work in Britain: Review, Reflection and Development*. London: David Fulton Publishers.

Wolfendale, S. (1996b) 'The relationship between parental involvement and educational achievement', in C. Cullingford (ed.) *Parents, Education and the State*. Aldershot: Arena Books.

Wolfendale, S. (1998) *All about Me* (Second edition). Nottingham: NES-Arnold.

Wolfendale, S. and Cook, G. (1997) *Evaluation of Special Educational Needs Parent Partnership Schemes* (DfEE Research Report 34). London: DfEE.

Wolfendale, S. and Topping, K. (eds) (1996) *Family Involvement in Literacy: Effective Partnerships in Education*. London: Cassell.

# Part III

# Methods and practices

# Chapter 11

# The moral maze of image ethics

*Jon Prosser*

## Introduction

Visually orientated educational research, relative to orthodox educational research, is a 'newcomer' to the qualitative research field. As such it lacks a history of accepted ethical practice or a range of theoretical positions on which to base ethical judgements. This chapter does not focus on a general set of ethical principles that are the benchmark for 'wordsmiths' but instead considers common ethical predicaments that result from applying an image-based approach to qualitative research. Those involved who make and use images in a research context are ethically obligated to their subjects. There are moral and political reasons for this. Future visual researchers require access to images and image-making possibilities if image-based research is to make a significant contribution to qualitative research. To gain and maintain that access, to stay in potentially stimulating visual contexts, there is a need to secure the *confidence* of respondents and fellow researchers. Establishing respondents' confidence means assuring them that they will not be 'damaged' misrepresented or prejudiced in any way; in terms of researchers' confidence it means agreeing ethical procedures that protect respondents yet ensure the trustworthiness of findings. Image-based research, being a relative newcomer to interpretative studies, needs theoretical and methodological tenets on which to base its credentials. However, confidence in image-based investigations will be generated only when ethical principles are agreed between researchers and researched, and within the research community, and adhered to by visual researchers across a range of visual contexts.

Identifying what constitutes an appropriate ethical practice, as the title of the chapter suggests, is not easy. In order to explore the twists and turns of the ethical maze this chapter is divided into two parts. The first part considers *still photography* and provides examples from my own work to illustrate ethical dilemmas that face practitioners of image-based research. The second part considers *moving images*, and emphasis is placed on documentary-type film and video. This is an artificial division, as many issues, for example those of access, political pressures and aesthetics, discussed within the *still photography* subheading, are equally applicable to *moving images*, and the converse is also true. Hence, ethical issues should be considered as operating across this divide and encompassed by the more general term 'image-based research'.

## Image-based research

Image-based research is comprised of moving images in the form of film and video, and still images, for example, photographs, cartoons, and drawings. It thus does not form a homogeneous set of technologies, techniques or practices. This divergence is compounded by different analytical procedures and differently generated data used for different ends. Researchers using images may draw on a diverse range of disciplines which, potentially at least, apply a different set of ethical practices. The diversity of theory and practice within image-based research does not suggest a particular field of educational research which constructs and applies its own set of ethics. What makes image-based research differently situated as compared with other forms of research lies in the obvious: visual images are quite different in nature from words in their allusion to 'reality', and participants see themselves and can be seen by others.

Image-based research is often perceived by academics and practitioners alike as having a lower status (Prosser 1998) and operating on the margins of qualitative research. Orthodox, word-orientated researchers relate, methodologically and ethically, to their respective disciplines of sociology, history and psychology. Image-based researchers, on the other hand, derive their methodological and ethical inspiration from visual sociology and visual anthropology. However, with this alignment comes a new set of problems, especially for film-makers and photographers. Although photographs, for example, were used in early sociological journals, their use damaged any hope of academic integrity. Riis and Hine, for example, the most prominent protagonists in the use of photography to bring about social change, were seen by many as 'muck-raking' (Stasz 1979: 134). Equally, documentary photographers of this period such as August Sander's portraits of German social types (Sander 1986) and Eugène Atget's survey of Paris (Atget 1992) were perceived as lacking a methodological framework. Hence not only did early practice undercut the acceptability of image-based research in the eyes of social scientists, more importantly it failed to provide an initial ethical framework. Indeed, visual sociology emerged as a subdiscipline only around 1970. Consequently, few role models of acceptable ethical practice have been debated, let alone established for others to follow. All this has repercussions for image-based educational researchers and ethical practice who rely on visual sociology, visual anthropology, films of the documentary genre or media reportage for methodological models. Given the matrix of adoption and the paucity of role models for those educational researchers using images, there is little in the way of ethical consensus.

## Still photography

Photographs have numerous uses in educational research and at different phases of the research process different ethical principles come to bear. The period prior to making images, the act of constructing images, and issues arising after they are made, each carry discrete ethical implications. (This also holds for moving images.) In practice the process begins by negotiating access for image-making. This means negotiating with the head of an educational institution – as prime 'gatekeeper' – what can and cannot be photographed, how photography is to take place, and how resultant images are to be used. Of course both researcher and 'gatekeeper' have reasons for seeking permission or agreeing (or otherwise) that photography may occur. The researchers have their agenda: to add to sociological knowledge, to increase career prospects; and the 'gatekeepers' too have their agendas: to be treated fairly and to use the research activity to their own advantage. Becker (1988: xv) reminds us that contracts with a visual locus are rarely based on philanthropy but rather on some potential usefulness to both parties:

> Remember that the heads of . . . institutions such as hospitals, jails or schools, who need not participate in having films of themselves made, generally think there is something in it for them: perhaps a chance at reform, perhaps some public relations benefit. They may well think they are smarter than the film-maker or researcher. Is it unethical for image workers to pretend to be dumber than they are to take advantage of that arrogance? Others, less powerful, also have their own reasons for co-operating with image-makers, so the bargain is seldom one-sided.

There is no straightforward answer to Becker's question. Balanced against the pos-sibility of unbridled researcher deception is the potential for participants to behave 'unnaturally' if the focus of the study is made explicit. But implicit in Becker's statement is another ethical dilemma: that 'gatekeepers', during negotiations for access to schools, may set parameters or limitations on the research enterprise. The headteacher, being in a position of power, can influence how staff and students are portrayed by controlling access to him- or herself and therefore images (by, for example, insisting on photographing in 'formal settings' or 'staged' shooting), while allowing and directing access to those less powerful. This is borne out in the paucity of visual studies of powerful leaders of institutions and organizations as compared with the multitude of studies of less powerful groups such as teach-ers and schoolchildren. During negotiations for access, general guidelines have the potential to be made specific and formal or non-specific and informal. However, the underlying ethical issues are the degree to which the aims of the project are made clear and the extent to which academic freedoms are curtailed by censorship.

Stereotypically, a photojournalist appears in Hollywood films as 'standing on the hood of a tank as it lumbers into battle through enemy fire, making images of war as he risks his life' (Becker 1998: 85). Photographers seeking to document events in educational institutions need to be more wily in their approach. The introduction of a camera to participants can take place on the first day as a 'can opener' (Collier and Collier 1986) or over a period of time using a 'softly softly' approach (Prosser 1992: 398). The 'softly softly' approach entails walking around an institution with the camera in an 'out of the case over the shoulder like a piece of jewellery' mode, followed by 'safe' photography of buildings or positive publicity-type images suitable for inclusion in the institution's prospectus. Only much later is 'serious' photography normally attempted. There is a delicate dividing line here between being sly, deceitful and furtive, and being sensitive and judicious. The final arbiters of ethical decisions may lie not with the visual researcher, nor the research profession who are not in a position to know, but with participants who, in accepting or rejecting the investigator, signal their response.

Images can be obtained openly or covertly. To act covertly, for example, would be to hide from the subject, use a telephoto lens that allows recording of a scene from a distant position, or to use a 'snooper' which allows the photographer to point their cameras in one direction while actually taking a photograph at right angles to the apparent angle of shooting. Such techniques are rarely practised in educational contexts. Nonetheless, since cameras may incite suspicion and discourage naturalistic behaviour, disputable tactics are used, such as shooting 'from the hip' or setting a camera on 'auto' to give the impression the camera is not functioning, when it is. Visual sociologists would justify, this practice by arguing that if permission to take photographs had been granted, emphasis shifts to applying techniques that are appropriate to obtaining trustworthy data, and this may entail shooting when subjects are unaware. Nevertheless, few image-orientated educational researchers would countenance outright covert or clandestine photography, as it more often reveals researchers' discomfort with their own photographic activity than it does insights into the daily lives of their subjects.

During the opening phase, prudent photographers identify no-go areas and those participants not previously excluded by the 'gatekeeper' who do not want their photograph taken. This is a question of privacy made ambiguous by territory, motive and consequence. Educational establishments are neither private nor public places, making the legal position even more unclear than is normally the case (the law on privacy and intrusion with regard to photography in public and private places is vague in the United Kingdom). Besides, teachers and managers feel 'ownership' of their spaces that comes from a deep sense of professional autonomy. To assume they are not 'private' places would be a mistake on the part of the photographer. Of course, the most dramatic, even sensational, images may be of those not wanting their photographs taken, but that is no reason for taking photographs. Such actions are not only dishonest, but also counter-productive to the enhancement of sociological knowledge. Ultimately the reason for not taking photographs of participants if they are hostile to the idea is not a matter of privacy or morality but the likelihood of such action compromising rapport – a necessity for any researcher hoping to remain in the field.

Although access provides initial ethical problems, these can normally be anticipated. Any problems at this stage are precursors to more substantial dilemmas, anticipated and unforeseen, that attend the photographic activity that follows. Given that all photographs are constructions, it is important to know something of the context of creating an image if the implied promise of truthfulness to the subject,

*Figure 11.1* 'The Ritual of Knock and Wait' (Photo by Jon Prosser).

the audience and the research profession is to be upheld. I will use examples of weaknesses in my own work to illustrate how the serendipitous nature of photography can compromise not only the face validity and the veracity of images but also the ethical status of the photographer.

Figure 11.1, 'The Ritual of Knock and Wait', used in a study of school culture, shows a teacher knocking at the headteacher's door, bending, listening for a response from within. The objective – to illustrate a taken-for-granted ritual – was planned and drew on the work of Cartier-Bresson (1952) in isolating a 'decisive moment' for its visual arrangement. The context of taking the photograph is interesting because it highlights a range of ethical issues. The first is the possibility of misrepresentation stemming from the polysemic nature of images, for even a single image has many legitimate interpretations. My intended meaning of the photograph was simply 'this is the everyday ritual of knocking and waiting'. However, the aesthetic device (more on this later), the inclusion in the frame of a visual clue (the painting on the left), potentially implies a 'Big Brother is watching you' relationship between the teacher outside and the headteacher inside. This would be one interpretation, but a misrepresentation, since observations and interviews showed that such an implication would be quite unfounded. The aesthetic device, used to make a more dynamic, and implicit but consequential statement, detracts from the original objective of the image. It demonstrates the importance of using images in conjunction with words to project an intended meaning. Equally, it illustrates that while the researcher-created images may be attributed a meaning by others, their intended meaning is best signalled in relation to the socio-political context of how and why the image was made.

The second ethical issue is concerned with fabrication. The first time Figure 11.1 was taken, the film was damaged in processing and could not be printed. When I came to repeat the photograph, the lens, film, time of day, angle of shooting and the scene were the same but the painting (it having been returned to the pupil who painted it) and the teacher were missing. The pupil agreed to bring the painting into the school for one day – the day the head was away from the school. Teachers, aware that he was away, did not knock on his door. After I had waited for two hours a teacher, out of sympathy for my plight, pretended to knock and I got my picture. The second image replicated the first in many respects, but is nonetheless artificial, a 'set-up' with little in the way of the naturalism so central to documentary photography and qualitative research. The photograph, used as an illustration, was included in reporting the findings of the study without mention of the context of taking.

Is all deceit morally equal and to be equally condemned? My feeling is 'no'. It depends, for example, on the mode of communication. Would it be considered deceitful if, during an interview, a tape recorder failed and the interview were repeated? Probably not. However, as the mode of communication in the case of 'The Ritual of Knock and Wait' is a photograph, there is a stronger case to argue that deceit has taken place. Image-based researchers frequently state that photographs are not and will never be an objective witness of reality or a 'window on the world'. Nevertheless, many audiences expect an unrealistically high level of 'objectivity' and 'truthfulness' of photographs, more so than would be expected of verbal or written forms of communication. The problem of photographs being perceived by audiences as 'telling us what the world is really like' (Beloff 1985: 100) is long-standing, as Gross *et al.* (1988: 4) point out:

> The 'marriage of conviction' between our faith in the truthfulness of the photographic image and our belief in the possibility of objective reporting has lasted nearly a century and a half, and has been strengthened by the invention of motion pictures and television. Although both partners in this marriage have come under growing suspicion, undermined by our growing awareness of the inevitability of subjectivity in the selection, framing, contextualisation, and presentation of images and reports, their continuing acceptance in public discourse and belief testifies to their resilience.

Therefore, because image-based researchers are aware of the inherent problem stemming from the 'marriage of conviction', it is their moral responsibility to pass on information relating to the context of making which tends to support the so-called trustfulness of the photographic image (more on this later). Consequently, what makes 'The Ritual of Knock and Wait' ethically indefensible is that the context

*Figure 11.2* 'Pupil on Walkabout' (Photo by Jon Prosser).

of taking was not revealed, denying audiences informed interpretation and further enhancing the possibility of a false sense of trust in the photograph.

Figure 11.2, 'Pupil on Walkabout', illustrates a quite different ethical problem. One person's representation may be another's misrepresentation, and in photography aesthetic considerations are one way of shaping a truth. Aesthetic devices are important in documentary photography and are used in constructing powerful images which in turn encourage 'readers' not only to look but also to accept a particular meaning of an image. However, this is a two-edged sword since aesthetic qualities, knowingly or otherwise, can distract or disproportionately influence the photographer's meaning and the 'reader's' interpretation. 'Pupil on Walkabout' is an example of this problem. The boy was regularly found on a Friday afternoon hiding in the school's fuel storage area or in the cloakroom (usually under a mound of coats). He explained how each Friday the physics teacher told him to 'get lost', so he did. The photograph was taken to illustrate his predicament.

Two issues arise from the use made of this photograph in a research context. There is a dynamic relationship between words and images. Edward Weston, a famous American photographer, in discussing the relationship between photographs and titles, said, 'a poet can write a few words under it [a photograph] which will change how you see it. In this case words and picture will affect each other, they enlarge each other' (Danziger and Conrad 1984: 30). In the case of Figure 11.2

neither the title nor the text used in the report (Prosser 1989) support my intended meaning of the image.

A second and more significant failing compounds this weakness. In the past, documentary photographers, for example, Sander (1986), have developed what can be described as 'pseudo-objective' photography. They used standard lenses without filters, emphasized frontality of the subject and flatness of space, recorded people in their natural environment, and printed their negatives full frame to produce an aesthetic style known as 'standers and sitters'. This style was used in Figure 11.2 and raises a number of general ethical questions. As stated earlier, one ethical responsibility of researchers is to report conceptions and procedures on which a research report is based. However, given that photographs are constructions, to what extent is it possible for photographers to account reflexively for the influence of aesthetic considerations? I was aware that using the 'standers and sitters' style, coupled with chiaroscuro lighting, would produce an 'arty' image. Equally, I was aware that the central positioning of the boy, the pathos of the figure and the gloominess of the place would evoke an overly emotional response in the viewer. In conveying a sense of isolation and depression I was representing an interpretation that was unsupported by data and had no substantive basis. This was not a case of incompetence (I knew what I was doing), more a case of the artistic style, drama and sensationalism of an image being given priority over academic integrity. Limitations resulting from lack of reflection show ineptitude; limitations resulting from failing to act on reflexivity constitute unethical behaviour.

## Moving images

Although there are technical and procedural differences between moving and still imagery, in terms of ethical dilemmas there are many similarities. There are similarities between photographs and moving images as a result of similar technologies and modes of communication. The still camera and the movie camera each in their own way are technological devices that replicate accurately what is set before them. However, importantly, they do so at our bidding. Both are 'visual' but, being different in their mode of recording and presentation, pose different ethical dilemmas. Their similarity gives rise to similar ethical questions, and in the same way their differences give rise to a different set of ethical issues. Therefore, despite their interchangeable ethical problems, a contrast will be drawn between moving and still images.

The most marked differences between still and moving images are pointed out by Beloff (1985: 104), quoting Hopkinson:

> A newsreel has movement, but the still photograph has permanence. It is a moment of time frozen. The famous picture of the South Vietnam general shooting a terrorist with his own hand in a Saigon street would have meant little flashing by on television screens. As a still picture it stands forever – an accusation of mankind.

An alternative distinction is provided by Adelman (1998: 156), quoting Berger:

> The fact that a film camera works with time instead of across it affects every one of its images on both a technical and metaphysical level. . . . Most important of all, the eye behind the film camera is looking for development not conjuncture.

The implication that single images without accompanying words to provide context rarely fulfil the reflexive and internal validity afforded by moving images is an important one. Despite these critical distinctions, there are many interchangeable ethical dilemmas facing both still and moving image-makers.

Perhaps the most common ethical debate focuses on notions of the truth and veracity of still and moving images. Our belief in the capacity of photography to provide evidence of the external world is reflected in the saying 'the camera never lies'. We know this has never been the case. Shortly after photography was patented at the Academy of Sciences in Paris in 1839, for example, the inventor, Louis Jacques Daguerre, was experimenting by retouching photographs. Winston (1998) catalogues a large number of manipulations of the photographic image ranging from Gardner's rearrangement of bodies after the battle of Gettysburg (dragging them about forty metres and changing their clothes) to Robert Doisneau's famous picture 'The Kiss' in which the main protagonists were not photographed in the act of spontaneous gesture of affection but were a specially commissioned actor and his girlfriend. Kane (1994) provides an inventory of digital manipulation including *National Geographic Magazine's* moving two pyramids closer together for aesthetic reasons. Yet since we know that photography was never objective, why do we hold on to the authenticity of the photograph? Kane (1994: 10) suggests a reason:

> Even when photo-images are faked, they only confirm the essential power of the photographic. When Stalin infamously removed Trotsky from the picture of Lenin in Red Square, or when surrealists and avant-gardists fiddled with exposures and turned the photo into a phantasm, both parties were exploiting – for political and artistic purposes – our fundamental trust in the camera. We believe the camera's eye can bring us truth, whether subjective (the snapshot of a loved one, the performance of a great actor) or objective (pictures of weather forecasts, police suspects, lab experiments). The photographic is the way we moderns test that reality is *out there:* we rely on its veracity more than we readily admit.

Given that we invest images with an integrity 'more than we readily admit', how can we best stand outside of ourselves to judge them? To begin with, the trustworthiness of moving and still images depends on their contextual validity. In terms of the context in which images are *made*, transparency of the process is central; in terms of the context in which images are *viewed*, their mode of representation and the cultural and pictorial codes of their reception are central. Judgements and claims of contextual validity are best made essentially via *reflexive accounts* but also through their *representation*. Reflexive accounts attempt to render explicit the process by which data and findings were produced, and are the 'Achilles heel' of all film genres claiming academic integrity. It is clear that until recently anthropological film, for example, has been insufficiently reflexive or integrated. (Usually, reflexive accounts, where they do exist, are provided as an adjunct to the film.) Nonetheless, even in the case of a reflexive documentary account, the academic community will find fundamental faults since there is a widely held belief that 'reality' is distorted by directors' beliefs, sponsors' needs, artistic convention and for artistic reasons (Winston 1995). This argument is also applied to all forms of the realist mode of communication, including the 'photographic essay' and 'documentary photography'.

## Informed consent

The above-mentioned concerns are not abstractions, of interest only to academia. The problems resulting from the social and political milieu that are part and parcel of any film-making show themselves in a series of moral and ethical dilemmas. Consider the scenario of making a documentary film of a school. The relationship between the film-makers and their subjects is initiated within a framework of *informed consent*. This customarily means that subjects are free of coercion or deception; have an understanding of the process by which a film is to be made, the outcomes, and the uses to be made of the film; and, as individuals or groups, have the capacity and competence to consent (Anderson and Benson 1988). Even a cursory reflection on these criteria applied in an educational setting would pick up potential discrepancies. The hierarchy of the school, on understanding the potential advantages of making the film, could entice or inveigle the subjects (teachers, administrators and students) to take part for the school's common good. This would have direct repercussions since the subjects, not steeped in filmic knowledge, would be unaware of the techniques and ploys of directors going about their art. Moreover, as with any case study the outcomes of filming cannot be preordained. Only in editing can the final 'story' be told, which means that ultimate control lies with the film-makers, not the subjects. Also, pupils (minors requiring parental consent) and parents may be given only cursory information about the film and rarely have the luxury of 'opting out'. Finally, since the effects of the film on actors and audience can rarely be predicted by the film-maker, there can be no guarantees of negative repercussions on subjects.

These points exemplify how easy it is for ethical ideals to be subverted in practice. It should be borne in mind that 'informed consent' is more often a matter of individual conscience and rarely takes the form of a contract identifying particularities. Without acquiescence and the participation of teachers and pupils, observational films in educational settings would not exist. If truly informed consent were absent or lacking, the films' ethical integrity would be impaired. If directorial freedom were confined, constructive and artistic integrity would be limited. Clearly, for directors there is a tension between needing actors' co-operation during filming and wanting complete autonomy during editing. The view of participants, as cited by Becker (1988: xiii), highlights the irreconcilable ethical dilemma:

> I ought not to be able to sign away my rights to be treated, when someone collects images, in an ethical fashion, whether I want to or not. . . . I cannot give my consent unless I am truly informed, and that I know at least as much about the process of making photographs and films (or doing social research) as the people doing the work.

## Recurring themes

Generally, situated ethics constitute a set of dilemmas for film-makers that are not easily resolved. Where they are resolved, it is only by setting aside one set of values in preference for another. This is most obvious in the Griersonian documentary film tradition applied in the past to studies of education, health, welfare and housing. Directors used their creations for social reform, to expose bad or evil, and to bring about desirable change. However, in taking up the cause of social improvement by documenting social victimization, they put to one side any consideration of improving the lots of the subjects of their films. In paying little attention to the moral rights of participants they provide evidence for claims that 'most documentary film-makers have relatively little commitment to the subjects of their films' (Beauchamp and Klaidman 1988: 138). Moreover, in the past, the popularity of such films led to a recurrence of themes commonly termed 'victim documentaries' (Winston 1995). Brian Winston (1988: 34), in quoting a comment made by Basil Wright in 1974, exemplifies the recurring 'victim documentary' theme:

> You know this film (*Children at School*) was made in 1937. The other thing is that this film shows up the appalling conditions in the schools in Britain in 1937 which are identical with the ones which came out on television the night before last: overcrowded classes, schoolrooms falling down, and so on. It's the same story. That is really terrible, isn't it?

What Winston implies is that 'overcrowded classes, schoolrooms falling down' is a recurring 'victim'-type documentary that had media currency in 1937, 1974 and 1988. Given the combination of pressures from sponsors, the public's need for expose, and the enhancement of career prospects of the film-maker, it is little wonder that films of the less powerful in society are repetitious while case studies of the powerful are significant by their absence. Direct cinema, when aiming to show everyday comprehensive schooling, tends, at least in part, to focus on poorly performing or overwhelmed teachers. Not surprisingly, those in the 'spotlight' are unhappy when they view the film for the first time – usually much later, when screened on national television. This view is common in documentary work:

> how rare it is that image-makers show us to others as we would like to be
> seen, and, moreover, put in question the assumption that the image makers'
> perspective is more objective or valid than that of their (willing or unwilling)
> subjects.
>
> (Gross *et al.* 1988: viii)

Directors willing to discuss interpretation of their work are rare. One of the few
is Roger Graef, well known for his series of films in the early 1970s, 'The Space
between Words' – essentially about communication but encompassing comprehensive schooling. He accepts that his filming threw up unpredictable issues, that
teachers are not committed to accepting outcomes and should be in a position to
respond to both the record and the director's interpretation:

> my solution . . . is to provide as part of my rules for filming, a guaranteed
> viewing during the editing stage to all the key participants, with a firm promise
> to change anything that can be pointed out to be *factually inaccurate*. That
> extends to re-editing for *emphasis* as well [original emphasis]
>
> (Graef 1980: 171)

Graef has developed a set of procedures (Graef 1980: 175) to explain and guide his
ethical practice, though, as he himself points out, these do not themselves guarantee
ethical practice or fair treatment of participants. Nevertheless, his position represents
the 'high water mark' of ethical practice in observational filming of educational
institutions.

It is the director who has responsibility for the interpretation of data and the
presentation of findings. However, it is clear that a distinction should be drawn
between observational film that is governed by principles that underpin research
and documentary films which are shaped by the vagaries of mass audiences. The
ultimate ethical concern in documentary films, shared by Beauchamp and Klaidman
(1988: 183), is that truths are distorted: 'The search for "truth" fades and becomes
a search for a preconceived moment, a biased hypothesis that captures the "essence
of truth" in the mind of the documentary maker.'

The pressures on the makers of docu-soaps (often referred to as 'bubble gum
for the eyes') and documentaries, as a result of the need to please audiences of 10
million or more, are significant. It is clear from the extent of documentary frauds
at present that such 'investigative' films have major ethical implications concerning how they treat people and how they represent or misrepresent the 'truth' of
a situation. Contemporary documentary films about education, although methodologically and ethically flawed, are viewed by mass audiences as evidence of the
decline of schooling.

## Video-based classroom research

The use of camcorders by researchers to record classroom interaction is far removed from the pressure of documentary and journalistic enterprise and their compulsion for dramatic narrative. Video-based classroom research enhances the possibility of researcher–practitioner co-operation, decreases the theory–practice divide, and, where there is mutual 'close reading' of visual data (Mitchell and Weber 1998), provides respondent insight and validity. It is a particularly pure form of vérité, being without commentary and focusing on observational method. The resulting visual records provide extra-somatic 'memory'. The camera's reproductive and mimetic qualities can be used to systematically record visual detail with emphasis on reproducing objects, events, places, signs and symbols, or behavioural interactions. The ability of the camera to record visual detail without fatigue, to be organized, catalogued and analysed at a later date, is useful to fieldworkers.

Filming in classrooms necessitates a close working relationship being established between the participants and the researcher. The issue of ownership and control is central since disconcertingly, and unlike in word-orientated research, not only do participants have the opportunity to see themselves interacting with each other, but so too do others. Those who claim ownership, excluding the researcher, are not necessarily the actors themselves. Certainly the 'gatekeepers' who hold power have claim, as do governors and the heads who are responsible for their schools' good name. There are examples (Graef 1989: 1) of observational film benefiting those in positions of power yet 'blighting' the career of subordinate actors. This is because problems commonly occur when observational films and videos are shown to outside audiences (i.e. outside the immediate circle of researcher and actors). Graef (1989: 2) believes that 'Vérité brings out that viewers are very nosey about details of other people's lives, but disapprove of that noseyness in themselves and transfer this disapproval into disapproval of what they are looking at.'

The problem of judgemental audiences of video recordings is picked up by Busher and Clarke (1990: 121):

> It is perplexing why audiences rush to judgement about aspects of action, approaches to teaching and personality when viewing a video of a teacher in action. Video-extracts of lessons are void of all but immediate information about the action of the scenes on view while yet appearing to offer an adequate basis for the exercise of judgement by viewers. In this sense videos can be dangerous in easily causing a false sense of understanding of the truth of things as can glimpses of lessons snatched while walking down a corridor.

Since it is very difficult to predict outside audiences' reaction to observational film of classrooms, participants' awareness of potential hazards of external interpretation is integral to informed consent, and as important as who owns and controls the data is how data are to be used.

Videos of classroom interaction necessitate shots of the largest group in the frame: pupils. Not only is their performance most visible, but without their co-operation filming could not take place. Teachers in whose classroom video recordings are made usually tell their pupils that filming will take place but rarely discuss its meaning – perhaps because of the scale of the consensus-seeking exercise, which is more difficult to achieve as pupils' age decreases. This raises the common ethical question of 'How much information do subjects need to give "informed consent"?' (Graef 1980: 163), and signals a less frequently asked but important question: what about minors' rights? Pupils' 'voices' are absent and their disempowerment is complete if they (and their parents) are not invited to view their 'performance'. Busher and Clarke (1990: 144) make an additional point that 'some children seem to attract more attention in the classroom than do others', and that consequently the visual record 'is likely to be skewed both to over-display, and to overemphasize the importance of the attractive children'. This, coupled with Calderwood's findings (1988) that videos of classroom interaction incite colleagues' curiosity more than other forms of recordkeeping, and the unpredictability of audience reaction, makes empowerment of pupils an important ethical issue.

## Contemporary classroom video recording

The ethics of educational research has undergone modifications over the past decade, as a result of increasing complexity in the research process and challenges posed by critical theorists and postmodernism. Latterly, postmodern and narrative influences have brought a new meaning to reflexive accounts. Hence, depending on the stance taken, discussion of contemporary Visual ethics ranges from privacy, ownership, informed consent, to truth, transparency, reflexivity and realism. Modern documentary films can be viewed as the quintessential postmodernist media in that they attempt to depict reality, champion relativism and set little store by objective standards of truth. Winston (1995), in *Claiming the Real*, examines the continuum of principles, ethics, epistemology and practices of documentary work, offering an important insight into the essential differences between film as documentary, and the documentary as fiction. The issues of relative but conflicting ethics, of representing different 'voices' contrasted with notions of fictions and realism, are central in this type of work.

The postmodern and narrative approaches are also beginning to impinge on classroom video recordings. This is clearly illustrated through the work of Weber and Mitchell (1995) and Mitchell and Weber (1999), who use photographs and videos of themselves and colleagues as tools for narrating auto/biography of their professional lives and as an aid to help practising teachers examine their professional identity. Ethical obligations now take a different turn. To what extent should the sensitivities of participants be taken account of when film-makers turn their cameras on their own schools, own colleagues and own classes, whose agreement and trust they may take for granted?

These questions are not easily answered. There is the difficult reflexive question of procedural reactivity. Are film-makers sufficiently sensitive to predict the outcome of recording and, more importantly, replaying recordings of the taken-for-granted act of teaching? Video-based research allows participants to see themselves and reflect on their practice *but* it also has the potential to displace previously established self-images. This makes video-based research different from still-image research and quite different from word-orientated ethical considerations. Self-initiation or initiating others into video recording of classroom practice are acts that carry responsibilities. Teachers' initiating of colleagues into video recording of the relatively private intimacy of their classrooms is to confront them with a camera's unfaltering stare, to be caught 'looking in the mirror', requiring the teachers to open themselves to the public. Mitchell and Weber (1999: 199–200) and Busher and Clarke (1990: 120–2) both illustrate the potential pain from self-analysis to teachers as a result of unsupported or insensitive use of video recording.

Finally, autobiographical film and video are capable of going further by telling the stories of the repressed and under-represented, whose 'voices' are rarely heard in classroom documentaries. However, the degree of trust, confidence, faith and intimacy, so essential for this type of work, also brings with it particular moral issues. Katz and Katz (1988) describe how the ethics of autobiographical films, where close associates may be drawn in alongside the biographer to form a special relationship, differs from an orthodox ethical code. A strength of autobiographical studies and studies made from within communities as distinct from external agencies lies in their ability to act as an antidote to what Winston (1995) terms 'victim documentaries'. Victim documentaries are the focus by the powerful on the private and everyday lives of the less powerful. Rather than rely on pervading values of bodies that often fund documentaries, 'in-house' films and videos have the opportunity to give 'voice' to ethnic, religious and sexual groups that are external or peripheral to mainstream beliefs.

## A way through the moral maze?

There are innumerable examples of poor ethical practice by image-based researchers. This ethical 'black hole' is sustained because few experienced visual researchers have established a consistent set of ethical procedures and few image-based research students are taught ethics. As a result, important ethical issues are rarely debated and ethical knowledge seldom disseminated. There are additional reasons for the moral complexity of image-based research. It is a subdiscipline that is applied across a range of disciplines including sociology, anthropology and psychology. Ethics are situated differently according to each discipline's 'slant' on what comprises befitting moral behaviour. Add to this the relative newness of visual studies and the multiplicity of image-based research in terms of technology used and processes followed, and we begin to recognize the complexity of the moral maze within which it is situated. The ethics of visual research is in its infancy and, metaphorically speaking, located near the centre of a complex moral maze.

There are many false avenues to explore before escape from an ethical 'wilderness' is possible.

More established subdisciplines, such as educational psychology, have established a code of practice that in the past has acted as a focal point of debate and, potentially at least, consensus-based action. Image-based research lacks guidelines and codes of practice in its evolution. Of course guidelines and codes of practice in themselves do not amount to good practice, but they are important arenas of debate on the road to realization of moral behaviour in visual research. Consequently – and this may sound at odds with the views of other contributors to this book – visual researchers need to take a backward step, to reach a consensus on what constitute the principal ethical dilemmas of image-based research. The establishment of a 'checklist' of moral dilemmas is important because it will reflect the different nature of image-based research relative to other styles of research. The 'checklist' is a necessary evil that will act as a springboard to attaining ethical practices that are situated in image-based research as opposed to, for example, word-based research. Recognition of the distinctive ethical dilemmas posed by visual research is the first and most significant step in escaping the moral maze. What is important is that practitioners of visual research reflect on and report back their experiences in order to ground their situated ethics in actuality. It is difficult to avoid prescription at this point, but it seems clear that case studies of situated ethics should be widely disseminated to students of image-based research and those under the gaze of visual researchers. The situatedness of differing research styles is central to establishing enhanced ethical practice. It is equally important that situated ethics becomes a matter of public knowledge rather than remaining the domain of implicit professional knowledge.

## References

Adelman, C. (1998) 'Photocontext', in J. Prosser (ed.) *Image-based Research: A Sourcebook for Qualitative Researchers*, London: Falmer Press.

Anderson, C. and Benson, T.W. (1988) 'Direct Cinema and the Myth of Informed Consent', in L. Gross, J.S. Katz and J. Ruby (eds) *Image Ethics*, New York: Oxford University Press.

Atget, E. (1992) *Atget Paris*, Paris: Hazan.

Beauchamp, D. and Klaidman, R. (1988) 'The Uncounted Enemy: A Vietnam Deception', in L. Gross, J.S. Katz and J. Ruby (eds) *Image Ethics*, New York: Oxford University Press.

Becker, H.S. (1988) 'Foreword: Image, Ethics, and Organisations', in L. Gross, J.S. Katz and J. Ruby (eds) *Image Ethics*, New York: Oxford University Press.

Becker, H.S. (1998) 'Visual Sociology, Documentary Photography and Photojournalism: It's (Almost) All a Matter of Context', in J. Prosser (ed.) *Image-based Research: A Sourcebook for Qualitative Researchers*, London: Falmer Press.

Beloff, H. (1985) *Camera Culture*, Oxford: Blackwell.

Busher, H. and Clarke, S. (1990) 'The Ethics of Using Video in Educational Research', in *Using Video-Recording for Teacher Professional Development*, School of Education, University of Leeds.

Calderwood, J. (1988) *Teachers' Professional Learning,* London: Falmer Press.

Cartier-Bresson, H. (1952) *The Decisive Moment*, New York: Simon and Schuster.

Collier, J. and Collier, M. (1986) *Visual Anthropology: Photography as a Research Method*, Albuquerque: University of New Mexico Press.

Danziger, J. and Conrad, B. (1984) *Interviews with Master Photographers*, London: Paddington Press.

Graef, R. (1980) 'The Case Study as Pandora's Box', in H. Simons (ed.) *Towards a Science of the Singular*, Occasional Publication No. 10, Centre for Applied Research in Education, University of East Anglia.

Graef, R. (1989) 'Privacy and Observational Film', *Anthropology Today* 5, 2: 1–2.

Gross, L., Katz, J.S. and Ruby, J. (eds) (1988) 'Introduction: A Moral Pause', in L. Gross, J.S. Katz and J. Ruby (eds) *Image Ethics*, New York: Oxford University Press.

Kane, P. (1994) 'Putting Us All in the Picture', *The Sunday Times*, Section 10, 28 August.

Katz, J.S. and Katz, J.M. (1988) 'The Ethics of Autobiographical Film', in L. Gross, J.S. Katz and J. Ruby (eds) *Image Ethics*, New York: Oxford University Press.

Mitchell, C. and Weber, S. (1998) 'Picture This! Vernacular Portraits and Lasting School Impressions of School', in J. Prosser (ed.) *Image-based Research: A Sourcebook for Qualitative Researchers*, London: Falmer Press.

Mitchell, C. and Weber, S. (1999) *Reinventing Ourselves as Teachers: Beyond Nostalgia*, London: Falmer Press.

Prosser, J. (1989) 'The Nature of School: An Ethnographic Case Study', unpublished DPhil thesis, Department of Educational Studies, University of York.

Prosser, J. (1992) 'Personal Reflections on the Use of Photography in an Ethnographic Case Study', *British Educational Research Journal* 18, 4: 397–411.

Prosser, J. (1998) 'The Status of Image-Based Research', in J. Prosser (ed.) Image-Based Research: *A Sourcebook for Qualitative Researchers*, London: Falmer Press.

Sander, A. (1986) *Citizens of the Twentieth Century*, Cambridge, MA: MIT Press.

Stasz, C. (1979) 'The Early History of Visual Sociology', in J. Wagner (ed.) *Images of Information: Still Photography in the Social Sciences*, Beverly Hills, CA: Sage.

Weber, S.J. and Mitchell, C. (1995) *That's Funny, You Don't Look Like a Teacher! Interrogating Images and Identity in Popular Culture*, London: Falmer Press.

Winston, B. (1988) 'The Tradition of the Victim in Griersonian Documentary', in L. Gross, J.S. Katz and J. Ruby (eds) *Imagine Ethics*, New York: Oxford University Press.

Winston, B. (1995) *Claiming the Real: The Documentary Film Revisited*, London: British Film Institute.

Winston, B. (1998) ' "The Camera Never Lies": The Partiality of Photographic Evidence', in J. Prosser (ed.) *Image-based Research: A Sourcebook for Qualitative Researchers*, London: Falmer Press.

# Chapter 12

# Rants, ratings and representation

## Ethical issues in researching online social practices

*Michele Knobel*

## Introduction

The past ten years have witnessed a growing debate within the social sciences over what constitutes ethical research practice where cyberspaces and human interaction are concerned. Some researchers argue that codes of ethical conduct currently used in physical spaces – principally those endorsed by universities and influential professional associations (e.g. the American Psychological Association) – hold equally and immutably for cyberspaces. In other words, these researchers argue there is no difference between investigating human interaction and subjectivity offline or online. Others have argued for a more situated or negotiated approach to ethical research practice. For them, researching communities and practices on the Internet requires new approaches to ethical conduct because what holds in physical space – or *meatspace* – hardly ever translates directly into cyberspace, and may even hinder 'good' research because, for example, the insistence on informed consent from participants in the study may actually irreparably disrupt an online community or series of interactions, or because assurances of participants' anonymity in research reports are deeply problematic in the archived and searchable network of cyberspace.

This chapter focuses for the most part on education-related research – that is, research conducted with a view to informing education practices in some way. It engages directly with issues concerning ethical research conduct when investigating online practices, with reference to studies whose data is drawn solely from cyberspaces, as well as to studies that include an online investigation component (e.g. studies of what children do when participating in online social spaces outside school, compared with what they do in class in terms of Internet and computer use). The aim of this chapter is to develop a set of principles that will serve as a starting point for developing guidelines for ethical online research within education arenas. In keeping with this aim, the chapter is organised in the first instance by addressing front end, in process and back end ethical concerns within the research process. These 'points' of focus are applied directly to what Colin Lankshear and I have called in the past 'bearers of moral consequences' (Lankshear and Knobel 1997); that is, groups of people or communities most directly affected by ethical decisions in a given study. In the present case, 'the researched' or study participants are examined first, followed by the 'researcher's craft' and her responsibilities toward the research community as an effective practitioner of research relevant to education. These two sections are followed by a related discussion of ethical concerns and responsibilities where two other bearers of moral consequences are concerned: supervisors and their graduate students, and consumers of research. The chapter concludes with three maxims developed from these discussions that can act as useful guides in making decisions where ethical conduct, education research and cyberspace are concerned.

## Online research and ethical activity

Online research usually refers to two kinds of activity. The first is the analysis of online, public documents (such as newspapers, journals, letters, policies, books, etc.) which are treated as texts in the sense of texts used in a theoretical or historical study (cf. Knobel and Lankshear 1999). These texts can also be used to help to locate a study theoretically, historically, politically or socially in ways that do not require the author's anonymity to be preserved. Second, online research can refer to the study of Internet-worked cyberspaces. It is this second sense that is taken up in this chapter. Where researchers working within the field of education are concerned, this activity generally focuses on person-to-person interactions and communications on and over the Internet, and includes the study of websites, online chatspaces, instant messaging uses, e-mail discussion lists or messages, archived discussions and other types of person-to-person exchanges. Online research can be conducted entirely within cyberspace; that is, the entire corpus of data is located on the Internet. Online research can also form one component of a study that straddles physical space and cyberspace. [. . .]

In research circles, ethics is defined as the study of the formal or informal system of principles or standards that guide what is considered to be 'right' or 'proper' conduct, and the decision-making processes involved in the moral choices people make. Morality refers to the actual application of a system of principles or standards to conduct in a range of contexts and in ways that are, or can be, judged in terms of conformity or nonconformity to a generally accepted standard for or rule of conduct. In short, ethics is the study of moral activity. Some researchers argue that where ethics and online research are concerned, nothing has changed: the standards and principles that apply to physical space research apply equally to research in cyberspace. Others argue that ethical issues encountered in meatspace research are often amplified in cyberspace and require even more careful attention to the moral dimensions and consequences of gathering data from online interactions. For example, the Association of Internet Researchers (AOIR 2001: 1) identifies the following differences between online and offline research. In online research, there is

- *greater risk to individual privacy and confidentiality* because of greater accessibility of information about individuals, groups, and their communications – and in ways that would prevent subjects from knowing that their behaviours and communications are being observed and recorded (e.g. in a large-scale analysis of postings and exchanges in a USENET newsgroup archive, in a chatroom, etc.);

- *greater challenges to researchers* because of greater difficulty in obtaining informed consent;
- *greater difficulty of ascertaining subjects' identity* because of use of pseudonyms, multiple online identities, etc.;
- *greater difficulty in discerning ethically correct approaches* because of a greater diversity of research venues (private e-mail, chatroom, webpages, etc.);
- *greater difficulty of discerning ethically correct approaches* because of the global reach of the media involved; that is as CMC [computer-mediated communication] engages people from multiple cultural (and legal) settings. (original emphases)

This list of difficulties is not exhaustive, neither would all education researchers agree with what has been included in it. Nevertheless, these differences signal important interfaces or *points* where ethical problems can arise.

Despite a growing proliferation of guidelines for conducting ethical research in cyberspace, much of the existing ethical commentary concerning online research wrestles principally with three issues: (1) the distinction between public and private spaces; (2) obtaining informed consent from study participants; and (3) the assurance of participants' anonymity in research publications. A focus on the research context, informed and willing participation, and reporting issues, however, risks suggesting that once these things have been taken care of – along with every researcher's duty to respect those participating in the study and to treat and present them as dignified beings – then ethical considerations have been well satisfied. However, within education in particular, conducting ethically informed online research is a complex process. One of the key difficulties confronting researchers working within the field of education who engage in online investigations is the direct and indirect involvement of a wide range of people who have vested interests in each study conducted. Regardless of whether the study is concerned directly with education or aims at informing education by examining what people are doing technology-wise outside schools, education researchers usually need to take into account in their research planning, conduct and write-up their fellow researcher-educators, other educators, other researchers, policy-makers, students and parents who are either involved in the research or who will be impacted by the outcomes of a study, graduate students who are 'apprenticed' to the researcher, government bodies, and other interested people. Meeting the research needs of each of these parties can tempt education researchers into quantitative online studies that compute the amount of time people spend online, or that measure the effects of computer use by calculating coefficient variations between pre-test and post-test scores on school subject content matter, and the like. These types of studies place ethical considerations on familiar ground in terms of complying with standard university or other associations' ethical research procedures (e.g. respondent anonymity, informed consent from students and parents where minors are concerned, duty of care and beneficence). However, as more and more educators become interested in what young and not-so-young people are doing with computers and the Internet in school *and* out of school, we need to begin engaging with more complex considerations of what 'counts' as ethical research where cyberspaces are concerned.

## The moral consequences of what we do research-wise in cyberspace

In 1997, Colin Lankshear and I defined moral consequences in terms of those effects or outcomes for the good or harm of human beings within areas of human activity where people can reasonably be assigned rights and obligations (cf. Warnock 1970: Thomas 1996). In our argument we identified what we called *bearers of moral consequences*; that is, those people (and sometimes things, such as policy decisions, study outcomes and recommendations, or education programs) that need to be considered in any ethical/moral stocktake. These bearers included

(1)  the 'researched'; that is, study participants affected directly and indirectly by the consequences of various research decisions and outcomes;
(2)  researchers within the education community who are affected directly and indirectly by the quality of their academic colleagues' research work;
(3)  graduate students, who are apprenticed to conducting ethical education research by their supervisors and who are subject to the moral consequences of the decisions they make within the design and implementation of their (the students') investigations;
(4)  consumers of research – those people for whom the research has some kind of use or interest value.

Colin and I also distinguished between different 'points' of moral consequence within qualitative research studies in general and that were set against a backdrop of higher education in Australia. [. . .] We defined these points of moral consequence in terms of (gross) stages or phases within the processes and acts of doing research where what we do, or omit doing, generates consequences or outcomes that impinge on people (and things) directly and indirectly involved in a study. In reality, 'points' comprise practically every moment research is 'going on', but for purposes of heuristic convenience we distinguished broadly between 'front end', 'in process', and 'back end' points of research conduct and responsibility, which roughly correspond to planning, implementation, and end-of-project dissemination phases.

This same heuristic device proves useful for examining ethically informed approaches to online research that go beyond differentiating between public and private spaces on the Internet, engaging with obtaining informed consent and ensuring participant anonymity in reports.

# The researched

## *Front end concerns*

Commentaries on ethical action within online research tend in large part to focus on the participants in a study. Researcher treatment of participants – or those who are 'researched' – is discussed principally in terms of 'doing no harm', 'beneficence' or 'nonmalificence' (e.g. AOIR 2001; Johnson 2001). However, the front end concerns associated with participants in online research begin long before ethically responsible selection criteria and obtaining consent becomes an issue. Front end concerns include demonstrating *respect* for others online by participating in the community to be studied for an extended period of time prior to the start of formal data collection. The easy access to online communities afforded by the Internet makes it tempting to practise hit-and-run research, where the researcher spends a few days or even a few hours observing the interactions of online participants in a given community, then writes about them as though everything to be known about the community and its make-up has been observed and understood in that short period of time. This kind of snatch-and-grab approach usually provokes scathing comments from the community members studied. [. . .]

Despite the easy access to data afforded to researchers by online interactions, ethical practice in relation to obtaining informed consent still holds, even if argued over by online researchers themselves. Some investigators of online practices insist that obtaining informed consent from participants is an inalienable researcher responsibility – and if consent cannot be obtained readily, then the researcher should either change the study's design, or abandon the project altogether (e.g. Bruckman 2001). Indeed, some online researchers set themselves very specific rules for obtaining consent. Amy Bruckman, for example, proposes that consent can be given via e-mail if the participant is over 18, but that signed parental consent needs to be mailed or faxed to the researcher if participants are less than 18 years old. However, her position suggests it is possible to ascertain beyond a shadow of a doubt that the person targeted as a participant in a study is indeed aged 18 years or more. The Internet is, of course, rife with children masquerading or avataring as adults and vice versa.

Other researchers suggest studying the online practices of young people to whom one has in-person access and can obtain their written consent in a face-to-face mode before observing their interactions online (e.g. via strategically placed video cameras, tracking and recording software; e.g. Leander 2003). Kevin Leander's study of young adolescents and their online practices involves observing them in person in meatspace while the participants are communicating online, as well as conducting online participant observations of their public and semi-public online group interactions (e.g. in chatspaces). In the online participant observations, Leander and his colleagues obtain signed consent from their target participants, and from friends with whom the participants interact online *and* offline. In addition, in those cases where 'e-friends' (those people whom key participants know only online) participate in ways deemed important to the project, they are contacted online and asked to sign *post hoc* research consent forms that give permission to Leander and his research team to use their postings as data (Leander 2003; see also Leander and McKim 2003).

In most cases, arguments over whether informed consent should or should not be obtained from participants in an online community boils down to arguments over which online, spaces are public and which are private. Within the humanities, most people agree that research conducted within public spaces (e.g. parks, shopping centres, in the street) does not require the researcher to obtain informed consent from all observed participants (cf. Goffman 1963, 1974). However, few researchers of online practices appear to agree on what criteria should be brought to bear on a space in order to judge it 'public' or 'private'. Some argue that the publicness or privateness of an online space should be judged according to how it is perceived by the people who interact within it. Allison Cavanagh, for example, points out that public space metaphors abound online – such as: village, cafe, town hall, town square – and indicate the non-private status of these different spaces (1999: 1). Cavanagh also points out that 'lurkers' or non-contributors to online interactions are tolerated, if not expected or assumed, in online communities or discussion groups. She observes that when lurkers change their status to more active participation, they generally are welcomed warmly by the community or group. Cavanagh attributes this to a shared cultural assumption about life online that 'internet interactions occur within a public arena and are therefore matters for public consumption' (p. 3).

Some researchers suggest the best response to the public–private dilemma is to create purpose-built research spaces online, such as a room in a MOO or e-mail discussion list which is established explicitly for collecting interactional data, with the purpose of the room written into its publicly available description (Bruckman 2001). Other strategies include setting up websites and the like that signal the researcher's status and to which participants in an online community can be directed. Other researchers, however, call for the *physical nature* of the space to be taken into account when judging whether an interaction is public or private (Frankel and Siang 1999). For example, password protected communities – such as some online cafes and salons – are generally assumed to be private spaces. On the other hand, archivable discussions – such as those generated on web-based discussion boards – are generally presumed to be public spaces (cf. AOIR 2001). However, these distinctions do not always hold, and it is the responsibility of the researcher to make reasoned judgements concerning the nature of the space. This usually involves participating in an online community prior to the start of a formal study so that the researcher can ascertain what kind of community – public or private, or a mix of both – members assume the space to be and act accordingly.

Public declaration of one's role as a researcher of online practice is important, although this is not always an easy undertaking even in meatspace. Part of this public declaration includes establishing means for participants and non-participants alike to contact the researcher about his or her research work. This kind of openness contributes to a researcher's credibility as someone with nothing to hide from study participants. [. . .]

Again, as with offline studies, the researcher needs to be aware of the social dynamics in which people to be targeted for interviews are located and what role or roles they usually play within a community. This once again underscores the importance of the researcher spending an extended amount of time observing, and perhaps participating within, the community to be studied prior to formal data collection. For example, if a researcher interviews or studies the talk of only newcomers to the community, the insights offered will not be as 'experienced' or as historically informed as insights garnered from long-term members. Moreover, selecting a troublemaker or 'troll' as a key participant in a study can skew the researcher's interpretations in unjustifiable ways. In short, the researcher is served well by spending a substantial amount of time getting a 'feel' for the kinds of interactions that take place within the targeted online community. This includes getting to know who the regular participants are, what some of the contentious issues are for community members, who the troublemakers are and who they tend to target (and why, if possible), and the like. These insights enable the researcher to treat all participants with the respect to which they have a right, to conduct himself or herself as an informed and non-threatening member of the community once formal data collection begins, and to build into the study right from the start measures for obtaining balanced insights into the community's interactions and practices.

### In process concerns

Once formal data collection has begun, the researcher must continue to maintain participants' confidence in the project and trust in the researcher herself. This includes maintaining a consistent online persona, not flaming other members for something they did, avoiding long-winded rants, and generally paying attention to the social needs of others by not being overly intrusive or persistent in asking questions or even always being online.

The relative physical anonymity of online spaces makes it all the more important for a researcher to use only one identity within a researched space. Even within public spaces such as eBay discussion lists and participant commentary website, posters who use more than one online alias or username are always criticised and suspected of deeper duplicities, regardless of their reasons for doing so (e.g. wanting to use one alias to post a certain kind of message, to avoid receiving personal e-mails from others or to avoid becoming a target for negative ratings). An online researcher who interviews under one alias, but participates within discussions under another not only interferes needlessly with the data to be collected, but risks publicly alienating others should they discover the deceit. Online researchers are served well by thinking through and even pre-planning the public identity he or she will project onto the online space to be studied and how this identity will be communicated to others (e.g. through careful choice of an alias, a judiciously worded character description, an avatar that carries a magnifying glass and note-book). Education researchers who study children and young people online are under particular pressures to project an online identity that is both credible, sustainable, and defensible (e.g. ethically speaking, it would be difficult to justify a 40-year-old male researcher projecting a 12-year-old girl identity within a teen-targeted chatspace).

Demonstrating respect for participants by practising restraint online is a key element in ethical research behaviour. In meatspace, ethical self-monitoring requires classroom researchers to avoid interjections while observing teachers and students. Likewise, online researchers need to take care that the seeming anonymity the Internet generates does not lead them into dominating an interactional space, or chastising participants, or taking offence at something said (within reason, of course. Cases where researchers have been forced to intervene in hurtful activities or identity thefts taking place in chatspaces are well documented: e.g. Turkle 1997; Dibbell 1998). Studying eBay once again provides fruitful insights into how researchers should, or rather should *not*, behave within this particular space. At one stage, contributors to the feedback discussion list were clearly fed up with one member who advertised the fact he was writing a book about eBay, but who dominated many of the interactions taking place within this particular interactional space. He would admonish newcomers for not reading previous posts where questions similar to the ones they had asked had already been addressed, criticised some of the contributors for being mean or rude, and submitted screeds of advice on how to participate effectively within eBay auction interactions. Participants put up with this for some time before exploding into scathing calls for him to hurry up and finish his book so that he would then leave the list and everyone alone.

Employing a reciprocity factor in online studies seems to be one way of demonstrating ongoing respect and of minimising accusations that only the researcher will benefit from the study. The kinds of reciprocity that online researchers can offer study participants include helping them with some online task such as writing 'bot' programs (e.g. a small program that acts as butler in a MOO room, welcoming people as they enter the door), helping solve HTML dilemmas encountered in setting up a personal website or a personal profile page within an online community, offering lists of URLs for relevant information on a topic or issue needed by a participant, and suchlike. [. . .] Researchers do not have an inalienable right to expect people to want to be researched for nothing in return. In many ways, die reciprocity factor reminds the researcher to appreciate the time and effort outlaid by each participant in responding to questions, agreeing to be observed while using a computer or the Internet, and suchlike.

### Back end concerns

One representational issue particular to cyberspace is the researcher's commitment to participants' anonymity within research reports. Indeed, the very ease of access to data on the Internet also makes it possible for readers to locate much of the data used in a study for themselves, effectively blowing any pseudonym cover the researcher may have attempted for participants within published reports.

Researchers studying archived data (e.g. web-based and e-mail-based discussion lists) or websites *cannot* ensure anonymity for participants. Some researchers rightly point out that using pseudonyms for participants with well-established online identities actually interferes with the integrity of the study because it removes an important data layer concerning the online alias people choose to use and the identities they craft via these aliases (cf. accounts in Cavanagh 1999; Frankel and Siang 1999). Other researchers argue that aliases are part and parcel of a 'consciously "public" performance for others' (AOIR 2001: 1) in which users participate willingly and openly, and thus cannot be subjected to the same pseudonym rules that apply in meatspace (although pseudonyms are no guarantee of anonymity for participants in meatspace either; see Lankshear and Knobel 1997). Still others problematise the issue of aliases and pseudonyms even further by pointing out that 'much of the conversation analysed in these [online] contexts involves references to others' pseudonyms – and thereby their character, behaviours, etc. Hence to change nicknames or pseudonyms would dilute – if not render unintelligible – the meaning of specific exchanges' (AOIR 2001: 1). And of course, the danger with replacing an alias with a pseudonym is that the pseudonym could prove to be the alias of someone else in another space – or even the same space – which makes for untold confusion and possible embarrassment. My own approach to this issue is to weigh up the extent to which readers of texts about my research can readily access the data I draw on in my accounts when deciding whether or not to use pseudonyms in reporting online interactions. In cases where hiding the participant's identity is close to impossible, I advise the participant of this and obtain their consent to use their 'real' alias. In other cases, I either ask participants to nominate a pseudonym for themselves, or I invent one that is as close in nature to the original as possible – always running Internet checks to see if the alias is already in use by someone else.

The representation of online identities is another dimension of ethical concern for educational researchers. Regardless of personal feelings, researchers are duty bound to represent study participants fairly, respectfully and with dignity. Many representation concerns from meatspace research transfer directly into cyberspace. These issues include decisions about whether or not to edit participant-generated texts copied from e-mails, discussion boards, websites and the like in order to smooth out dialect, class or other differences represented by poor grammar and spelling. Producing a text worth reading is also a sign of respect for the time and data participants gave to the study, as is drawing logical, informed, and well-argued conclusions from the data, and so on.

Fairly and respectfully representing study participants can be difficult at times because cyberspace is not always a harmonious social sphere, and often the most intriguing or culturally revelatory events are those where the ugly underbelly of being human is exposed to public viewing (cf. accounts in Dery 1995; Dibbell 1998). Many online researchers point out that this obligation extends to researching hate websites or hate speech – websites or discussion lists devoted to usually fascist commentaries on the supremacy of one race over another, or one set of beliefs and/or values over another (e.g. anti-gay websites, websites belonging to white supremacist groups). For example, Bruckman advises:

> You can respond to hate speech or other undesirable behaviour online as a netizen or as a journalist, and there are few restrictions on your ethical conduct – email their website manager, publish letters decrying their behaviour, do whatever you can. But as soon as you put on your researcher hat, you owe them the same treatment you do any other subject.
>
> (Bruckman 2001: 3)

Of course, the danger with this approach is that

> Research *on* specific behaviours (pornography, hate speech, etc.) *may* work to *legitimate* those behaviours. That is, if re-presented carelessly in research, these behaviours may be 'packaged' in such a way (e.g. through the neutral, ostensibly objective language of social science) as to make them seem more acceptable for the broader society.
>
> (original emphases; Elgesem, cited in AOIR 2001: 1)

Increased access to a wide range of morally problematic activity online means researchers need to pay careful attention to issues concerning the representation of participants and their interactions. One proposed solution to this dilemma is to structure the study in such a way that the linguistic choices made by participants, the interactional rituals they enact, or the cultural meanings they share via their language use become the focus of the study, rather than the actual content of the website or discussion list per se.

My own position on this issue is that demonstrating respect for others requires the researcher to represent each major participant as fully *dimensional* as possible. In other words, in any defensible online study of groups whose values and world views are very different to those of the researcher, the researcher needs to describe the complexities that make up the online identities of key participants and which locate them within a complex web or context of enacting a particular identity online (and usually offline, as well). Representation as an ethical concern is, in many ways, not something which is attended to once data have been collected and the time has come to write up interpretations, but needs to be considered right from the start of planning the study so that the right kinds of data are collected – such as detailed character descriptions, detailed context descriptions, and so on.

In addition to considering ethical responses to front end, in process and back end points of concern where participants are concerned, online researchers also have duty of care responsibilities towards other researchers and to their own academic field of endeavour.

## The researcher's craft

### Front end concerns

Online researchers have ethical responsibilities that relate directly to the practice of research within their field.

What is often overlooked where ethics and online research are concerned is the exclusionary nature of the medium itself. Regular and sustained physical access to computers and the Internet of the kind that enables medium- to long-term participation in web-based activity remains generally confined to the middle and upper classes throughout the world (Pastore 2001; Victory and Cooper 2002). When ethnicity is taken into account, the marginalising properties of the Internet become even more pronounced. In September 2001 in the USA, for example, 71.2 per cent of Asian Americans and 70 per cent of non-Hispanic Whites were found to have ready access to computers at home, while only 55.7 per cent of African Americans and 48.8 per cent of Hispanics had similar access (Victory and Cooper 2002: 21). This same national study found that 'Internet use [at home] among Whites, Asian American [*sic*] and Pacific Islanders hovered around 60 per cent, while Internet use rates for Blacks (39.8 per cent) and Hispanics (31.6 per cent) trailed behind' (Victory and Cooper 2002: 21). Recent income statistics released by the US Government indicate that the median income for Hispanic *households* is currently $30,439 per annum and for African American households it is $33,447 per annum, while non-Hispanic White households and Asian households have an annual median income of $45,904 and $55,521 respectively (Bush 2002). Outside the USA the differences between those who can afford to access and use computers and the Internet on a regular basis and those who cannot is even more marked (cf. Warschauer 2003).

Although marginalised groups are making effective use of community-based computing centres and facilities and shared neighbourhood computing resources, they remain marginalised on the Internet and in online research (Kolko *et al.* 2000). This throws into question whether online research can ever be ethical when already marginalised groups are automatically excluded from participating (Steinberg 2002). To complicate matters, physical markers of ethnicity can generally be hidden or invented online if a person chooses to, making it difficult – if not impossible, or at the very least highly complicated – for researchers to assign ethnicities to participants with any conviction beyond what participants claim and enact online. There are no easy answers where marginalised groups and the Internet are concerned. One possible, albeit limited, response researchers can make is to draw overt attention to the inequities inherent in online research in their published work (Steinberg 2002).

In terms of the researcher's craft itself, one key, but often overlooked, element in maintaining the reputation of researcher craft – the act of carefully planning, carrying out and disseminating research. [...] A well-planned study indicates in advance the time frame to which participants will need to commit upon agreeing to take part in the study, the extent to which participants will be required to contribute data, and will signal what kind of data will be expected from participants (e.g. two e-mail interviews over a period of four weeks, a participant's set of postings to a discussion list over the period of six months), and so on.

A poorly planned study will appear ad hoc to participants and may even undermine their confidence in the researcher as someone who knows what she is doing, with subsequent poor reflections onto the institution or area in which the researcher works. Participants may feel put out if the researcher changes her mind and instead of conducting the one interview the participant agreed to, asks for responses to five different sets of questions at five different times. Collecting gigabytes of data from people without a clear plan in advance of how the data will be analysed and written up simply wastes people's time, and makes them loath to participate in future research (regardless of who is conducting it). Even specific tools and techniques for collecting online data come with a range of ethical issues. For example, one popular method for keeping tabs on the websites children visit at home or school is tracking software, which records the URLs visited, the order in which they were visited, and even the amount of time each webpage was up on the screen. This kind of software has enormous implications where a researcher's duty of care towards children and children's rights to privacy are concerned. Although some schools make use of such software to monitor improper uses of the Internet, this does not necessarily make this software a good thing, nor does it mean that researchers have a right to make use of the data such software generates, or to employ such software elsewhere. One way of addressing this dilemma is offered by Leander in his study of young adolescents' online practices. Leander and his research team use tracking software that can be turned on and off at will by the key participants. This ensures as far as is possible that each study participant's right to privacy and to control their degree of participation within the study is respected.

Research in schools has regularly been a victim of poorly planned projects, with many teachers feeling 'researched out' by participating in studies that have dragged on for longer than expected or have fizzled out altogether. Research in cyberspace that aims at informing education with insights gained from observing online practices and interactions, needs to be carefully thought through and rigorously planned in order to avoid similar problems within online communities.

### In process concerns

Common sense should prevail in research conducted online where practising the researcher's craft is concerned. It stands to reason that education researchers are ill-advised to solicit offline contact information from online participants – regardless of participants' claimed age – or to arrange to meet online contacts face to face. In addition to security issues for the researcher, society and the law does not look kindly on adults who meet children or adolescents online and then arrange to meet them offline. Playing with identity online is a common practice (cf. Hine 2000) and naively assuming people are who they say they are can prove costly to online researchers interested in following up their cyberspace observations with face-to-face interviews.

## Back end concerns

Demonstrating that a study is both valid and trustworthy is an important ethical concern for researchers. Researching online interaction and activity brings with it particular issues concerning the validity or credibility of interpretations and the trustworthiness of the project overall. It is generally well accepted in research circles that qualitative-type research projects attend to verification criteria other than traditional, quantitative processes of ensuring the reliability and validity of a study. These criteria centre on the *communicative validity* and the *trustworthiness* of the study (Kincheloe and McLaren 1994; Knobel and Lankshear 2001). Communicative validity is concerned with judging soundness of the overall argument put forward in research reports (Carspecken 1996).

There are a number of well-recognised strategies for communicating the validity of interpretations and claims in research reports. These include cross-examining multiple sources of data or evidence, using negative cases, member checking, outsider audits, and so on. In terms of research online, employing communicative validity measures can actually be facilitated by the very nature of the online data. For example, data collected over a given period of time can be compared and contrasted with previously archived data from the same chatspace, discussion list or website in order to add further weight to an interpretation. Ready access to negative cases can be provided through search engine functions within the website being studied, or across the Internet in terms of drawing negative cases from similar sites or services. [...]

The trustworthiness of a study is concerned with the degree to which a reader can trust and believe in the quality of the study itself (cf. Lincoln and Guba 1985; Denzin 1998). The key to collecting high quality data is constructing a sound and coherent research design (Knobel and Lankshear 1999; Lankshear and Knobel 2000). Believability depends on the online researcher clearly demonstrating that she has collected data that are *sufficient* for her research needs (and determined in large part by the research question she has asked). Producing a *credible* study means that the overall coherence of the research question(s), the theoretical framing, and the data collection and analysis designs are explicit, justified and appropriate. As with meatspace studies, researchers cannot take what people say at face value, but need to cross-check it with things they have said in the past in order to ascertain the degree to which the participant is or is not 'pulling their leg' or deliberately providing misinformation. Credibility takes on additional dimensions when data collected online are involved. This is not so much because readers can often access the very data used in the report to check and verify claims and interpretations made by the researcher, but because this accessibility is assumed by researchers and readers alike (except where non-archived chatspace is involved) and generally is treated as another (potential) verification checkpoint within a study. Herein lies an interesting paradox. Despite general and widespread recognition that the Internet is an amorphous, ever-changing network, when the data used in a study have been removed or are no longer archived or accessible for one reason or another, the credibility of a study can be thrown into disarray.

[. . .]

## Graduate students and supervision of their research

Increasingly in Education, research supervisors are expected to take on more research students, ensure these students graduate, and continue with their own teaching, researching and publishing efforts. As Colin Lankshear and I have written elsewhere (1997), in Australia many postgraduate Education students come to qualitative research from under-graduate teaching degrees which are often content-dominated, have been short on meta-level teaching and learning, and where prior exposure to serious engagement with research methods and literature often approximates to zero.

Research supervisors within Education thus need to pay extra attention to the knowledge base of their students and to ensure that these students know how to engage in online research that is ethically, theoretically and methodologically informed and coherent, well designed, rigorously conducted, and so on. Indeed, online research with its relative ease of access to well-defined groups of people or sets of texts, the abundance of data and the flexibility opened up by easy access via any computer almost anywhere, and the appeal of investigating cyberspace per se because it has a default 'cutting edge' feel to it, risks lulling supervisors into sanctioning smash-and-grab student research. Supervisors face on a daily basis myriad pressures that take attention away from overseeing each student's research planning and design processes, ensuring that students are paying full and careful attention to their own ethical responsibilities as researchers, checking students are sure that the site or community they plan to study will not suddenly disappear before their data collection has been completed, and apprenticing students to conducting theoretically informed research that addresses a genuine problem and/or set of well-formed and sound research questions. A large part of supervisors' ethical responsibilities towards their research students is to ensure these students are addressing the kinds of front end, in process and back end ethical concerns mentioned earlier.

## Consumers

Consumers of research – that is, those for whom the research has use value – include the researcher and her wider community of inquirers, theorists, and commentators; study participants; groups of people who have a stake or vested interest in the phenomena under study (e.g. schools, parents, students, community, teacher educators, education departments, the media, etc.); and organisations which have identified a research 'need' and provided funding for researching it (e.g. universities, local, state and federal bodies/agencies) (Lankshear and Knobel 1997). [. . .] The needs of consumers of research who have vested interests in the studies conducted by academics and consultants, either because they are funding the studies, or participating in them, or hope to gain educationally from them, generate a number of ethical dilemmas for education-oriented online researchers. Decisions need to be made as to how far to participate in research that focuses on technology in education contexts, and to what extent online research should be conducted outside school contexts so that education can be brought more closely into line with what young people can already do, as well as what they will need to be able to do and be once they have left school.

For example, one ethical issue of increasing concern involves decisions about what to research in education. In the USA at present, for example, websites devoted to teachers and students that present testing and practice exercises aligned directly with national and/or specific state education standards are beginning to proliferate around the nation. Schools are investing heavily in online services that automatically assess students' essays; test reading comprehension; and provide web-based lesson plan generators (complete with lists of learning objectives to select from and automated cross-references to state or national standards indicators and assessment rubrics). Other online investments are teacher–student interfaces that include message boards, spaces for posting assignment grades, homework texts, etc., learning portals similar in kind to the UK's National Grid for Learning, and so on. Most of these applications merely automate existing classroom practices (e.g. multiple choice tests, spelling tests, drill worksheets), with little to recommend them in terms of real engagement with important forms of self-directed learning, high-order thinking, research skills, information evaluation, and the like. The funding available for studying the take-up and use of these technologies is on the rise; however, education researchers interested in the ways in which new technologies can be used to address existing inequities between certain groups of children will need to reflect carefully on how to best research these applications without contributing further to maintaining existing school-generated inequities among children. This can become particularly vexing when permission to conduct research in a school is predicated on an evaluation of a web-based learning system in which the school has invested heavily. Indeed, ethical approaches to studying new technologies, cyberspaces and education require the 'end users' or targeted consumers of the research outcomes to be factored into the project right from the start.

## Conclusion

To sum up, researching cyberspaces does bring with it a distinct set of ethical issues a researcher needs to attend to while planning and designing a project, while conducting the investigation, and while writing up and disseminating a report of the study. For every ethical rule someone puts forward, someone else can find a situation online where the principle cannot possibly hold (e.g. the principle of ensuring anonymity, or the principle of obtaining informed consent). Nonetheless, running through the front end, in process and back end points of ethical consideration discussed so far have been at least three key precepts or maxims that I find particularly useful in guiding ethical decision-making within my own research. In addition to practising the general maxim of doing no harm in any research study, these maxims are as follows.

*Maxim 1: be informed*    A key element of conducting ethically defensible research online is to spend a substantial amount of time observing, or participating, in a community in order to get a sense of how it operates, how members choose to represent themselves, and the like. This includes becoming closely familiar with the discourse rules for participating, learning how to spot newcomers, troublemakers and long-term members, researching the history of the community, and the like. This will help ensure fair and respectful representation of the online context and study participants.

*Maxim 2: be honest and open*    Honesty and openness are always the best policy where online research is concerned. This includes advertising one's researcher status to study participants and non-participants alike within the targeted online community. It includes asking permission of the owner of the website and/or the community to conduct research in that space. This maxim also calls for researchers to post contact details in open and accessible ways so that participants and non-participants may ask questions at any time about the research process. Being honest and open extends to maintaining a consistent online identity when participating in a community or discussion list, etc. Preferably, this identity is one that is close to at least one of the identities practised by the researcher in meatspace. Online education researchers are ill-advised to pretend to be something they are not while conducting online studies as it compromises the integrity of the researcher's interactions with others as well as the credibility of the study overall.

*Maxim 3: be prepared to invest in online communities*    Researching online communities often requires the researcher to be prepared to invest in the moral compass of that community. For example, many online communities make use of a ratings system that is used to judge a member's 'good standing' in the community. This system operates by means of members or moderators rating a transaction (whether it be between a buyer or seller, or in terms of the quality of a posted response to a topic or new item). The higher one's rating, the greater one's respectability or trustworthiness, and the like. In such cases, the researcher should take seriously a community's rating system as a 'character reference' and work at establishing a reasonable rating (and thus, credibility and trust within the community). The online researcher should also be prepared to commit to the community for longer than the data collection period alone in order to pay due respect to the community itself, as well as to ward off criticisms of smash-and-grab research that may alienate participants and make them wary of participating in subsequent studies with other researchers.

Simply attending to front end concerns such as obtaining participant consent is never enough where ethical online research conduct is concerned. Paying constant attention to the key points of potential ethical concern and to the bearers of moral consequences associated with each study is crucial to ensuring to the best of one's ability that the study has been designed, implemented and written up with all due attention to the well-being of others, to the betterment of education as a field, and to one's own development as an ethically aware researcher.

## References

Association of Internet Researchers (AOIR) (2001) *AOIR Ethics Working Committee: A Preliminary Report.* aoir.org/reports/ethics.html (accessed 16 March 2002).

Bruckman, A. (2001) Ethical guidelines for research online: a strict interpretation. Unpublished position paper. www.cc.gatech.edul/~asb/ethics (accessed 28 February 2002).

Bush, G. (2002) Economic Statistics Briefing Room. www.whitehouse.gov/fsbr/income.html (accessed 12 April 2002).

Carspecken, P. (1996) *Critical Ethnography in Educational Research: A Theoretical and Practical Guide* (New York, Routledge).

Cavanagh, A. (1999) Behaviour in public? Ethics in online ethnography, *Cybersociology*, 6. www.socio.demon.co.uk/magazine/6/cavanagh.html (accessed 28 February 2002).

Denzin, N. (1998) The art and politics of interpretation, in: N. Denzin and Y. Lincoln (Eds) *Collecting and Interpreting Qualitative Materials*, pp. 313–344 (Thousand Oaks, CA, Sage).

Dery, M. (1995) *Flame Wars: The Discourse of Cyberculture* (Durham, NC, Duke University Press).

Dibbell, J. (1998) *My Tiny Life: Crime and Passion in a Virtual World* (New York, Owl Books).

Frankel, M. and Siang, S. (1999) *Ethical and Legal Aspects of Human Subjects Research on the Internet* (Washington, DC, American Association for the Advancement of Science).

Goffman, E. (1963) *Behavior in Public Spaces: Notes on the Social Organization of Gatherings* (New York, Free Press/Macmillan).

Goffman, E. (1974) *Relations in Public: Microstudies of the Public Order* (Harmondsworth, Penguin).

Hine, C. (2000) *Virtual Ethnography* (London, Sage).

Johnson, D. (2001) *Computer Ethics*, 3rd edn (Upper Saddle River, NJ, Prentice-Hall).

Kincheloe, J. and McLaren, P. (1994) Rethinking critical theory and qualitative research, in: N. Denzin and Y. Lincoln (Eds) *Handbook of Qualitative Research* (Thousand Oaks, CA, Sage).

Knobel, M. and Lankshear, C. (1999) *Ways of Knowing: Researching Literacy* (Newtown, NSW, Primary English Teaching Association).

Knobel, B. and Lankshear, C. (2001) *Maneras de Ver: El Analisis de Datos en Investigacion Cualitativa* (Morelia, Instituto Michoacano de Ciencias de la Educacion).

Kolko, B., Nakamura, L. and Rodman, G. (2000) Race in cyberspace: an introduction, in: B. Kolko, L. Nakamura and G. Rodman (Eds) *Race in Cyberspace* (New York, Routledge).

Lankshear, C. and Knobel, M. (1997) The moral consequences of what we construct through research, paper presented at the *Australian Association for Research in Education Annual Conference*, Brisbane, November. www.geocities.com/c.lankshear/moral.html (accessed 27 February, 2003).

Lankshear, C. and Knobel, M. (2000) *El Estudio Crítico-Social del Lenguagje y la Alfabetización* (Morelica, MI, Instituto Michoacano de Ciencias de la Educación).

Leander, K. (2003) Researching digital literacies as situating practices. Article in preparation.

Leander, K.M. and McKim, K.K. (2003) Tracing the everyday 'sitings' of adolescents on the Internet: a strategic adaptation of ethnography across online and offline spaces. *Education, Communication & Information*, **3**(2), 212–240.

Lincoln, Y. and Guba, E. (1985) *Naturalistic Inquiry* (Beverley Hills, CA, Sage).

Pastore, M. (2001) Online consumers now the average consumer, Cyberatlas, 12 July. cyberatlas.internet.com/big_picture/demographics/article/0,5901_800201,00.html#table (accessed 12 April 2002).

Steinberg, S. (2002) Response to the research methodology and social practice in online and offline spaces: the challenge of digitization symposium, paper presented at the *Annual Meeting of the American Educational Research Association*, New Orleans, April.

Thomas, J. (1996) Introduction: a debate about the ethics of fair practices for collecting social science data in cyberspace, *The Information Society*, 12, 107–117.

Turkle, S. (1997) *Life on the Screen: Identity in the Age of the Internet* (New York, Touchstone).

Victory, N. and Cooper, K. (2002) *A Nation Online: How Americans are Expanding their Use of the Internet* (Washington, DC, National Telecommunications and Information Administration, the Economics and Statistics Administration, and the US Census Bureau).

Warnock, G. (1970) *The Object of Morality* (London, Methuen).

Warschauer, M. (2003) *Technology and Social Inclusion: Rethinking the Digital Divide* (Cambridge, MA, MIT Press).

# Chapter 13

# Ethics in quasi-experimental research on people with severe learning disabilities
## Dilemmas and compromises

*Mary Kellett and Melanie Nind*

## Introduction

Debates about research ethics are shifting in the current climate which focuses on inclusion and human rights. The question of how people with learning disabilities can be meaningfully involved in research continues to be topical, particularly for researchers working with qualitative approaches. Kiernan (1999) reviewed the recent relevant literature and the present authors will not repeat this work. However, we do acknowledge the fine examples of research projects which have attempted to empower people with learning disabilities and give them a voice (e.g. Ward and Simons 1998). Oral history approaches (in which people tell their stories in their own words) and participatory action research (in which people identify problems and act together to bring about change) are well suited to addressing the power imbalances between people with learning disabilities and those who have traditionally 'researched them'.

This chapter responds to the call for studies addressing ethics in other kinds of research. Quasi-experimental research involves different assumptions from qualitative research. It is less concerned with multiple truths and more concerned with testing hypotheses. As experimental researchers, the current climate can make us feel somewhat uncomfortable and certainly vulnerable. With the rights and voices of people with learning disabilities seen as so important, we could come to see ourselves as an anachronism. This leaves us with (at least) three options: (1) We change the type of research that we do and the type of questions which we ask. (2) We could give up and go home! Or (3) we could accept out vulnerability and limitations, and join the debate with honesty and an open mind. It is this last option that we are interested in exploring.

In this chapter, we use the example of our own ongoing quasi-experimental research to explore the ethical issues which arise and how we might respond to these in ways which are appropriate for our values' position as well our research design. We also explore the issues of research involving individuals who are preverbal and who have profound intellectual impairments. This is timely because the concept of people with learning disabilities as partners in research brings with it the danger of omission in research of those with the greatest disabilities. These individuals may be left outside research efforts because they are perceived as too difficult to include. We do not think that some people with (learning) disabilities can effectively represent all people with learning disabilities, including those who are profoundly intellectually impaired, but we do not yet have models for involving people with profound learning disabilities as real partners in research. This leaves us with the (non)option of being tokenistic or with a dilemma. Do we compromise with whom we do our research or do we compromise the ideal of dialogue in our methods?

Our research is an evaluation of Intensive Interaction (Nind and Hewett 1994). In Kiernan's (1999: 43) terms, this is 'research *on* rather than research *with*' people with learning disabilities. A central aim of the present study was to identify what happened to the social and communicative abilities of six young children when Intensive Interaction was used. The first matter of ethical debate is whether the research is worth doing and whose interests are served by it. There has been a call for research that pursues the agenda of people with (learning) disabilities themselves, rather than research pursuing the agenda of non-disabled academics (Morris 1992; Oliver 1992; Barnes and Mercer 1997). For people with profound intellectual impairment, this can be a double bind since research leading to enhanced lifestyles for this group may not be a priority on either agenda.

Intensive Interaction is an approach for enabling people with profound or complex learning disabilities to be more effective communicators, and those who work with and care for them to be more effective 'listeners'. It has evolved from analysis of the characteristics of the natural model of caregiver–infant interaction. A set of working principles, rather than any prescribed content, is employed in both everyday incidental interactions and regular quality sessions which are subjected to critical reflection. The intervention involves daily, recorded one-to-one inter-actions in which the teacher takes the learner's lead, responds contingently to the learner's behaviours, and treats them as if they have social or communicative intent. The teacher's interpersonal behaviours are modified, and sensitive use is made to timing, rhythm, playfulness, watching, waiting and adapting based on non-verbal feedback. The approach itself could be subjected to ethical scrutiny, particularly considering its element of offering developmentally appropriate interactions, some-times in the face of chronological age, which has been passionately debated (Nind and Hewett 1996; Smith 1996; Samuel and Maggs 1998).

Intensive Interaction is concerned with the interactive processes that occur and is not bound up with a medical model. Therefore, evaluative research that furthers professionals' and families' understandings of the efficacy of the approach clearly stands to benefit people with profound learning disabilities by reducing the barriers to their effective communication. Indeed, although this research may not be eman-cipatory or empowering in the ways often currently called for (Kitchen 2000), it does seek to both change the views of the wider society and enable change of the individuals involved.

Checking ourselves in the way that Barton (1998: 34) modelled does not make us too uncomfortable in terms of: Who is this work for? What right do we have to undertake it? and What responsibilities come with it? We do not doubt that we, the academics, and other professionals will benefit from the research, but this is in addition to people with learning disabilities and their families, and not at their expense.

The present evaluation of Intensive Interaction with children is a replication/adaptation of an earlier study with adults in a long-stay hospital (Nind 1996). The replication element limited the choice of research design, but with a new researcher leading the project, new ethical questions were asked of the methods, and the design and tools were put under new scrutiny.

## Quasi-experimental research design

We encountered many ethical (and practical) dilemmas when we embarked on this project, not least in the research design itself. A means of evaluating the effectiveness was needed and we did not have the option of pupils explaining how it was for them in their own words. An option was to measure progress in two groups, one getting Intensive Interaction and one not, in a 'control group' design. However, on a practical level, it is impossible to find a 'typical' or 'representative' group, and a satisfactory sample match (Hogg and Sebba 1986). A pragmatic alternative would have been to use a 'reversal phase', with one group getting the intervention for a period before it was withdrawn to see if progress was halted or reversed.

Both the models present serious ethical concerns. Based on previous research (Nind 1996; Watson and Fisher 1997), we hypothesized that Intensive Interaction would facilitate social and communication development. To withhold or withdraw something of benefit in order to prove its effectiveness would be unethical and potentially damaging to the welfare of the research participants.

To overcome these problems, we opted for a multiple-baseline interrupted time-series design (Cuvo 1978; Cook and Campbell 1979; Nind 1996). This meant a series of assessments throughout a baseline and intervention phase (and the intervention continuing beyond the duration of the study). While participants began the baseline phase together, the start of the intervention was staggered. Thus, the approach was delayed for a few weeks rather than withheld or withdraw. The design was strong in that a pattern of individuals making progress around their intervention start-times would indicate a relationship between progress and intervention. The most plausible explanation of outcomes would be that the intervention was responsible for change (Glass *et al.* 1975; Borg 1987). In effect, the participants would become their own controls, enabling a workable compromise to be reached between experimental rigour and ethical considerations.

## Informed consent

In collaboration with staff, six children from two primary special (severe learning disabilities) schools and one integrated nursery were selected for the present study. Before proceeding, the informed consent of the children, or at least, their parents/guardians was required. We took steps to give parents full and honest information, and to ensure that our consent was not pressured or coerced, but this did not fully discharge our ethical responsibilities. We were going to be working with preverbal children with severe learning disabilities aged between 4 and 11 years: How could we ensure that the subjects were participating with informed consent? While we could not construe the subjects as partners in research, we still had a duty to ensure that these individuals were comfortable with participation and we could not ascertain this through dialogue. Like Stalker (1998), we could find no precedents for this in the literature and we found that we had to devise our own framework.

Starting with the children as their focal point, we involved the network of people who understood the subjects, cared about them, and knew when they were unhappy, distressed or uncomfortable. We sought open dialogue with this network with the aim of being assured of the ongoing consenting status of the children. Such approaches to consent issues involve expanding traditional researcher–teacher–parent relationships to include other concerned individuals such as siblings, friends and support staff. We wanted to make real the notion of the participants' right to withdraw at any point. Like Knox et al. (2000), we saw consent in terms of an ongoing process involving a network of advocates who would allow for functional informed consent in a complex situation.

The effects of this were to make the researcher who gathered the observational data on a weekly or fortnightly basis much more involved in the lives of those involved with the project than she might otherwise have been. It was necessary to forge good relationships and trust such that open dialogue was made possible. Face-to-face contact, phone calls, home–school books and home visits were all used. In this way, not only did the successful implementation of the intervention rely on the interpersonal qualities of the practitioners, but also the evaluation itself relied on the interpersonal qualities of the researcher. This perhaps blurred the boundaries between a quasi-experimental approach and more interpretative approaches. There was also compromise because the additional sharing and cooperation required in this model inevitably diluted the power and control of the researcher.

## Duration of baseline

The intervention and design for evaluating it were known to have been effective with adults in a long-stay hospital (Nind 1996). However, the practical implementation of this design in a community special school raised some unforeseen issues. This concurs with the growing concern in recent years about ethical practice in special education research (Shakespeare 1996; Gray and Denicolo 1998; Stalker 1998).

The design element of a staggered start to the intervention meant that one child in each school would start Intensive Interaction after 4 weeks, one after 8 weeks and one after 12 weeks. However, following Intensive Interaction training, the teachers were enthusiastic to begin. As they got going with other pupils, they became increasingly confident of the benefits of the approach and increasingly frustrated at the delay in its use with the research participants. At the design stage, a multiple baseline of 4, 8 and 12 weeks seemed reasonable. In practice, it proved difficult for the first teacher to delay for 4 weeks, frustrating for the second teacher attempting to delay for 8 weeks and virtually impossible for the third teacher, who regarded 12 weeks as a whole term of lost opportunity.

This raises real dilemmas. From the researcher's perspective, multiple baselines avoid the need for a control group or reversal phase, while providing stronger evidence than a simple series of case studies. This allows for more comprehensive dissemination, and ultimately, wider benefits. From the teacher's perspective, the baseline period represents lost opportunities for progress. At what point does one choose between potentially greater benefits for greater numbers and probable benefits to an individual being delayed? Opting for the rigorous design still leaves the problem of the duration of the baseline phase. How long is long and how long is ethical? If 12 weeks is acceptable, but 20 weeks unacceptable, should the line be drawn at 12 weeks or at 19 weeks and 6 days? Who should make that judgment? The decision is likely to be a compromise, as it was for us, reached through dialogue between the researcher, steering group or supervisor, and the network of advocates called for earlier in this chapter. Following concern at the first 12-week baseline, the baselines in the second school were made 4, 5 and 6 weeks long, rather than 4, 8 and 12 weeks as planned.

## Measuring tools

The present research also required a means of measuring social and communicative behaviour that could be used frequently, was non-intrusive and could show tiny changes. Several measures were needed for richness of data and triangulation (findings from different perspectives and means). Two published assessments, Kiernan and Reid's (1987) Pre-Verbal Communication Schedule and an adaptation of Brazelton's (1984) Cuddliness Scale were used alongside systematic observation. This allowed for a more standardized and long-term view alongside the detail of social behavior intricately coded second-by-second from video recordings. Participants were filmed initially weekly and then fortnightly over a period of one year.

Video data were analysed for typical classroom behaviour when alone; any attempt to initiate social contact; responses to the proximity and physical contact of the teacher; interactive behaviour; and engagement in a one-to-one teacher–pupil interactive session. Once again, the measures appeared reasonable, but as the pupils began to make progress, teachers and researcher felt increasingly uncomfortable with 'passive' situations where the teacher purposefully did not initiate interaction. Observation of positive responses to proximity and physical contact was originally sought as an early sign of progress. Nevertheless, these pupils seemed bewildered as to why teachers sometimes interacted intensively with them and sometimes passively.

Again, there was tension between rigorous method and contextual research ethics. For us, although such a rich source of experimentally valid data could strengthen the study, the potential distress to pupils was too high a price to pay. This inevitably lead to another compromise and a need to sacrifice some of the neat, tidy study in pursuit of rather messier but more ethical data. The passive condition for the assessment was abandoned for the first pupil–teacher pairing as soon as concern about its negative impact emerged. It was then dropped for the later pupils before concern emerged.

## Ownership of data

A further issue arising from the project, but not necessarily linked to its experimental nature, concerned ownership of data. This project involved video recording of pupils and teacher in one-to-one social interactions. Who should own the data: the pupils, teachers, parents, researchers or funding source? Should ownership be shared jointly between all parties concerned? Or should the raw data be destroyed when analysis is complete so that these are not owned by anyone? The desire to extend just rights to participants may need to be tempered by logistical realism in order to protect data which could prove valuable in future studies. We were made to compromise again, and opted for a solution in which the researcher acted as 'banker' or unofficial archivist of the video data, storing it safely and enabling participants and their families to have their entitlement to view the material.

## Conclusion

Conducting quasi-experimental research in current learning disability contexts raises many ethical dilemmas and exposes possible conflicts of interest between researchers and research participants. We fully recognize the limitations of any study in which the researcher has power and the researched are a separate vulnerable group, and we have shown how this power may be handled responsibly and perhaps shared. In experimental as well as interpretative research, there is potential power to do good, even to empower, as well as potential to do harm. Ethics committees and procedures should perhaps ask whether there are alternative designs in which the researched individuals can more actively become the researchers, but not rule out studies where this is not possible.

The growing number of groups involved in qualitative, participatory and emancipatory research may lead the way on research ethics in a new era, but they cannot be left to take the responsibilities which all researchers in the area of learning disabilities must share. The changing context of demands for inclusion, for evidence-based practice and for respect for all human rights should lead us to reflect on the practical benefits and ethical issues associated with our research. Having reflected on this study, we conclude that, like any research, it is not perfect that all researchers need to seek compromises, and that dialogue is needed on purposeful ways forward.

# References

Barnes C. and Mercer C. (ed.) (1997) *Doing Disability Research*. Leeds, Disability Press.

Barton L. (1998) Developing an emancipatory research agenda: possibilities and dilemmas. In: Clough P. and Barton L. (eds) *Articulating with Difficulty: Research Voices in Inclusive Education*. London, Paul Chapman: 29–39.

Borg W.R. (1987) *Applying Educational Research: A Practical Guide for Teachers*. New York, NY, Longman.

Brazelton T.B. (1984) *Neonatal Behavioural Assessment Scale*. London, Heinemann Medical Books.

Cook T.D. and Campbell D.T. (1979) *Quasi-experimentation: Design and Analysis Issues for Field Setting*. Boston, MA, Houghton Mifflin.

Cuvo A.J. (1978) Multiple baseline in institutional research: pitfalls of measurement and procedural advantage. *Am. J. Mental Deficiency*, **84** (3): 219–228.

Glass G.V., Wison V.L. and Gottman, J.M. (1975) *Design and Analysis of Time Series Experiments*. Boulder, CO, Colorado Associated University Press.

Gray D.E. and Denicolo P. (1998) Research in special needs education: objectivity or ideology? *Br. J. Special Education*, **25** (3): 140–145.

Hogg J. and Sebba J. (1986) *Profound Retardation and Multiple Impairment*, Vol. 1: Development and learning. London, Croom-Helm.

Kiernan C. (1999) Participation in research by people with learning disabilities: origins and issues. *Br. J. Learning Disabilities*, **27** (2): 43–47.

Kiernan C. and Reid B. (1987) *Pre-verbal Communication Schedule*. Windsor, NFER-Nelson.

Kitchen R. (2000) The researched opinions on research: disabled people and disability research. *Disability Soc.*, **15** (1): 25–47.

Knox M., Mok M. and Parmenter T.R. (2000) Working with the experts: collaborative research with people with an intellectual disability. *Disability Soc.*, **15** (1): 49–61.

Morris J. (1992) Personal and political: a feminist perspective on researching physical disability. *Disability, Handicap Soc.*, **7** (2): 157–166.

Nind M. (1996) Efficacy of Intensive Interaction: developing sociability and communication in people with severe and complex learning difficulties using an approach based on caregiver–infant interaction. *Eur. J. Special Education Needs*, **11** (1): 48–66.

Nind M. and Hewett D. (1994) *Access to Communication: Developing the Basics of Communication with People with Severe Learning Difficulties through Intensive Interaction*. London, David Fulton.

Nind M. and Hewett D. (1996) When age-appropriateness isn't appropriate. In: Coupe O'Kane J. and Goldbart J. (eds) *Whose Choice? Contentious Issues for Those Working with People with Learning Difficulties*. London, David Fulton: 48–57.

Oliver M. (1992) Changes the social relation of research production. *Disability, Handicap Soc.*, **7** (2): 101–114.

Samuel J. and Maggs J. (1998) Introducing Intensive Interaction for people with profound learning disabilities living in small staffed houses in the community. In: Hewett D. and Nind M. (eds) *Interaction in Action: Reflections on the Use of Intensive Interaction* London, David Fulton: 119–148.

Shakespeare T. (1996) Rules of engagement: doing disability research. *Disability Soc.*, **11** (1): 115–119.

Smith B. (1996) Discussion: Age-appropriate or developmentally-appropriate activities? In: Coupe O'Kane J. and Goldbart J. (eds) *Whose Choice? Contentious Issues for Those Working with People with Learning Difficulties.* London, David Fulton: 70–80.

Stalker K. (1998) Some ethical and methodological issues in research with people with learning difficulties. *Disability Soc.,* **13** (1): 5–19.

Ward L. and Simons K. (1998) Practising partnership: involving people with learning difficulties in research. *Br. J. Learning Disabilities,* **26** (4): 128–131.

Watson J. and Fisher A. (1997) Evaluating the effectiveness of Intensive Interaction teaching with pupils with profound and complex learning difficulties. *Br. J. Special Education,* **24**: 80–87.

# Chapter 14

# Owning the story

## Ethical considerations in narrative research

*William E. Smythe and Maureen J. Murray*

[...]

### Limitations of regulative principles in narrative research

The narrative study of lives is a growing, multidisciplinary tradition of research based on the in-depth autobiographical interviewing of research participants; it involves 'listening to people talk in their own terms about what had been significant in their lives' (Josselson 1993: ix). Narrative research is situated within the broader domain of qualitative social science research, which, in turn, is a subset of all research conducted with human participants. The main data collection instrument in narrative research is the research interview, which is often conducted in a naturalistic setting over an extended period of time and might require some significant personal involvement of researchers in the lives of those they study. Methodologically, narrative research is an essentially interpretive enterprise in that the researcher is engaged actively in formulating meanings for participants' narrative expressions, often in quite different terms than the participants themselves would. Thus, narrative researchers often are conflicted ethically about how to do justice both to their own and their participants' very different understandings of their life experiences – indeed, how to maintain any balanced ethical perspective in the context of such an intrusive style of research. It is widely agreed by now among narrative researchers that traditional ethical principles in research offer insufficient guidance in this respect. In the introduction to a recent volume on ethical issues in the narrative study of lives, Josselson (1996a) wrote

> There are no easy answers to these questions. Merely waving flags about confidentiality and anonymity is a superficial, unthoughtful response. And the concept of *informed consent* is a bit oxymoronic, given that participants can, at the outset, have only the vaguest idea of what they might be consenting to. Doing this work, then, requires that we find a way to encompass contradictions and make our peace with them.

> (pp. xii–xiii)

[. . .] What emerges, quite plainly, is the general inadequacy, for narrative research, of the ethical principles that guide more traditional nomothetic social science research. [. . .]

## Informed consent

Informed consent is problematic, given the idiographic nature of narrative inquiry. What happens during the course of a narrative interview very much depends on the individuality of the research participant and the quality of rapport that develops between participant and researcher. In contrast with nomothetic research, where people are processed in cookie-cutter fashion through standardized methodological protocols, it is often impossible to forecast with any degree of accuracy what will happen during the data gathering phase of a narrative research project. By virtue of its *emergent* or *discovery-based* methodology, significant methodological decisions often are made on the fly (Price 1996). Hence, narrative research participation is something one has to experience firsthand to make an informed decision about. Chase (1996) wrote

> I think we need to remind ourselves as well as prospective participants that narrative research is a contingent and unfolding process, the results of which we cannot anticipate or guarantee. An informed consent form cannot possibly capture the dynamic processes of interpretation and authorship.
>
> (p. 57)

Moreover, as in other forms of qualitative research, the nature of the relationship that develops with research participants might seriously compromise the meaning and purpose of informed consent, especially in its legalistic overtones (Rubin and Rubin 1995; Rossiter *et al.* 1996). The open-ended nature of what people consent to can often lead to problems securing ethical clearance; given the highly personal nature of narrative data, the use of a signed consent form might sometimes compromise participants' rights to privacy and confidentiality (Price 1996).

An alternative to the traditional, static, one-shot approach to securing consent that often is recommended to qualitative researchers is the notion of *process consent*. In process consent, informed consent is a mutually negotiated process that is ongoing throughout the course of the research rather than something obtained just at the outset (Grafanaki 1996; McLeod 1996; Balfour 1999). In our view, this should include the option for participants to withdraw their data following participation. Minimal provisions for mutually negotiated consent are incorporated in traditional informed consent insofar as participants are informed that they may withdraw at any stage of the research without penalty. In process consent, explicit procedures are provided for mutually negotiated consent and the process is initiated by the researcher rather than the participant.

## Privacy and anonymity

The information collected from participants in narrative research typically is so detailed and individually specific – that disguising the identities of research participants becomes extremely difficult. [ . . . ]

True anonymity generally is a problematic requirement to meet whenever a person's story is presented and analysed as a whole and in detail. In such cases, as Chase (1996) observed, 'research participants easily recognize themselves in our texts and readers who know them may recognize them, too, even when pseudonyms and other forms of disguise are used' (p. 45). Hence, the debate over whether the use of pseudonyms renders narrative and historical research less 'authentic' (Etter-Lewis 1996) is rendered moot, as the individuals normally are identifiable anyway. Given the very real possibility of such breaches of privacy, it is incumbent on narrative researchers to take steps to protect individuals, and the third parties who figure in their narratives, from undue exploitation in the process of telling their stories (Graves 1996).

## Protection from harm

This brings us to the issue of avoidance of harm. The potential risks invoked by narrative research have to do with the subtle and often unforeseeable consequences of writing about people's lives. In her study of life in a kibbutz, for example, Lieblich (1996) noted that some of her participants used the research interview as an opportunity to vent old grievances and even perpetuate distortions of the truth. Other members of the community felt hurt by these revelations once the study was published and the identities of participants became known. Etter-Lewis (1996) also raised the issue of 'airing dirty laundry' in narrative research. Participants also might make themselves vulnerable in their own narrative revelations. Hence, extensive precautions often are necessary to protect the integrity of participants' reputations and their ongoing relationships with the others who figure in their stories (Chase 1996). However, given the inherent problems with confidentiality in narrative research, such precautions are not always successful. In addition, narrative researchers, like other qualitative researchers, must confront the potential risks involved in inadvertently touching on highly charged emotional issues in the course of an interview, especially when dealing with individuals from highly vulnerable populations such as the terminally ill (Raudonis 1992; Grafanaki 1996; McLeod 1996; Balfour 1999).

Perhaps the most pervasive risk for participants in narrative research has to do with the emotional impact of having one's story reinterpreted and filtered through the lenses of social-scientific categories. The problem is that, once the researcher's account is taken as the authoritative interpretation of an individual's experience, the individual's own understanding of their experience inevitably is compromised. Narrative research can in this way become intrusive and subtly damaging, even when participants respond positively to the researcher's account. Reflecting on her own experience with one such participant, Josselson confessed

> I felt that even though Lydia found my comments useful to her, I had intruded on her and on her life in a powerful way. Whatever sense she was making of her life was, after all, her sense. What right had I to impose my meaning making on her?
>
> (p. 66)

More generally, Josselson (1996b) observed

> The renarrating we do when we write about someone is a form of psychotherapy, cloaked not in the authority of the therapist–patient relationship but in the authority of the written word. To renarrate a life unasked, therefore, robs the Other of a piece of his or her freedom no matter how exhilarating an experience it may be . . .
>
> (p. 67)

[…]

In sum, the assessment of risk in narrative research is a highly sensitive and idiosyncratic matter, one that resists any obvious formulation in terms of principles of minimal risk or uniform procedures for risk–benefit analysis.

## Conflict of interest

Conflicts of interest due to multiple relationships are virtually unavoidable in narrative research, especially when the research takes place in a naturalistic setting. Lieblich (1996), commenting on her study of Israeli kibbutz life, pointed to her inevitable involvement in the lives of those she studied, from the perspective of her multiple roles as researcher, expert resource person, and friend. With respect to the last of these roles, she wrote

> What started as a research became a relationship . . . as I have asked my 'subjects' to cooperate with me on deep and meaningful levels, I have become indebted to them in many ways, more than I had ever imagined. Many became friends. Is this good or bad? Could I anticipate this development?
>
> (pp. 172–173)

Toward the end of her article, she stated:

> Today, my contacts with the kibbutz are less frequent, yet the relationship is sound and solid. I am there for them in certain ways, as they are for me. Is this ethics or friendship? I believe that a researcher who resents this entanglement

should not start a narrative research about people who belong to his or her own culture and society.

(p. 184)

[...]

However, the distinctive and most pervasive role conflict that narrative researchers face is between serving as their participant's confidant, on the one hand, and then going public with their stories, on the other hand. Josselson (1996b) aptly characterized the type of conflict of interest that these conflicting roles can lead to as that of 'talking about people behind their backs'. She wrote

My guilt, I think, comes from my knowing that I have taken myself out of relationship with my participants (with whom, during the interview, I was in intimate relationship) to be in relationship with my readers. I have, in a sense, been talking about them behind their backs and doing so publicly. Where in the interview I had been responsive to them, now I am using their lives in the service of something else, for my own purposes, to show something to others. I am guilty about being an intruder and then, to some extent, a betrayer.

(p. 70)

### Deception and debriefing

Deception normally is not a significant ethical issue for narrative research. Narrative researchers generally have no reason to systematically mislead their research participants at any stage of the research process. They are interested in people's stories, told in their own words, about some aspect of their life experiences, and participants are told this at the outset of a narrative interview. Hence, there is no need for debriefing, in the usual sense of clarifying the 'true purposes' of the study, following people's participation. Narrative researchers typically are forthright and explicit about the purposes of the research from the outset of participation. However, there is debriefing in the sense of sharing the results of the researcher's narrative analysis with participants at some stage of the process. There are as yet no well-established guidelines governing when and to what extent (if at all) participants should be involved in the process of analysis. In some studies, participants are actively involved in the process of narrative interpretation itself; in others, participants' comments, clarifications, and permission to use their data are sought only after the analysis is complete but before the study is published; sometimes participants' reactions are solicited only following the release of the published report, if at all. Peer debriefing – the sharing of one's findings with a disinterested peer researcher – is sometimes recommended as a way of ensuring honesty and reducing researcher bias; however, no widely accepted standards and procedures for such debriefing have been worked out yet (Price 1996).

### Narrative ownership

Debriefing raises another important ethical issue – the central ethical problem in narrative research, in our view – narrative ownership. Who owns the research participant's narrative? That is, who wields the final control and authority over its presentation and interpretation? The issue of the ownership of data scarcely arises in traditional psychological research, where (as pointed out earlier) one simply gives away one's data to the researcher as part of the standard research participation contract. However, can one give away one's own story in this fashion, especially when it is so heavily invested with one's personal meaning and sense of identity? A common reaction of narrative research participants to researchers' analyses of their stories is that the analysis fails to capture them fully in their personal uniqueness and individuality. As one of Josselson's (1996b) research participants put it succinctly, the researcher's account just did not 'feel' like her. Associated with such reactions, there is often a subtle sense of betrayal, a feeling that the researcher has undermined participants' authority to speak for themselves about their own experiences.

Such reactions are perhaps inevitable when people's stories are transformed into instances of larger social or psychological phenomena. The narrative researcher approaches a life story from a radically different perspective than that of the individual who tells the story. The purpose of narrative analysis normally is not to clarify what participants intended to say but, rather, to interpret the underlying, implicit meanings behind what they say. Ochberg (1996) stated

> When I interpret a life story, I try to show what an informant accomplishes by recounting his or her history in a particular fashion. To succeed, I must undermine the usual assumption: that people say what they mean and mean only what they say. I lead a reader through the account showing how everything that has been said has other meanings, ulterior purposes.
>
> (p. 98)

Moreover, it is incumbent on the narrative researcher, as a social scientist, to relate the meanings of an individual's story to the larger, theoretically significant categories that they exemplify, an objective quite foreign to that of the individual telling a purely personal narrative.

Hence, it is widely agreed among narrative researchers that, given their unique perspective on people's stories, it is imperative that they claim some ownership and control over the narratives they study. Chase (1996) addressed the matter in the following way:

> Who should control the interpretive process in any particular case depends in large part on the aim or purpose of the research and thus what kind of material needs to be collected and what kind of interpretation best suits that material. Moreover, as long as decisions about these questions are made by the researcher . . . the researcher continues to exercise authority not shared with participants. . . . I believe that claiming and acknowledging one's interpretive authority is imperative.
>
> (pp. 51–52)

Price (1996) also agreed, but with the following qualification: 'This acknowledge-ment of ownership is the foundation for an ethical study when accompanied by the recognition of one's own biases and prejudices' (p. 213).

However, how does one distinguish such acknowledgment of ownership from exploitation or 'colonization' of the participant's story by the researcher? Further-more, not all narrative researchers agree that their own interpretive perspective is the final one. Etter-Lewis (1996), for example, defended the contrary position that

> The narrator's outlook must prevail. Researchers lose nothing in sharing the process (reaffirming the narrator's authority of self), which naturally is inter-active and collaborative rather than autocratic. In other words, narrators must participate in this alliance with the power to know, correct, and teach, whereas the interviewer must be a willing learner whose external knowledge (i.e., information outside of the narrator's experience) guides (not dominates) the elicitation process.
>
> (p. 127)

Issues of ownership, interpretive authority, and betrayal are subtle, complex, and pervasive. [. . .] These issues cannot be dealt with adequately by uniform proce-dures such as offering to remove participants' data from the study, at their request, following debriefing (MRCC et al. 1998). As is evident in the previous examples, people still can feel that they have been misrepresented and that their 'say' has been taken away even when they otherwise agree with the researcher's account. We need an entirely different way of thinking through ethical dilemmas of this kind. In the next section, we argue for an epistemological approach to this issue.

## Narrative epistemology and ethics

One of the unique features of narrative research is the intimate entanglement of ethical issues with epistemological ones. The issue of narrative ownership strikes to the heart of the matter. When researcher and participant are at odds in their narrative accounts of a given life experience, whose account is to be considered the more credible and on what grounds? Participants enjoy a certain epistemic privilege by virtue of the fact that the story is about their own experience and no one can know an experience as intimately as the one who has lived it. Researchers, on the other hand, have theoretical knowledge and access to literature that can frame the participant's experience within a much larger context. On the basis of such knowl-edge, researchers often can aspire to an understanding of an individual's experience that goes beyond the individual's own understanding in some respects. However, how do we know, in a given instance, who is right? This is an epistemological question. It is a question that simply does not arise in more traditional nomothetic research, where people are employed as data sources and almost never are asked to interpret their own data (although the data, themselves, might consist of interpre-tation or judgements of various kinds). In nomothetic research, disputes about the interpretation of evidence typically are between different investigators and are to be settled, ultimately, by an appeal to methodological and theoretical considerations; they are separate from the ethical treatment of research participants. In narrative research, the ethical cannot be bracketed so neatly from the epistemological, as participants have an essential stake in the interpretation of their own stories.

It has been argued that narrative has its own distinctive epistemology, that it is a mode of knowing fundamentally different from the *paradigmative* mode more characteristic of logical and scientific arguments (Bruner 1986; Polkinghore 1988). Narrative discourse is structured more temporally than conceptually, concerns relations among particulars rather than abstract generalities, addresses the vicissitudes of human intentions and motivations, and aims to be convincing more by virtue of its believability than in terms of its logical coherence or empirical testability (Bruner 1986). Most important for out purposes, narrative accounts are told from multiple perspectives (Bruner 1986). There is no single best way to tell a story. There are at least as many perspectives from which to tell a story as there are key characters within it; literary and journalistic narratives often switch between several such perspectives. The epistemological import of multiple narrative perspectives is the suggestion that narrative meaning must be multiple as well. Rather than aspiring to a singular account of reality – the ultimate aim of paradigmatic inquiry – the narrative domain requires that we live with multiple interpretations of reality.

## Three types of narrative

Another consideration that contributes to the multiplicity of narrative meaning is that there are fundamentally distinct types of narratives. The one that is most familiar to modern readers is the *personal narrative*. This mode, typified by contemporary biography and autobiography and many works of modern fiction, is centred on the individuality of a central main character or person. The narrative is told from a consistent, personal perspective and is aimed at revealing the unique, idiosyncratic character and life circumstances of a particular individual. This is exemplified in the way that modern biographical and autobiographical works tend to focus on presenting the life circumstances and influences on their characters in their unique particularity.

A more archaic narrative form is the *archetypal narrative* of mythological and religious texts. Here, the focus is not on human individuality as such but on timeless human motifs that reflect fundamental spiritual, existential, and moral concerns, such as human mortality, the stages of life, love and war. [. . .]

The narratives that social scientists construct in the narrative study of lives fall somewhere between the personal and the archetypal. These are narrative accounts that bear on psychological and social themes, such as emotional abuse, healing from trauma, racial discrimination, needs for achievement and affiliation, and interpersonal dynamics in the family, among many others. We call these *typal narratives* because they attempt to subsume individuals and their life experiences within broader types that are of theoretical interest to social scientists. Its principal aim is neither to capture the individuality of persons in detail nor to bring out archetypal human themes, but rather to concretely exemplify the theory-laden categories of contemporary social science. To the extent that these themes depend on current social and cultural contexts, typal narratives are not as timeless and invariant as archetypal narratives, but neither are they as individually specific as personal narratives.

### Narrative typology and ownership

The three types of narrative we have identified are neither exhaustive nor mutually exclusive. However, our typology allows some leverage on the ethical issue of narrative ownership. As we noted earlier, perhaps the most common complaint voiced by narrative research participants in reaction to what is written about them is that the narrative researcher's account fails to jibe with participants' views of themselves; it fails to capture their sense of their own individuality and uniqueness. We can now understand this reaction as a response to the essential tension between the requirements of the personal versus the typal narrative. When people react negatively to being 'typed' (Bakan 1996; Bar-On 1996), when they feel that the way they are portrayed in the researcher's narrative is just not 'them', perhaps this is what they are responding to. Yet, this type of reaction is inevitable in what Chase (1996) termed

> the interpretive process of transforming particular stories into examples of larger social phenomena. If a participant expects that the researcher will capture fully who she is, then it must be disconcerting to have her story analyzed for the social processes it reveals rather than preserved in its uniqueness.
>
> (p. 50)

Josselson (1996b) concurred and is prepared to take full ethical responsibility for the intrusiveness of this mode of interpretation:

> That we explore people's lives to make them into an example of some principle or concept or to support or refute a theory will always be intrusive and narcissistically unsettling for the person who contributes his or her life story to this enterprise. I don't think that there is any measure one can take to prevent this (beyond the usual safeguards, of course). No matter how gentle and sensitive our touch, we still entangle ourselves in others' intricately woven narcissistic tapestries. When we write about others, they feel it in some way.
>
> (p. 70)

As Chase (1996) pointed out, there can therefore be no simple division of labour in narrative research between the participant as narrator and the researchers as interpreter. Both are tellers of tales and moralizers, both narrators and interpreters.

However, they spin their tales according to fundamentally different narrative requirements. Participants seek to present and promote views of themselves and their lives that they can make sense of and live with, whereas researchers are looking for vivid exemplifications of theoretically significant social and psychological categories. When the two come into conflict, it is because they are constructing two entirely different types of narratives based on the same material.

## Recommendations for practice

[...]

What are the implications of our understanding of ethics for actual research practice in the narrative domain? In particular, how does an awareness of multiple narrative meanings impact on ethical practice in narrative research? In this section, we offer some practical recommendations for ethical conduct in narrative research based on the ideas presented earlier and our own experience as narrative researchers. These recommendations are, to some extent, idealization of practice that might not always be possible to implement in a given situation. Furthermore, they are presented as a framework of possible options rather than as prescriptive rules. We organize this discussion sequentially, in terms of the main phases of the research process: recruiting, obtaining consent, interviewing, analysing the data, and writing the report.

### Recruiting

In our view, ethical responsibility for research participants begins at the recruitment stage of narrative research. Participants in narrative research are asked to share more personal and identity-laden data than in traditional, nomothetic research. As a result, they incur particular kinds of risks. Participants might not always be the best judges of the potential consequences of their participation. We believe the onus is on the researcher to use discretion in determining the suitability of specific individuals as research participants. This could be done by way of an informal conversation with potential participants prior to the invitation to participate in research. Three areas of concern are potential vulnerabilities of participants, participants' ability to understand the concept of multiple narrative meanings, and the researchers' power and influence with respect to participants.

In recruiting participants, the researcher needs to be aware of vulnerabilities that might affect their contribution to the research. Some individuals might not respond well to the exigencies of narrative inquiry – that is, to the consequences of being open and reflective about their experience. Likewise, an individual's ability to grasp the notion of multiple narrative meanings might be limited. In out view, understanding this notion is essential to narrative research participation. Although the degree of such understanding can never be ascertained with certainty, as narrative researchers we must be prepared to exclude individuals who we believe might have considerable difficulty dealing with the issue. Finally, researchers need to be aware of their power and influence with respect to participants and of their participants' motives for wanting to participate in narrative research, which might not always be in their best interest. [. . .] Many participants, especially those with the more altruistic motives, might divulge much more than they are really ready to disclose and thereby make themselves vulnerable. Researchers should not abuse their authority to encourage people to participate in research that might adversely affect them in this way. If the researcher suspects that a person will be harmed by what they disclose, then the researcher is obligated to raise this concern with the individual prior to obtaining their consent to participate.

### Obtaining consent

We endorse Munhall's (1989) concept of process consent – that is, consent to participate in research is not an all or nothing, one-time agreement but rather a mutually negotiated, ongoing process between researcher and participant. This approach to obtaining consent is mandated by the open-ended, unpredictable character of narrative inquiry and the dept the self-disclosure that participants might communicate. One never knows when a narrative interview might threaten to move beyond the boundaries of what is safe for the participant; hence, the researcher must be continually vigilant regarding participants' consent. Among the possible ways to implement such process consent would be the use of multiple consent forms, an initial consent form followed up by multiple verbal or signed authorization to continue, or informal periodic conversations regarding consent. However implemented, fundamental to process consent is that it is something initiated by the researcher on an ongoing basis.

In our view, participants need to be sensitized to the issue of multiple narrative meanings from the outset. Part of the process of consent should involve clarifying this issue for potential participants. This can help alleviate the common misunderstanding among narrative research participants that the researcher will ultimately convey the participant's own story just as the participant understands it. Specifically, prospective participants should be made aware that their personal narrative will be renarrated by the researcher in the course of the analysis. When individuals are invited to participate in narrative research, do researchers clearly say, 'I want you to tell me your story so that I can interpret it and retell it from my perspective?' One way to raise this issue would be with reference to journalism and the common practice of journalists putting their own spin on a story and changing it from the way the teller related it. Although narrative research is normally more collaborative than this, final interpretive authority still tends to rest with the researcher. A brief statement to this effect should be included on the consent form and the issue periodically revisited during process consent.

### Interviewing

Having addressed the issue of multiple narrative meaning during the consent process, the issue now should be set aside as the interview begins. The researcher needs to clarify that the focus is now on the participant's personal narrative and bracket any consideration about its subsequent interpretation or renarration. That is, it is important to encourage participants to tell their story in their own words from their own perspective. For this reason, it is advisable not to schedule research interviews immediately following the discussion of consent, where issues of multiple meaning are highlighted. Ideally, a brief interval of time should elapse between discussion of consent issues and the research interview. One way to mark separations of this kind is to invoke the distinction between what is considered 'on camera' (i.e. part of the research data) and what is 'off camera' (i.e. discussion of consent and other issues that are not part of the research data). Participants should always be directed to be aware of when their remarks are being recorded as research data and when they are discussing other matters.

As the interview proceeds, the researcher needs to monitor continually the vulnerability and consent of the participant, for the reasons pointed out earlier. Researchers also need to monitor the development of trust with the participant to ensure that this trust is not abused inadvertently. One of the factors that is paradoxically problematic in this respect is that narrative researchers generally have developed the skills to be good listeners, which encourages others to trust them with their stories. Often, researchers will hear more than the participant consciously might be comfortable telling them. Researchers have to be aware of that possibility and watch for it; they have to be able to discern, during the interview, when a participant is telling them things that they are perhaps not yet ready to share. Researchers need to use their intuition and judgement to avoid harm and maintain informed consent throughout the process.

### Analysing the data

The key ethical issues, from out perspective, arise during the analysis and interpretation phase of the research, because this is the phase in which the multiplicity of narrative meaning becomes evident. When they leave the interview phase to analyse the data, researchers must continue the reflexive process that helps them determine how they feel about what they have learned regarding the meanings that participants have shared with them. Following the transcription of the interview, there are at least four separate phases to the analysis. First, researchers consult with participants to ensure their transcripts accurately reflect what they said. Second, researchers code the transcripts according to their own intuitions and analytic methodologies. During this stage, researchers should journal their personal reflections and feelings about the analysis. Specifically, they should reflect on their own perspectives and interpretations as they might impact on the analysis and participant. Third, researchers review their interpretations in conjunction with their personal reflections and address any ethical concerns that might arise. For example, a researcher might be concerned that communicating an interpretation about a participant's low self-esteem might further damage that individual's self-esteem. Finally, and most important, comes the stage of soliciting participants' feedback on the researchers' interpretations. As pointed out earlier, the narrative research literature presents numerous options for different degrees of participant involvement in the analysis, ranging from no involvement to collaborative input to final interpretative authority for the participant. From our point of view, the more significant issue, beyond the extent to which participants are involved at this stage, is that the degree of their involvement in the analysis be negotiated carefully with the researcher and that the process of negotiation be documented appropriately. Given the inherent multiplicity of narrative interpretation, we believe it is important to offer participants the opportunity to have their interpretation stand along with the researchers' interpretation, especially when there are significant discrepancies between the two. This is consistent with our conviction that there is no one privileged interpretation of any narrative.

### Writing the report

In writing the research report, researchers must continue to monitor their internal hunches about how their interpretation will impact their participants. Interspersed with this process is their continued consultation with the participants. The relationship of the researcher with participants does not end once the interviews are completed. Researchers must decide at this stage whether to show all or portions of the report to participants for their approval. This is the final opportunity to review participants' consent; if either the researcher or participant has any remaining misgivings about publishing the participant's data, this may be grounds for excluding it.

After the report is published, researchers have yet a further opportunity to solicit participants' reaction, even though issues of consent are moot at this point. Although this practice is not common, researchers who have sought such feedback have discovered some unexpected consequences for individuals who subsequently read what researchers write about them. [...] Researchers need to recognize that when they publish their research, their participants are invited to read what they have written about them. Hence, researchers must spend some time carefully thinking about the impact that their view of their participants, as portrayed by the researcher's lens, will have on the participants. Perhaps one of the best ways they can prepare both their participants and themselves for this is by looking at the example and the impact made by journalism and the media, as journalists are also in the business of telling other people's stories. In light of these powerful influences, it becomes imperative to clarify the issue of multiple narrative meanings for the readership. The researcher's analysis should be presented, not as a privileged account, but as conditioned by a certain perspective that should be made as explicit as possible. This leaves room for participants and readers to interpret the narrative in their own terms subsequent to publication.

## Conclusions

Our analysis of narrative research ethics has highlighted narrative ownership as a key issue, which we have addressed by appealing to the multiplicity of narrative meaning. In the previous section, we made a number of practical recommendations based on our understanding of the unique features of narrative ethics and epistemology. In keeping with this focus on multiple narrative perspectives, we conclude this chapter by situating our approach, with respect to the broad range of contemporary perspectives on research ethics. Just as we have advocated the idea of multiple narrative perspectives, so we endorse a multiplicity of ethical perspectives.

Recent discussions of ethical issues in qualitative research have criticized traditional, regulative approaches to ethics on the grounds that they are too procedurally driven, normative, rationalistic, principle centred, individualistic, and utilitarian. They have recommended that qualitative research ethics should be more reflexive than procedural (McLeod 1996), descriptive rather than normative (Hasselkus 1991), intuitive versus exclusively rationalistic (Rave and Larsen 1995), aspirational as opposed to principle centred (Rossiter *et al.* 1996; Corey *et al.* 1998), intersubjective versus individualistic (Rossiter *et al.* 1996), and more deontological than utilitarian (Munhall 1989). These approaches are consistent with what has been called the 'narrative turn in ethics' (Widdershoven and Smits 1996) and with the overall orientation of this chapter.

However, a dichotomous approach to these issues is, in our view, unrealistic. It presents the options for ethical decision making as mutually exclusive alternatives. In practice, we find that these dichotomies expand into distinct dimensions of ethical choice. Ethical issues in narrative research are best rendered in shades of grey rather than in black and white. For example, both poles of the intuitive–rational dimension of ethical decision making come into play in an ethical dilemma such as whether to remove a participant's data following completion of a study. From a rationalist perspective, the researcher will consider the ramifications of removing the data in terms of general considerations such as consent and anonymity. From an intuitive perspective, the researcher will rely on their personal feeling about what best serves the needs of the participant. Neither ethical standard is, in our view, privileged; they both need to be taken into account in practice, even if this involves attempting to satisfy seemingly mutually contradictory demands. A similar argument could be made with respect to the ethical dimensions of descriptive–normative, aspirational–principle centred, intersubjective–individualistic, and decontological–utilitarian ethics.

Thinking about research ethics in the narrative domain opens up a multitude of considerations for ethical decision making that tend to be overlooked in conventional research. This chapter is only a first step toward dealing with these complexities. We encourage a more encompassing, transtheoretical approach that blends ethics with epistemology, an approach that balances knowledge issues with ethical practice in a critical and self-reflective way. The challenge for future formulations of research ethics is to articulate a framework for ethical decision making that addresses the increasingly diverse methodologies of contemporary social science.

## References

Bakan, D. (1996). Some reflections about narrative research and hurt and harm. In R. Josselson (Ed.), *The Narrative Study of Lives: Vol. 4. Ethics and Process in the Narrative Study of Lives* (pp. 3–8). Thousand Oaks, CA: Sage.

Balfour, G. (1999, February). *How Qualitative Researchers Manage Ethical Dilemmas: Investigating the Connections between Ethics and Theory*. Paper presented at the First Annual Conferences on Advances in Qualitative Research Methods, Edmonton, Alberta, Canada.

Bar-On, D. (1996). Ethical issues in biographical interviews and analysis. In R. Josselson (Ed.), *The Narrative Study of Lives: Vol. 4. Ethics and Process in the Narrative Study of Lives* (pp. 9–21). Thousand Oaks, CA: Sage.

Brock, S.C. (1995). Narrative and medical genetics: on ethics and therapeutics. *Qualitative Health Research*, 5, 150–168.

Bruner, J. (1986). *Actual Minds, Possible Worlds*. Cambridge, MA: Harvard University Press.

Chase, S.E. (1996). Personal vulnerability and interpretive authority in narrative research. In R. Josselson (Ed.), *The Narrative Study of Lives: Vol. 4. Ethics and Process in the Narrative Study of Lives* (pp. 45–59). Thousand Oaks, CA: Sage.

Corey, G., Corey, M. and Callanan, P. (1998). *Issues and Ethics in the Helping Professions* (5th ed.). New York: Brooks/Cole.

Etter-Lewis, G. (1996). Telling from behind her hand: African American women and the process of documenting concealed lives. In R. Josselson (Ed.), *The Narrative Study of Lives: Vol. 4. Ethics and Process in the Narrative Study of Lives* (pp. 114–128). Thousand Oaks, CA: Sage.

Grafanaki, S. (1996). How research can change the researcher. The need for sensitivity, flexibility and ethical boundaries in conducting qualitative research in counselling/psychotherapy. *British Journal of Guidance and Counselling*, 24, 329–338.

Graves, P.L. (1996). Narrating a psychoanalytic case study. In R. Josselson (Ed.), *The Narrative Study of Lives: Vol. 4. Ethics and Process in the Narrative Study of lives* (pp. 72–79). Thousand Oaks, CA: Sage.

Hasselkus, B.R. (1991). Ethical dilemmas in family caregiving for the elderly: implications for occupational therapy. *The American Journal of Occupational Therapy*, 45, 206–212.

Josselson, R. (1993). A narrative introduction. In R. Josselson and R. Lieblich (Eds.), *The Narrative Study of Lives: Vol. 1.* (pp. ix–xv). Newbury Park, CA: Sage.

Josselson, R. (1996a). Introduction. In R. Josselson (Ed.), *The Narrative Study of Lives: Vol. 4. Ethics and Process in the Narrative Study of Lives* (pp. xi–xviii). Thousand Oaks, CA: Sage.

Josselson, R. (1996b). On writing other people's lives: self-analytic reflections of a narrative researcher. In R. Josselson (Ed.), *The Narrative Study of Lives: Vol. 4. Ethics and Process in the Narrative Study of Lives* (pp. 60–71). Thousand Oaks, CA: Sage.

Liebich, A. (1996). Some unforeseen outcomes of conducting narrative research with people of one's own culture. In R. Josselson (Ed.), *The Narrative Study of Lives: Vol. 4. Ethics and Process in the Narrative Study of Lives* (pp. 172–184). Thousand Oaks, CA: Sage.

McBurney, D.H. (1998). *Research Methods* (4th ed.) pacific Grove CA: Brooks/Cole.

McLeod, J. (1996). Qualitative approaches to research in counseling and psychotherapy: issues and challenges. *British Journal of Guidance and Counselling*, 24, 309–316.

Medical Research Council of Canada, Natural Sciences and Engineering Research Council of Canada, and Social Sciences and Humanities Research Council of Canada (1998). *Tri-council Policy Statement: Ethical Conduct for Research Involving Humans.* Ottawa: Medical Research Council of Canada.

Munhall, P.L. (1989). Ethical considerations in qualitative research. *Western Journal of Nursing Research*, 10, 150–162.

Ochberg, R.L. (1996). Interpreting life stories. In R. Josselson (Ed.), *The Narrative Study of Lives: Vol. 4. Ethics and Process in the Narrative Study of Lives* (pp. 97–113). Thousand Oaks, CA: Sage.

Polkinghorne, D.E. (1988). *Narrative Knowing and the Human Sciences.* Albany: State University of New York Press.

Price, J. (1996). Snakes in the swamp: ethical issues in qualitative research. In. R. Josselson (Ed.), *The Narrative Study of Lives: Vol. 4. Ethics and Process in the Narrative Study of Lives* (pp. 207–215). Thousand Oaks, CA: Sage.

Raudonis, B.M. (1992). Pearls, pith, and provocation: Ethical considerations in qualitative research with hospice patients. *Qualitative Health Research*, 2, 238–249.

Rave, E. and Larsen, C. (1995). *Ethical Decision Making in Therapy.* New York: Guilford.

Rossiter, A., Walsh-Bowers, R. and Prilletensky, I. (1996). Learning from broken rules: Individualism, bureaucracy, and ethics. *Ethics and Behavior*, 6, 307–320.

Rubin, H.J. and Rubin, I.S. (1995). *Qualitative Interviewing: The Art of Hearing Data.* Thousand Oaks, CA: Sage.

Widdershoven, G.A.M. and Smits, M.-J. (1996). Ethics and Narratives. In R. Josselson (Ed.), *The Narrative Study of Lives: Vol. 4. Ethics and Process in the Narrative Study of Lives* (pp. 275–287). Thousand Oaks, CA: Sage.

# Chapter 15

# Methodological challenges in researching inclusive school cultures

*Melanie Nind, Shereen Benjamin, Kieron Sheehy, Janet Collins and Kathy Hall*

## Introduction

The recent attention given to systematic reviews (such as Dyson *et al.* 2002) has drawn attention to the lack of detail about methodology reported in much of the literature. Lack of methodological information limits our trust in a study's outcomes, but also limits the richness of our growing understanding of the methodological challenges related to such complex areas as inclusive education. This chapter tells the story of the methodological challenges that have arisen within one research project spanning a year and in doing so both problematises method and addresses some fundamental issues in the field. The chapter tells, in chronological order, the story of the research from its original conception through to the data analysis phase. This chronological sequence both allows and requires us to map the challenges and dilemmas as if they took place in discrete chunks of time, and then were resolved, allowing us to move on. The reality of course is less simple. Certain phases of the research were characterised by specific dilemmas, such as finding appropriate schools and negotiating entry. Other dilemmas, such as those around defining what we collectively mean by particular terms and concepts, continue to challenge us. Perhaps the pleasure, as well as the problem, of a story such as this, is that some tensions and differences cannot be resolved. Our task is one of making the most creative use we can of the challenges – for ourselves, our research participants and those who engage with our research.

## Getting started

When five of us got together with a desire to research inclusion in schools our first challenge was to know what it was we really wanted to focus on and do. We spent a good deal of time discussing this and in particular two main dilemmas: did we want to examine 'good' practice or 'everyday' practice, and did we primarily want to enhance inclusive practice or enrich our own understandings about the processes of inclusion. Without extensive dialogue on the tensions arising from our distinct backgrounds and perspectives we could not proceed.

Early discussions pursued what each of us understood by inclusion and the communities of learners that most concerned each of us. Inclusive education is, after all, contested territory with competing definitions. Gradually our focus sharpened to an interest in inclusive cultures and practices. While research has begun to illuminate and illustrate the processes that sustain inclusion/exclusion practices and the importance of inclusive school cultures within this (e.g. Hunt *et al.* 2000), we were interested in delving into those processes to better understand them. The systematic review of Dyson *et al.* (2002) identified a relative lack of observational evidence in the existing literature as well as an inadequacy of the research base regarding students' experiences of inclusion. Our intention was to foreground student voices and experiences and to offer portrayals of inclusive schools that are grounded in extensive observational evidence. What held us together was our interest in what goes on in classrooms (and playgrounds, assemblies, etc.) in interactions *between* teachers and pupils, and pupils and pupils, and teachers and teachers. It is this common agenda that steered us toward the research questions:

- What do inclusive school cultures look and feel like to year six pupils and the staff working with them?
- How are processes of inclusion/exclusion produced through the daily interactions of pupils and teachers in schools?
- How do these processes relate to teachers' stated classroom intentions, to school policy, and to the larger context of national policy/rhetoric on 'inclusive education'?

Our decision to adopt a case study approach drawing on ethnographic methods was relatively straightforward in that we shared a general agreement about the fitness of this for our purpose. Less straightforward was our next challenge of communicating our intentions to others. This meant establishing a common language amongst ourselves, and a way of describing our project and key concepts that was meaningful for the schools, parents and children. We grappled somewhat with others' desire to know precisely our definitions and concepts when we were comfortable with these still being very fluid. We wrote different introductory documents to engage our different audiences and what we originally conceived in terms of 'school cultures', we presented to our potential research partners in schools as 'school ethos'. This, and other such elisions, posed an acute problem for us; how far should we assume that teachers would be unwilling or unable, given the constraints of time that characterise teaching, to engage with our research questions in the terms that we ourselves found most meaningful? Were we guilty of 'dumbing down' our aims in order to appear credible and feet-on-the-ground (Blythman 1996), or were we simply being careful of our language for the sake of clarity? Somewhere between these two poles, we developed some working definitions of inclusion, inclusive schools, inclusive practice and inclusive ethos and found two primary schools who were willing to engage in this project with us, St Blythes Primary in the Midlands and George Holt Community

Primary in London. (Pseudonyms are used for the schools and people within them.)

The methodological challenges that followed ranged from the pragmatic to the ethical and more often than not combined the two. For example, 'how might we interview the children?' incorporated how can it feasibly be done and how can it be done responsibly, as equitably as is possible, and without causing harm. Similarly, 'when will the teachers find time to talk to us?' meant both finding the actual time and judging whether it was acceptable to take time away from teachers' contact with pupils and time for solitary reflection or recovery. We discussed such challenges with the luxury of space and distance from the classrooms, but ultimately some decisions were made in isolation but in context – on the spot. This meant that some good intentions were de-railed and explaining the project to pupils in one school, for example, became less than ideal. Many of the issues we faced are those that any ethnographically oriented classroom researcher faces, but some of the issues we regard as more acutely framed by the nature of our study are a study of inclusive cultures and practices. Clearly, there is nothing mutually exclusive in this categorisation, but it is largely these latter issues that we dwell on in this chapter.

## Overview of the study

First, we offer a brief summary of what our methods were and the questions we asked of the data, in order to present the methodological challenges within a more holistic context. We worked with two urban English primary schools, one in London and one in the Midlands. Two members of the research team took on the fieldwork role, one in each school. A week was spent in a year six class in each school, followed by a series of day visits. Alongside field notes, the data gathered included interviews with the headteacher, class teacher and groups of children, and audio and video recordings of lessons. In addition to unstructured thematic analysis of the data, some pre-specified questions were used to prompt data collection and analysis:

- What characterises the children who are most at risk of exclusion in these schools?
- Where do we see barriers to their learning and participation?
- What are the exclusionary processes going on?
- Where do we see evidence of inclusive cultures?
- Where do we see evidence of inclusive processes or actions?

## Choosing inclusive schools to research: inclusive – says who?

Corbett (2001) says of her decision to choose Harbinger school for her study of inclusive pedagogy, that it was because the school was already known to her and that, through discussion with teachers, she knew it to be inclusive according to a set of criteria. Similarly, Dyson and Millward's (2000) selection of schools was based on prima facie evidence that they were moving or seeking to move in an inclusive direction. In finding our schools, whose inclusive cultures and practices we were keen to understand, we did not have this straightforward clarity but instead faced all kinds of quandaries. One option was to study practice in schools whose inclusiveness was already in the public domain, but there was something uncomfortable about over-researching these schools at the expense of others doing equally good but under-explored inclusion work. To somehow build up 'hero schools' seemed to undermine the concept that processes of inclusion (and exclusion) go on, in everyday schools, every day of the week. Alternatively, we could devise our own criteria for deciding that a school is inclusive and therefore worthy of our study. This, however, felt a little like answering our own research question without even entering a school! Moreover, it went against our understanding that at classroom level inclusion is a process, a series of choices made throughout the day, thus pre-ordained benchmarks could be misleading and detract from our focus on learning about these intricate choices. We could instead opt out of having to set our own criteria of inclusivity and instead use official criteria, leading us to schools deemed inclusive by OFSTED (the inspection body) or the LEA (Local Education Authority). Or we could seek schools that self-identified as inclusive.

Ultimately we decided on a mixture of recommendation by others – senior advisory staff in LEAs, combined with self-identification – schools with an interest in further understanding their own inclusive practices. Nonetheless, finding schools was not easy. Our interest in year six classrooms meant we were competing against the school's assessment agenda and largely loosing out. (English schools have national tests, routinely known as SATs, at four key points, one of which is the end of primary schooling in year six.) Our approaches to schools were also made in the context of a culture of surveillance created by the inspection regime (Morley and Rassool 1999), which may have added to their wariness. We found ourselves trying to sell the idea of the study to the schools, flattering the headteachers with comments about their recommended status, and promising a supportive process focused on the good things going on in the schools. (This had more impact on the study than we could have anticipated; we found later that we had not constructed an ideal context in which to constructively share the data about the processes of exclusion we found.) Eventually, though, potential partner schools were identified, and their participation confirmed following a visit in which the fieldworker made some subjective judgement about the schools' openness and responsiveness to the project.

## Collecting and analysing data: how do we look and how do we know?

The next challenges concerned how we should look for inclusive cultures and practices and how we would recognise them. For Peters' (1995) research on inclusion, the decision to use ethnography and participant observation was an obvious choice, but as a disabled researcher she could avoid studying 'other' and make good use of her 'personal baggage' as a disabled person. Like her, we wanted to look at the flow of behaviours and at the attitudes and emotions interacting with the behaviours. We wanted the 'holistic, thick description of the interaction process' (Lutz 1981: 52) that ethnographic methods offer and we had the ethnographic desire to understand cultures on their own terms. But we recognised the tension of creating the culture by studying it and articulating it.

We faced the challenge of seeing through the layers of what we found in schools: the official culture, the school culture, classroom culture, playground culture, sub-cultures related to class, ethnicity, gender, sexuality and so on. Moreover, we needed to see through the pressures upon the schools that shape their culture, such as the pressure of financial survival in the market-economy. Whilst needing to be aware of the bigger picture, we sought to examine the microcosm of school interactions. Corbett (2001: 400) argues that 'school culture can be felt in the general atmosphere of the building, in the way people speak to each other, what is visible and valued, where images and artefacts are placed and how the school projects its "self"'. We were interested in these aspects and in Corbett's (1999: 129) notion of deep culture as 'the intangible process whereby children are taught to see themselves as either valued or devalued group members'.

A way forward for researching inclusive school cultures must, it seems to us, address not only the shared language that helps to identify the culture (Zollers *et al.* 1999) but also the different levels of culture. For Schein (1984) these are visible artefacts (such as the built environment, dress code, public documentation), values (the espoused reasons and rationalisations for behaviour) and basic underlying assumptions (the beliefs that are taken for granted and which are difficult to question or to change). Unpicking the interconnective structure between assumptions, values and artefacts enables us to evaluate the extent to which they are in tune with each other and with inclusive principles. One might hope to find few contradictions between what is seen, what is stated and what is fundamentally believed, and to uncover artefacts, values and assumptions that benefit the development of all pupils (Rix and Simmons 2003). By observing in action the routines, rituals, stories, symbols, structures and systems (formal and informal) (Johnson 1992) that testify to the cultures in schools that are inclusive, we can better understand inclusive educational processes and practices. The challenge, though, is to gain insight into the multitude of cultures that exist in schools as organisations (Deering 1996; Dyson and Millward 2000) and not to assume that enhancing inclusive practice is a matter of altering just one set of underlying assumptions.

There is an attractive simplicity to the idea that we can study schools with an inclusive policy framework and examine the policies enacted in the classroom. As Clough (1995: 131) explains, 'we have come to see teachers as sorts of indifferently "black boxes" whose actions can be explained in terms of policies, and there is at work here an assumption that we can explain what teachers do in terms of the policy contexts in which they work'. But teachers and policies function in context and we need to understand these contexts which include the thoughts, experiences and policies of other times. As our two main teachers offered us such different classrooms to explore, we were drawn to consider what Clough (1995: 131) described as the 'the complexity of jointly implicated personal and professional life events' and the need to research the 'seam of subjective experience' that relates to attitudes *in context*. Like Dyson and Millward (2000) we were conscious of the complexities, competing imperatives and micropolitics we would need to understand.

## How can we keep children and their experience at the centre of our research?

Morrow and Richards (1996) contend that the problem of unequal power relationships between research and children is the biggest challenge for researchers working with children. Mauthner (1997: 20) argues that we can address this by 'foregrounding children's subjective experiences', letting the children lead in interviews, encouraging story-telling and anecdotes, and considering children's experiences of the research itself. In aspiring to keep children and their experience at the centre of research on inclusion, as stressed by Corbett (2001), we sought to talk to the children, incidentally and in interview, so that we might build connections with them that could give us insights into their perspectives. We could see practices, such as George Holt's 'bottom six' going to literacy/numeracy with the deputy head/Special Educational Needs Coordinator, that we could judge as excluding, but we wanted to know if these were actually experienced as such by the children. We assumed, like Thomas and O'Kane (1998: 341) that 'children's own understandings of their situation may be as valid as any other'. Our reflections on the pilot study indicate that we may need more of this kind of 'participatory research' in the main study with more time and space to talk with children and more opportunities for them to control the agenda of our conversations. Pickett's (1994) comparison of an inclusive and traditional school used focus groups to elicit the views of students but in a more ethnographic study one would need to keep the conversation and the observation more tightly linked.

We asked the question of the data 'who is at risk of marginalisation and exclusion in this classroom/school?' This allowed us to explore the processes at work for a broad community of learners: those who went unnoticed in class, loners, children who were assessed as having special educational needs, and all those children cast as 'other' to a 'normal' frame of reference. The methodological advantages of this approach, however, had to be balanced with the risk of pathologising children, of joining in with and somehow condoning the problematising of some while making others the normative group (Moore *et al.* 1998: 73). Mizra (1995) and Mauthner (1997) warn of the need to avoid objectifying children (and teachers) and this methodological challenge continues to test us.

## Emancipatory research? How much do/should we change what we find?

Clough and Barton (1995) make it painfully explicit that inevitably to research special educational needs is to construct special educational needs. The very act of using the concept brings it alive. We could not research processes of inclusion/exclusion without being a part of their construction. We would be a part of the understandings we developed not separate from them. Our very involvement as researchers in the schools meant that we changed them (Goodey 1999); we could accept this passively or we could seek to make a difference.

If our research was to have an emancipatory dimension, then when we found processes of exclusion, we would need to seek 'some redress of the issues we describe, rather than just reproduce them' (Moore *et al.* 1998: 72). As Goodey (1999) contends, 'like it or not, research is participation in social change and in mutual reflexive exploration' and we needed to be responsible with our power. We had to decide not once, however, but over and over again, whether to answer the 'call for action' we felt from seeing exclusionary practice. Moreover, we had to think about how we might make taking action to be 'empowering' rather than 'threatening' for the teachers. Our desire to see school processes as they were had to be weighed against not only our desire to raise awareness, but our responsibilities to the participants within our study. We had responsibilities to the teachers who were placing trust in us and to the children who had the least power in the situation. These methodological tensions were not just rhetorical matters for philosophical debate, they were brought sharply into focus during the fieldwork. The researchers were faced with many day-to-day decisions about whether to intervene when, for example, the children called each other 'spastic' or there were playground incidents, or more frequently when there was an obvious need for helper work to be done in the classrooms. Should a researcher in the field observe while pupils struggle?

We dwell here on one such example from St Blythes where the fieldnotes record many instances of one pupil's lack of participation and the growing frustration about this for the researcher:

Third visit
Literacy
*Miss P (classroom assistant) sits at the table closest to me and asks the 12 children seated at the table who had done their homework. . . . It is striking that for the next hour Nita sits without her textbook, her homework or any access to the text that is being read. I am surprised how little attention is paid to her either by the classroom assistant or the other pupils.*

PE
*Nita has not got her kit and so was sent to another room with a book.*

Science
*Nita puts her hand up a couple of times but on both occasions just as Sonya [teacher] chooses someone else. . . . Nita plays with her 'secret diary' as the 2 girl monitors give out the books. Nita says she will choose the pictures first but the girl sitting next to her suggests she needs to do the writing first. 'Do you just have to write all that?' asks Nita with incredulity. Nita writes the date and title in the same time as it takes others*

*to write 4 or 5 sentences. . . . By 3.03 Nita has finished copying the writing from the board but has not begun to copy or sort the images on the worksheet.*

We see here an initial interest in a pupil who avoids participation. Over the period of the next four visits the researcher constructs her as a 'non-participator' as she describes some of the processes that serve to exclude Nita, including the ones she herself plays an active part in. As Allan (1999) has been powerful in illustrating, pupils are not just subject to exclusionary and inclusionary processes – they are active agents in these processes.

### Fourth visit

*During the course of the afternoon Nita approaches every adult in the room and several children to ask for help in copying her design. All attempts to help and suggestions are rejected and Nita becomes increasingly silly as the lesson progresses. I offer to help but what she really wants is for someone to do it for her and I don't think that is fair. When the lesson is coming to an end and Sonya asks the class to place their masks in the corner of the room Nita puts hers in the book corner on its own. I wonder why this is and hope I have a chance to talk to her about it sometime.*

### Fifth visit

*This is now the third literacy lesson I have had the opportunity to watch Nita. In contrast to the 2 previous lessons Nita becomes a real nuisance. She is clearly not engaging with what is going on and becomes quite vocal. She sighs and groans and is very visibly not doing what she has been asked to do. She is told off by both Mrs S and by Sonya and is sent to sit on her own where she is clearly not doing as she has been asked. In contrast to Monday she seems deeply unhappy as if this is no longer a game. I ask Sonya if I can work with Nita who then comes to read to me. Sonya's construction is that 'Nita is really out of sorts and she doesn't know what has got into her'.*

*9.45 Nita struggles over the text that the class have been working on all week. She has some grasp of the story but I suspect this is the first time she has actually read the text. I praise her for attempting words she does not know and for pausing at full stops. Nita seems cheered by the fact that she is getting some individual attention and is experiencing some success. By the end of the lesson we are only half way through and I ask if she would like to finish the story and she says yes. Sonya comes over to check that everything is OK. She asks Nita what's wrong and, in sharp contrast to her previous statement, comments on the fact that Nita always seems to behave like that for Mrs S. I wonder if this is anything to do with the fact that Mrs S has been the first to demand participation in the literacy lesson but I say nothing.*

*The lesson ends before Nita has a go on the computer but no one seems to notice. Everyone seems reasonably occupied with the predictable copying of text and pictures. Nita has spent the whole of the lesson copying out the contents list of a book. My frustration mounts.*

There are many occasions when the researcher judges it inappropriate to intervene. She has to balance the research agenda of learning about the processes with a moral agenda of responsibility to the child and a pragmatic agenda of not upsetting the teachers involved. She does, however, make this on-the-spot decision to intervene in what she is observing by volunteering to work with Nita and this eases the frustration a little, but only temporarily.

> Sixth visit
> *Back in the classroom the literacy lesson begins with a spelling test. I notice Nita is away and wonder if the two are connected in any way. Sonya later tells me Nita was naughty the day before and had been sent to [the headteacher].*

Decisions about whether and how to 'seek some redress of the issues we describe' did not just take place on-the-spot. We decided that we would adopt an approach of trying to enable the teachers to see the exclusionary practices for themselves, in this instance for Sonya to seize the agenda of reversing Nita's non-participation. This, we hoped, would offer some redress for the pupil whilst empowering rather than threatening the teacher. To this end, the researcher used checklist items from the Index for Inclusion (Booth *et al.* 2000) and local equivalents as tools in the joint process of analysing video excerpts of classroom practice. This did enable the teacher to come to her own conclusion that Nita was not as actively engaged as she would have liked.

Classroom practice in St Blythes, and to a lesser extent George Holt, was dominated by the impending formal assessment (Hall *et al.* 2002). Directly related to this, much of the practice failed to include or engage learners who, like Nita, were not motivated by the promise of SATs success or the threat of SATs failure. This presented real challenges for our work with the school staff. From the outset we were aware of the danger of making use of the school for our own ends, and the lack of reciprocity this would imply. We wanted to be able to give something back to the schools, both in recognition of their help, and to construct the school and the research team as equal partners in the enterprise of researching inclusive practice. We wanted the schools to get something from the project – honest feedback of the findings at the very minimum. The trust invested in the researchers by school staff was illustrated by some of their comments; one class teacher commented 'I feel now that you are part of our class, you know what I mean, because you have been there for five days – its got into the routine now.' As it became clear that we were finding more evidence of exclusive than inclusive cultures and practices, the issue of honest feedback became much more problematic as we were then faced with questions of how this could be tempered.

Our agenda was not to find out 'what works' in inclusive education and to report back on this, although because of current expectations of research it could easily read as such (Siraj-Blatchford 1995; Atkinson 2000). Ours was a much more exploratory and reflexive agenda, but it was harder than we anticipated to operationalise this set against a surveillant regime that leads teachers to expect judgement. In Sonya's teaching career she had only known this context and her expectations were shaped by it. It felt to us that she had wanted the study, like her OFSTED inspection, to affirm her as good teacher; she did not seize the opportunity to reflect on practice with us. This made the issue of analysing video data together too challenging to contemplate and, apart from some superficial work, we backed off from the challenge.

Our initial vision of involving the school staff in the project as fellow gatherers and analysers of data had already emerged as unrealisable due to their time constraints and different agendas. There were cultural and structural impediments to the sense of partnership we regarded as ideal, as the university and school staff had different pressures, priorities and roles. Grundy (1998) maintains that such differences can be a strength within trusting research communities, but in this pilot project we failed to invest the time in building such communities.

Rather than being a project in which we found out together, our study became one in which we had to give feedback to the schools on what we found. This very much suited St Blythes' headteacher who wanted feedback on the school's 'fit' with the researchers' 'ideal' or 'utopia' for inclusion. His agenda was still more reflexive than the teacher's, though he was less exposed by the study in many ways. He wanted 'to move to a situation where maybe we have talked it [inclusion] through more' and being involved in the study was part of pursuing this agenda.

There were times when the headteacher blatantly invited our support on an issue – to go along with his agenda. He raised the issue of his intervention group for pupils with difficult behaviour being 'predominantly black'. He explained that he had 'been trying for a long time' but couldn't find someone to 'stand up' with him and 'say let's recognise that this is a group of black children and explore why and try to deal with it'. Whilst it is tempting to move on from the school and treat the pilot study as a huge learning experience, if there is to be some reciprocity in our research relationship then perhaps we must be drawn into what could become a shared agenda? As a research group mainly comprising white women academics, there are though, difficulties of distance and power in us commenting on this group of 'naughty black boys'. We can, however, continue a dialogue and use the literature of Blair (2001), Majors (2001), and Searle (2001) on this very issue to assist in seeking redress of this institutionally racist practice.

Over and above the issue of how much feedback to give to the schools and how to give it, we face the challenge of how to share and publish 'interesting material'. We do not wish to cover up findings about exclusionary processes as these emerged as a strong theme in the data, but nor do we want to take advantage of the school's trust. The marketisation of schools means that 'bad publicity' can be tangibly damaging, which makes the need to ensure anonymity very real. This is a challenge that is very current for us as we write for conferences and publication.

## Conclusion

Facing the challenges in the pilot study helped us in our fundamental conception of what we are trying to do. Themes that arose from our data included the ways in which the physical environment contributed to non-participation, notions of ideal class/pupil/parent which were exclusive, within-child notions of ability and (unjustified) faith in tests which were used to categorise and separate pupils. As these leapt out of the data at us we faced the problem of keeping faith with the idea that this was a study of *inclusive* practices and cultures. While inclusive practices were to be found (with other emerging themes being children supporting each other's inclusion, discourses of community and rights, and teachers' awareness of pupils as people), it was easy sometimes to loose sight of these amid the exclusive practices and cultures. It is the latter that we inevitably see more of, but the former that we really need to understand.

It is very tempting, at this point, to conclude the story with the ending we would wish for. Now that we know the dilemmas and pitfalls – organisational, interpersonal and intellectual – that lie in wait for us, we can construct, if not the perfect methodology, a study that avoids whatever difficulties *can* be avoided, and puts those that cannot be eliminated to best creative use. Sadly, this is not going to be the case. This was a pilot study, and there is much we have learnt from it. As we have shown in this chapter, we faced a host of difficulties, some of them resolvable, but many of them not. There are many things we will do differently, or not do at all, in future projects of this kind. But cultures, attitudes, policies and practices are interwoven with complex contexts and it is also true that a new set of contexts will present us with another set of dilemmas with which to engage.

## References

Allan, J. (1999) *Actively Seeking Inclusion: Pupils with Special Needs in Mainstream Schools* (London, RoutledgeFalmer).

Atkinson, E. (2000) In defence of ideas, or why 'what works' is not enough, *British Journal of Sociology of Education*, 21, pp. 317–330.

Blair, M. (2001) *Why Pick on Me? School Exclusion and Black Youth* (Stoke-on-Trent, Trentham).

Blythman, M. (1996) Factoring teachers into the research equation, in: G. Lloyd (Ed.) *Knitting Progress Unsatisfactory: Gender and Special Issues in Education* (Edinburgh, Moray House Institute of Education).

Booth, T., Ainscow, M., Black-Hawkins, K. and Vaughan, M. (2000) *Index for Inclusion: Developing Learning and Participation in Schools* (Bristol, Centre for Studies in Inclusive Education).

Clough, P. (1995) Problems of identity and method in the investigation of special educational needs, in: P. Clough and L. Barton (Eds) *Making Difficulties: Research and the Construction of SEN* (London, Paul Chapman).

Clough, P. and Barton, L. (1995) Introduction: self and the research act, in: P. Clough and L. Barton (Eds) *Making Difficulties: Research and the Construction of SEN* (London, Paul Chapman).

Corbett, J. (1999) Special needs, inclusion and exclusion, in: A. Hayton (Ed.) *Tackling Disaffection and School Exclusion* (London, Kogan Page).

Corbett, J. (2001) *Supporting Inclusive Education: A Connective Pedagogy* (London, Routledge-Falmer).

Deering, P. (1996) An ethnographic study of norms of inclusion and cooperation in a multi-ethnic middle school, *Urban Review*, 29, pp. 21–40.

Dyson, A. and Millward, A. (2000) *Schools and Special Needs: Issues of Innovation and Inclusion* (London, Paul Chapman).

Dyson, A., Howes, A. and Roberts, B. (2002) A systematic review of the effectiveness of school-level actions for promoting participation by all students (EPPI-Centre Review, version 1.1*), in: *Research Evidence in Education Library* (London, EPPI-Centre, Social Science Research Unit, Institute of Education).

Goodey, C. (1999) Learning disabilities: the researcher's voyage to planet Earth, in: S. Hood, B. Mayall and S. Oliver (Eds) *Critical Issues in Social Research* (Buckingham, Open University Press).

Grundy, S. (1998) Research partnerships: principles and possibilities, in: B. Atweh, S. Kemmis and P. Weeks (Eds) *Action Research in Practice* (London, Routledge).

Hall, K., Collins, J., Nind, M., Sheehy, K. and Benjamin, S. (2002) Assessment and inclusion/exclusion: the power of SATs, paper presented at BERA conference, University of Exeter, September 2002.

Hunt, P., Hirose-Hatae, A., Doering, K., Karasoof, P. and Goetz, L. (2000) Community is what I think everyone is talking about, *Remedial and Special Education*, 21, pp. 305–317.

Johnson, G. (1992) Managing strategic change – strategy, culture and action, *Long Range Planning*, 25, pp. 28–36.

Lutz, F. (1981) Ethnography – the holistic approach to understanding schooling, in: J. Green and C. Wallat (Eds) *Ethnography and Language in Educational Settings* (Norwood, NJ, Ablex).

Majors, R. (Ed.) (2001) *Educating Our Black Children: New Directions and Radical Approaches* (London, RoutledgeFalmer).

Mauthner, M. (1997) Methodological aspects of collecting evidence from children: lessons from three research projects, *Children and Society*, 11, pp. 16–28.

Mizra, M. (1995) Some methodological dilemmas in fieldwork: feminist and antiracist methodologies, in: M. Griffiths and B. Troyna (Eds) *Antiracism, Culture and Social Justice in Education* (Stoke-on-Trent, Trentham).

Moore, M., Beazley, S. and Maezler, J. (1998) *Researching Disability Issues* (Buckingham, Open University Press).

Morley, L. and Rassool, N. (1999) *School Effectiveness: Fracturing the Discourse* (London, Falmer).

Morrow, V. and Richards, M. (1996) The ethics of social research with children: an overview, *Children and Society*, 10, pp. 90–105.

Peters, S. (1995) Disability baggage: changing the educational research terrain, in: P. Clough and L. Barton (Eds) *Making Difficulties: Research and the Construction of SEN* (London, Paul Chapman).

Pickett, R. (1994) The relationship between school structure and culture and student views of diversity and inclusive education: a comparative case study of two middle schools (Unpublished PhD thesis, University of Wisconsin).

Rix, J. and Simmons, K. (2003) *A Culture for Inclusion. Unit 14 Inclusive Education: Learning from Each Other* (Milton Keynes, The Open University).

Schein, E. (1984) Coming to a new awareness of organizational culture, *Sloan Management Review*, 25, pp. 3–17.

Searle, C. (2001) *An Exclusive Education: Race, Class and Exclusion in British Schools* (London, Laurence and Wisheart).

Siraj-Blatchford, I. (1995) Critical social research and the academy: the role of organic intellectuals in educational research, *British Journal of Sociology*, 16, pp. 205–220.

Thomas, N. and O'Kane, C. (1998) The ethics of participatory research with children, *Children and Society*, 12, pp. 336–348.

Zollers, N.J., Ramanathan, A.K. and Yu, M. (1999) The relationship between school culture and inclusion: how an inclusive culture supports inclusive education, *Qualitative Studies in Education*, 12, pp. 157–174.

# Chapter 16

# A guide to ethical issues and action research

*Jane Zeni*

## Introduction

Action research has become a major mode of inquiry in American education. However, as classroom teachers discover the intellectual excitement of studying their own practice and the power of collaboration on an action research team, many decide to pursue their work in a formal graduate programme, culminating, perhaps, in a dissertation.

Most universities and school districts conduct a review of research proposals using questionnaires designed for traditional scientific experiments. Researchers are asked if their tests are dangerous, if their subjects will be given drugs, etc. They are asked to spell out precisely which data they will collect. However, in action research – as in most qualitative inquiry – we pursue a question through an often-meandering route, finding appropriate data sources as we go along. When a teacher is studying his or her own practice, many of the traditional guidelines collapse. Yet action research raises it own, often sticky, ethical issues which may never be addressed.

In my graduate classes, where many of the participants are doing classroom inquiries, I find it helps teachers to locate action research in the whole array of research methods (see Table 16.1).

Action research draws on the qualitative methods and multiple perspectives of educational ethnography. When challenged, we take pains to distinguish our work from traditional *quantitative* research: We explain that we don't deal with big numbers, random samples or manipulated variables, but with the human drama as lived by self-conscious actors. Perhaps it is just as important to distinguish action research from traditional *qualitative* research: we aren't outsiders peering from the shadows into the classroom, but insiders responsible to the students whose learning we document.

Table 16.1 illustrates modes of research across two dimensions: qualitative/quantitative and insider/outsider. Action research usually falls in the lower-right quadrant of the matrix: qualitative research by insiders. Such 'insiders' may be primary literacy teachers, assistant principals, high school math teachers, curriculum coordinators, coaches – any of us who study our own practice as educators. We find the ethical safeguards of the outsider doing a classic experiment (random

*Table 16.1* Education research: a methodological matrix

| Quantitative | Qualitative |
| --- | --- |
| *Traditional research* | |
| Outsider: researcher investigating a teacher's practice | |
| Classic experiment (techniques of natural science, agriculture) | Classic ethnography or case study (techniques of anthropology) |
| Goal: To change/improve someone else's teaching/learning | To document someone else's teaching/learning |
| *Action research* | |
| Insider: teachers documenting their own practice | |
| 'Small-n' statistics (test scores; surveys; word counts; syntax measures) | Classroom ethnography; case study; autobiography; curriculum development and field testing |
| Goal: To change/improve one's own teaching/learning | |

Note:
Most, but not all, classroom action research is qualitative.

selection, control groups, removing the personal influence of the researcher) either irrelevant or problematic for us as insiders. In the same way, the ethical safeguards of the outsider doing qualitative research (anonymous informants, disguised settings) may defeat the action researcher's goal of open communication and dialogue with colleagues, students and parents.

When does good teaching become research? The line may be hard to draw until a study is well underway. Action research tends to involve:

1  more systematic documentation and data gathering;
2  more self-reflection in writing;
3  a wider audience (collaboration, presentation, publication).

It is this third feature that most often leads to ethical dilemmas. If our journals remain private and our videotapes aren't played, we can inquire with equanimity. However, in action research, though we document our own practice, we rarely work in isolation. We need the support and collaboration of a colleague, a seminar group or an outside researcher. Often this partnership creates an opportunity for sharing the work with a still larger audience at conferences or in print. Dilemmas of ownership and responsibility arise, and our academic codes of conduct are silent.

This Guide emerged from discussions in the Teacher Educators Seminar of the Action Research Collaborative.

[. . .]

Drafts were discussed by ARC teacher educators at four seminar meetings. Feedback came from a wider audience of teachers and administrators at several conferences, and in my own graduate courses.

What at first seemed a rather straightforward exercise in translation proved a formidable task. The more I tried to account for the different contexts and communities in which action researchers pursue their inquiries, the more complicated and muddled our ethical guidelines became. As teacher educators, we began to see that a 'new paradigm code of ethics' would itself become 'procrustean' (Gregory 1990: 166).

[. . .]

Instead, the following document provides a set of more-or-less provocative questions as a heuristic for reflection. An action research team or university thesis advisor can work through the Guide with a practitioner developing a plan for research. Most of the questions ask the researcher to discuss a potential ethical problem, to consider alternative actions and to explain his or her choices.

The *Guide to Ethical Issues and Action Research* uses the categories of a traditional 'human subjects' review only as a point of departure. Part I requests an overview of the project. Part II asks whether the activities fall within the everyday decision-making of a teacher or whether there is some further intervention. Part III examines the 'subjects' and the notion of subjectivity in action research. Part IV considers ways to reduce risks to participant – either through informed consent and anonymity, or through openness, dialogue and acknowledgement. Parts V and VI pose questions which, though generally ignored in an HSR, have been especially problematic for action researchers.

## Guide to ethical issues and action research questions for review and reflection

### Part I: overview

1  Briefly describe your project as you see it today.
2  What is the time frame of your project? Is it a one-shot enterprise or does it involve several cycles? Have you already done a pilot study?
3  What problem does your research address? What (initial) action will you take? What do you hope to accomplish?
4  List the research questions as they appear at this time.

(Questions will be revised or refocused during your project.)

### Part II: methods and setting

1  Are you, the researcher, also a participant in the setting where this research will take place? Specify your role (teacher, supervisor, principal, counsellor, social worker, etc.)
2  For this research, will you gather data on your normal educational practice and on changes in curriculum, instruction and assessment that you could make

in your role (above) according to your own professional judgement? Explain briefly.

3    What kinds of data will you collect (e.g. field notes, taped interviews, writing samples)? Explain any changes from the way you normally document your practice. Consider how else you could get data on your question. (Can you discuss three alternatives?)

4    What does your research aim to understand? What does your research aim to change?

*Comments on Part II*    Traditional academic research in education is conducted by outsiders who intervene in the instructional process to answer questions that may benefit themselves or the profession in general. While there is often a goal of improving teaching, rarely do the teachers or students under investigation benefit directly from the findings.

Action research involves practitioners studying their own professional practice and framing their own questions. Their research has the immediate goal to assess, develop or improve their practice. Such research activities belong to the daily process of good teaching, to what has been called the 'zone of accepted practice'.

The concept of a zone of accepted practice is often used to determine whether research is exempt from formal review. If a researcher answers 'yes' to questions 1 and 2, the project does not need a full review by a university or district research board. Most educational action research would thus seem to be exempt.

We urge academic institutions to support reflective teaching and to minimise the bureaucratic hurdles that discourage research by teachers to improve their own practice. However, research in the 'zone of accepted practice' may still involve risks to participants. As a precaution, we suggest grappling with question 3 and consulting people who can speak from a variety of perspectives:

- An action research project must conform to local school policy; discuss any troubling issues in this Guide with a principal, supervisor or district director of research.
- Action research is best developed through collaboration; review the questions with a team leader, professor or consultant.

Question 4 begins a closer look at how we choose to change our own practice. According to many reviews, 'subjects' are 'not at risk' if the research is merely 'unobtrusive observation' of behaviour not 'caused' by the researcher. However, action research is never detached; a teacher inevitably causes things to happen. (The classic ethnographer observes change, but does not usually try to cause it. On the other hand, the action researcher consciously tries to change and improve his or her own teaching.)

## Part III: 'subjects' and subjectivity

1   Describe the individuals, groups or communities you plan at this point in the research to study. Estimate the ages of the people involved.
2   Analyse the power relations in this group. Which people (e.g. students, parents) do you have some power over? Which people (e.g. principals, professors) have some power over you?
3   What shared understandings do you have with these people? Do you have personal bonds, professional commitments? Will your research strengthen this trust or perhaps abuse it?
4   Will your study attempt to read and interpret the experience of people who differ from you in race, class, gender, ethnicity, sexual orientation or other cultural dimensions? How have you prepared yourself to share the perspective of the 'other' (coursework, experiences, other sources of insight)?
5   Will an 'insider' review your questionnaires or teaching materials for cultural bias? Have you provided for consultation by adult members of the community? How will you reduce or correct for your misreading of populations who differ from you?
6   Does your inquiry focus on people with less power than you? Children in classrooms are always vulnerable – especially if their families have little money or education. ('Where are the ethnographies of corporate boardrooms?' asks House 1990: 162) How does your project demonstrate mutual respect and justice?
7   What negative or embarrassing data can you anticipate emerging from this research? Who might be harmed (personally, professionally, financially)? What precautions have you taken to protect the participants?
8   Might your research lead to knowledge of sensitive matters such as illegal activities, drug/alcohol use or sexual behaviour of participants? How do you plan to handle such information?

*Comments on Part III*   We must examine the impact of our research on the people whose lives we document. A classroom teacher may write field notes in order to improve her own practice. However, what if her notes focus on certain members of the class ('at-risk'/'Black male'/'learning disabled')? Our students and colleagues are more than 'subjects'. The following distinctions are useful:

| | |
|---|---|
| *Subject*: | Observed by researcher; no active participation (Not applicable to action research) |
| *Informant*: | Knowingly gives information to researcher |
| *Participant*: | More involved; perspective considered in research |
| *Collaborator*: | Fully involved in planning and interpretation |

Perhaps most of all, we need to examine our own subjectivity as researchers. Since I cannot be a fly on the wall in my own classroom, I must deal with my own emotional and interpersonal responses as part of my data. Hammersly and Atkinson (1983) call this the principle of 'reflexivity'. Sullivan (1996) writes of the 'problem of the "other".' Teacher research is engaged and committed. It is appropriate – essential – for our discussions and writing to look at ourselves in relationship with other participants.

## Part IV: risks and benefits

How can we protect K–12 students but not inhibit teachers' right to gather and reflect on data from their own teaching?

1   Describe the possible benefits of your research – to students, teachers or other participants; to society or to the profession.
2   Describe any risks to people participating in this study. For example, will your current students be disadvantaged for the possible benefits of future students? What steps are you taking to minimise risks?
3   Show how you will protect the people from whom you collect data through surveys, interviews or observations. For example, participants are usually considered free from risk IF:

   (a)   they are first informed; they must know the general nature of the study and what is expected of them;
   (b)   they give informed consent;
   (c)   they can refuse to participate and they can withdraw without penalty after beginning the research;
   (d)   anonymity of persons and/or confidentiality of data are protected if appropriate.

4   Describe your method of obtaining informed consent. Who will explain the consent document to the participants? How?
5   Are different kinds of consent needed at different stages in the project?
   For example, many teachers use two consent forms:

   (a)   a blanket consent to be in the study; if you regard classroom inquiry as part of your regular practice, this blanket consent form may be given to all students at the start of each year;
   (b)   special consent to eventual publication; this will be needed when you prepare publish student writing samples, taped discussions, photographs, or field notes that focus on a recognisable student.

6   Do you wish to protect the anonymity of students, teachers, parents and other participants? If so, it is wise to use pseudonyms even in your field notes. If your report is eventually published, you can also interchange physical description, grade level, gender, etc., or develop composite rather than individual portraits.

7    On the other hand, instead of anonymity, it may be wiser to seek full partici-
     pation and credit for students and colleagues. Research by an educator in his or
     her own classroom is rarely anonymous. Even if names are changed, students
     will be recognised in a well-written case study or classroom scene. What are
     the gains and losses of open acknowledgement?

*Comments on Part IV*    These questions deal with the welfare of students and
colleagues. Most university definitions of 'informed consent' resemble this one
from the AERA's Qualitative Research SIG:

> a decision made free of coercion and with full knowledge [of] possible effects
> of their participation, their role in reviewing written accounts . . . , an under-
> standing that the researcher will protect them from potential harm, and that
> there will be a mutually respectful relationship. Informed consent is granted
> at the initiation of the study and codified in signed consent forms. Because
> informants may withdraw at any time, informed consent is ongoing, continual
> negotiation.
>
> (Mathison *et al.* 1993: 3)

How informed is 'informed consent?' Lou Smith argues that 'field research is
so different from the usual experimental approaches that many individuals, even
responsible professional educators, do not understand what . . . they are getting
themselves into' (Smith 1990: 151). He stresses the need for 'dialog', moving
beyond 'contract' relationships to 'covenants' of trust (p. 150).

    As teacher researchers, our primary responsibility is to our students. We need
to balance the demands of our research with our other professional demands. This
issue becomes far less troublesome when classroom inquiry becomes an intrinsic
part of how we teach, and when students take an active role in our research – and
their own.

## Part V: ethical questions specific to 'insider' research

These questions don't appear on most 'human subjects', reviews, but they are central
to research by K–12 and college teachers. Yvonna Lincoln (1990) says, 'privacy,
confidentiality, and anonymity regulations were written under assumptions that
are ill suited' to action research. Our colleagues, administrators, and parents might
better participate 'as full, cooperative agents', our co-researchers (pp. 279–280).

1    Which of the research participants at your school/college have read your pro-
     posal? Which ones have been informed of the research orally in some detail?
     Which ones know little or nothing of this project? Explain and justify the
     decisions behind your answers.

2   What do your students know of this project? Who told them? What are the risks to them or their families of their knowing (or not knowing) what you write or collect? Explain you decisions.

3   Who else will read your field notes or dialogue with you to provide multiple perspectives? Lather (1991) describes 'the submission of a preliminary description of the data to the scrutiny of the researched' (p. 53) as an emancipatory approach to inquiry and also as a way to establish 'face validity' (p. 67). Incorporating quotes from other participants, especially when their views differ from yours, can make your work richer, more nuanced.

4   You will inevitably gather more data than you 'need'. Consider why you choose to report some data to a wider audience and why you choose to keep some for your colleagues, your students or yourself. (What do you tell and what do you store?) Consider the political implications of the way you focus your story.

5   How will you store and catalogue your data during and after the study? Who will have access? Should you take special precautions with your notes and other data?

6   Will this study evaluate your own effectiveness or a method to which you are committed? Will your findings be confirmed by observers who do not share your assumptions? How will you protect yourself from the temptation to see what you hope to see?

7   Who is sponsoring this research through grants, contracts, released time, course credit, etc.? Will you evaluate the sponsor's programme, textbook, method, etc.? Can you protect yourself from pressure to report favourably on the sponsors?

8   How do your school administrators see your work? Is action research under suspicion or is it mandated from the top in a drive for organisational quality control? Is there protection for your own thoughts, feelings interpretations? How safe do you feel in this institutional environment pursuing this research? Reporting what you learn to a wider audience?

9   What data will be contributed by others? Will you be recording case studies, oral histories or other stories that may be considered the property of others? How have you arranged with colleagues or other participants for

- credit in your manuscript?
- publication rights?
- royalties?
- other recognition?

10  If your study is collaborative, how are you negotiating authorship and ownership?

11  Who is responsible for the final report? Will other stakeholders (teacher? principal? school board?) review your report in draft? Will this

(a)  improve your accuracy?
(b)  compromise your candor?

Participants may not agree with part or all of your interpretation. If so, you may revise your views; quote their objections and tell why you maintain your original view; or invite them to state alternative views in an appendix.

12 Have you decided on anonymity or on full acknowledgement if your study is eventually published? Perhaps you will identify teachers, but use pseudonyms for students. How and when have you negotiated these issues?

### Part VI: the Golden Rule

At the most basic level, (Smith 1990: 149) suggests that we, as classroom researchers, ask ourselves these questions:

- What are the likely consequences of this research? How well do they fit with my own values and priorities?
- If I were a participant, would I want this research to be done? What changes might I want to make me feel comfortable?

Teacher-researcher Marian Mohr states it this way: 'Teacher researchers are teachers first. They respect those with whom they work, openly sharing information about their research. While they seek knowledge, they also nurture the well-being of others, both students and professional colleagues' (Mohr 1996).

Action researchers need to discuss with their constituencies the role of classroom inquiry in their professional lives. For example, some teachers display for parents their own publications as well as the writing of their students informally printed, illustrated and bound. Teacher-researcher Kathryn Mitchell Pierce (1997) asks at an 'open house' for parents' support in gathering data for professional development. She adds, 'I'll come back to you again for more specific permission if your child appears in anything I plan to publish.'

In this way, parents and students are knowingly involved in the work from the beginning, with time to ask their own questions and make thoughtful suggestions. Open communication is the key to overcoming the split between researcher and researched, between theory and practice.

## References

Gregory, T.B. (1990) Discussion of ethics, in E. Guba (Ed.) *The Paradigm Dialog*, pp. 165–166. Newbury Park: Sage.

Hammersley, M. and Atkinson, P. (1983) *Ethnography: principles in practice*. London: Routledge.

House, E.R. (1990) An ethics of qualitative field studies, in E. Guba (Ed.) *The Paradigm Dialog*. Newsbury Park: Sage.

Lather, P. (1991) *Getting Smart: Feminist Research and Pedagogy Within the Postmodern*. New York: Routledge.

Lincoln, Y. (1990) Toward a categorical imperative for qualitative research, in E. Eisner and A. Peshkin (Eds) *Qualitative Inquiry in Education*. New York: Teachers College Press.

Mathison, S., Ross, E.W. and Cornell, J. (Eds) (1993) *Casebook for Teaching about Ethical Issues in Qualitative Research*. Washington: Qualitative Research SIG, American Educational Research Association.

Mohr, M. (1996) Ethics and standards for teacher research: drafts and decisions, in *Research in Language and Learning: reports from a teacher research seminar*. Fairfax: Northern Virginia Writing Project, George Mason University. (Informal publication distributed by the Writing Project.)

Pierce, K.M. (1997) Presentation at seminar on ethical issues in action research, Clayton (MO) Public Schools.

Smith, L. (1990) Ethics, field studies, and the paradigm crisis, in E. Guba (Ed.) *The Paradigm Dialog*. Newbury Park: Sage.

Sullivan, P. (1996) Ethnography and the problem of the 'Other' in P. Mortensen and G.E. Kirsch (Eds) *Ethics and Representation in Qualitative Studies of Literacy*. Urbana: National Council of Teachers of English.

# Chapter 17

# Reflections on interviewing children and young people as a method of inquiry in exploring their perspectives on integration/inclusion

*Ann Lewis*

## Introduction

This chapter takes as its starting point the idea that it is vital to explore the views of child participants in integrated or inclusive settings, but that doing so in valid and reliable ways is more problematic than is often recognised. The work is rooted in positivist paradigms, hence my use of terms like interviewee, validity and reliability, but I am conscious of their limitations. While I regard the pursuit of objective and verifiable truths as a reasonable goal for the researcher, I recognise too the often slippery, unstable and ambiguous nature of human interaction (Scheurich 1985).

Neither positivist nor ethnographic approaches are problem-free. The literature on interviewing young children, particularly those with learning difficulties, reflects divergent approaches. These encompass interpretive approaches (e.g. Allan 1999; Crozier 2000) often informed by a sociological perspective which stresses building a reciprocal and genuine discussion with the children. In contrast, work from a legal perspective (e.g. Aldridge and Wood 1998; Ceci and Bruck 1993) has been informed by developmental psychological theories, and stresses the importance of obtaining accurate information. Yet both sets of work share a concern with obtaining a fair view of the child's perspective. While the theoretical and philo-sophical roots of each are distinctive, practice should benefit from the lessons of each. Whether one's inclination is towards more structured and formal or less struc-tured and more reciprocal approaches to interviewing children, there are clearly more, and less, effective ways to encourage them to engage in discussion.

My examples are drawn from face to face interviews with primary school children in the context of integration because that is where most of my work has been located; clearly non-verbal or distance means may be preferred, and may avoid some of the attendant difficulties (but create others). I began work in this area in the mid-1980s, when conducting research interviews with children was much less widely accepted as feasible and reasonable than is now the case. Since then the Code of Practice concerning SEN (DES/WO 1994), and more strongly the draft revised Code (DfEE 2000)as well as the 1992 Home Office Memorandum of Good Practice (Home Office/Department of Health 1992) have brought to the fore the ethics and practice of seeking children's views. The increasing emphasis (justly) on the right of children to be heard has however tended to emphasise the fact of production over the complexities of interpretation.

Obtaining valid and trustworthy responses has been much debated in interviewing children generally (Grieg and Taylor 1999; Hill *et al.* 1996). Interview strategies for use with children with learning difficulties, contrasted with other interviewees, are likely to be similar; but there are particular issues that arise more sharply with the former group. The complexities have been highlighted by the recent need to obtain such evidence in cases of suspected child abuse, where a disproportionate number of these children and young people have learning difficulties (Aldridge and Wood 1998; Masson 2000). More widely workers in the fields of bereavement counselling, hospice work, police witness statements and health professional have been concerned with eliciting the views of, and providing support or information to, children and young people with learning difficulties (Dodd and Brunker 1999; Le Count 2000). In parallel with such professionals' concerns has been discussion about research methodology that has highlighted the involvement of people with learning difficulties as researchers (Kiernan 1999).

## Some ethical considerations in interviewing pupils about inclusion or integration

Some specific issues arise when interviewing children with learning difficulties about inclusion or integration. These are similar to those raised in other research contexts but are potentially particularly sensitive or difficult.

## Confidentiality and the ethics of openness

The child may feel betrayed if information is passed on, particularly as children with learning difficulties may be prone to believe (through experience) that their views will not be respected.

## Unintended repercussions of protocols

I heard recently of research involving pupils with severe learning difficulties in which the researcher had stressed that material (taped interviews, etc.) would be destroyed at the close of the research project. The pupils involved were upset about this as, to them, this reflected a lack of perceived worth in their material. What was of value was assumed to be kept as precious, not discarded. This underlines the more general point about the need to see the research enterprise from the child's/pupil perspective.

### Anonymity

This may be difficult to sustain when there are small and readily identifiable samples (e.g. a few pupils with SLD or their parents in a primary school).

### Consent/assent

Some writers have made a useful distinction between consent to participation in research (e.g. the parent gives consent on the child's behalf), contrasted with assent (the child agrees to participate). The two types of agreement may be conflated but disentangling them, particularly in this context, highlights the way in which a succession of consents on behalf of children with learning difficulties may profoundly influence sample and hence findings.

### Intrusion

The process of talking about how peers feel about particular aspects of inclusion may unwittingly present as potentially problematic an area that had not previously been perceived as unusual. For example, in asking children about a range of activities they would do with particular classmates, the researcher may create the impression that some of these activities would be unusual or unexpected.

## Some sampling considerations in interviewing pupils about inclusion

### Access to individuals

Samples will be limited in various ways: first, through the obvious power of gatekeepers (those who give consent on behalf of the child). The researcher will, virtually always, have to go through somebody else to reach the sample for interview. Allan (1999) ponders a particularly interesting illustration of how mainstream pupils may act as gatekeepers. In some contexts the gatekeepers will provide an 'all in' access, for example, where a head teacher agrees to researchers interviewing pupils and this is construed as part of the usual school curriculum. Then all pupils are, at the consent level, included. However gatekeepers may operate an 'opt in' policy. Alderson (1999) argues that this is exclusionary because opting in requires certain skills (e.g. communication) and attitudes (e.g. confidence). If the consent/assent processes are distinct then, after consent by others has been given, the pupil needs to give assent to participation in the research. Alderson (op. cit.) notes the importance of allowing informed dissent by the child. This links with issues about communication.

## Mode of communication

Samples of pupils for interview may be distorted by the mode of communication employed in the research. Begley (2000) acknowledges that her work concerning the views of pupils with Down's syndrome excluded those pupils who lacked verbal communication. These pupils would have needed a signer to translate to Begley, and she felt that the logistics and reliability of this would have invalidated findings. Similarly, in my work on children's attitudes to integration, the views of pupils with profound and multiple learning difficulties (PMLD) were excluded because I was not confident about being able to access their views reliably. However, this is possible: Detheridge (2000) has described research in which she explicitly involved similar pupils using technology-aided communication. Thus the selected mode of communication has implications for sampling and respondent validation.

## Selection of data for analysis

Another level of sampling occurs in the move from information to data. Material may be distorted by the sample of material chosen for coding, and this links with mode of communication (previous section). For example, indistinct speech may be excluded, leading to the systematic but inadvertent omission of the views of a particular subset of interviewees.

## Interview strategies

The main body of this chapter reviews a range of interview techniques that have application for researchers or practitioners who wish to find valid and reliable ways of obtaining children's views. They are particularly important when interviewing young children, or children/young people with learning difficulties. This material is divided into four main sections:

> Initiating the dialogue (use of questions compared with statements; using multiple questions)
>
> Sustaining the dialogue (use of pause, prompts, allowing 'don't know' responses and providing a résumé)
>
> Specific choices about phrasing (use of modifiers, pronouns and referents)
> Context (impact of background information and discussion).

### Initiating the dialogue

#### Use of statements, rather than a question, as a prompt

A range of work with children has shown the value of making statements that prompt a response, rather than a direct question, to elicit views. The tendency for adults, particularly teachers, to use question–answer feedback routines has been described by some writers as reflecting power relationships (Edwards and Mercer 1987). Through the use of questions, the adult keeps the 'upper hand'. Thus in the research context, the use of statements rather than questions also reflects an implied power relationship. The use of statements as prompts in research interviews can occur naturally in small group interviews with children (Lewis 1992; Lewis and Lindsay 2000). Here one child's comment may trigger a response from another child in the group. This is shown well in the following example in which 10–11-year-olds from a primary school were discussing among themselves the likely work in adulthood for pupils from a special (severe learning difficulties) school who visited the class regularly. The style of interaction is in marked contrast to the interview with Gwyn (on page 221).

*Kay:*      Kirsty's quite good at... [*pause*]... at um... stencilling; she can find the letters really quickly.
*Jo:*       Jeremy's quite good at jigsaws mainly.
*Stevie:*   Yeh... Kirsty's good at jigsaws.
*Kay:*      Yeh but there's no JOB to do with jigsaws.
*Jo:*       They could check all the pieces.

### Multiple questions

Multiple questions disguised as one question are a notorious trap in interviews. Even experienced interviewers may make this mistake, for example:

> If you could change anything you wanted about your present class or school, or the work you do at school, what changes would you make?
>
> (from Gross 1993)

This multiple questioning is particularly problematic for children with learning difficulties who may not seek clarification. One strategy to help deal with this is to permit and explicitly to encourage 'don't know' responses and clarification requests. This has emerged as important in legal contexts but has applicability for more general research situations. Saywitz (1995) notes that children with learning difficulties may be particularly liable to say 'don't know' (and/or not to ask for clarification). If they have had unsuccessful school or assessment experiences in which they have come to expect that they will not fully understand what is being asked, they may have learned that they can 'get away with' avoiding answering.

### Sustaining the dialogue

#### Use of pause

Some researchers (Bull 1995) have argued that in all interviews, but particularly those involving children or people with learning difficulties, it is valuable to allow long pauses (up to three seconds) in order to encourage a response. A good illustration of this is given by Julie Barsby (1990) in her research involving children with learning difficulties evaluating their work in collaboration with a friend:

(First interview)
*Interviewer:*   Could you make your writing better?
*Child:*         [nods]
*Interviewer:*   How could you do that?
*Child:*         Don't know.

| | |
|---|---|
| *Interviewer:* | You don't know? |
| *Child:* | No. |
| *Interviewer:* | [*pause*] What could you do to make your writing more interesting? How could you make your story better? |
| *Child:* | Write little. |
| *Interviewer:* | Pardon? Write small? |
| *Child:* | Yes. |
| *Interviewer:* | What about the story itself? |
| *Child:* | [*long pause*] |

This can be contrasted with Julie's third interview with this child, three weeks later:

(Third interview)

| | |
|---|---|
| *Interviewer:* | Could you make your writing better? How do you felt about your work? |
| *Child:* | It's not bad for me. I could've done a bit better but I did my best because I had a late night. |
| *Interviewer:* | How could you make your writing better? |
| *Child:* | I could have a little think about it and tell the truth why they were enjoying themselves. |
| *Interviewer:* | Mm. |
| *Child:* | Well I know you wouldn't tell me off 'cos you giggle too. I've seen you with Mrs C [*long pause . . .*] I could say that the kids have a good laugh and think it's well funny when teachers run and fall over and look through their glasses over their noses. If I put that then I'd really've painted a picture of the best sort of teacher in the world. All the, er, kids'd know then. |

### Effect of prompts

If a particular level of question is more effective than other levels then it is useful for all researchers to recognise this, whether they are approaching the interview through highly structured questioning or a more open style. The optimum degree of verbal prompting has been examined in seminal work by Dent (1986) and reviewed by Ceci and Bruck (1993): 'The focus has [thus] shifted from examining whether children are susceptible to determine under what conditions they are suggestible' (p. 16). A distinction was found between normally developing children and children with learning difficulties (8–11-year olds from a school for pupils with moderate learning difficulties). For the former, unprompted recall was the most accurate (but the least full), while for the learning difficulties group, general but not leading questions were most effective in terms of accuracy plus fullness. Specific questions were unhelpful for both groups and produced more information but this tended to be inaccurate. Similarly, Ceci has reported research in which children, having witnessed a classroom incident, were questioned about this. The more they were asked for elaboration – 'Who came in?' (a lady), 'What was she wearing' (a hat), 'What did the hat look like?' (it had feathers), 'How many feathers?' – the more that children supplied (incorrect) detail.

Dent concluded that if accuracy of recall is desired, then specific questions should not be used at all with children aged 8–14. General open-ended questions appeared to be best with children with mild or moderate learning difficulties. There has been debate since (see Bull 1995) about whether the rejection of specific questions in this context was justified, and a suggestion that clarification is needed about the types of specific questions which are associated with greater/lesser accuracy.

In my work on children's views about integration I was not primarily interested in accuracy but in the cognitive component of attitudes. I used mainly general questions with both primary school 7- and 11-year olds, and 9–11-year olds from a school for pupils with moderate learning difficulties.

In the following extract I was talking with a 10-year old about 12–15-year olds from a special (severe learning difficulties) school with whom he had worked in weekly art sessions during the preceding two terms.

Children has been describing the special school pupils:

| | |
|---|---|
| *Interviewer:* | Do you think they'll [special school pupils] always be like they are now? |
| *Gwyn:* | They might, it depends. |
| *Interviewer:* | What would it depend on? |
| *Gwyn:* | Depends if they were . . . being helped . . . or . . . just left. |
| *Interviewer:* | What sort of help would make them better do you think? |
| *Gwyn:* | Umm . . . if they had medical attention or something. |
| *Interviewer:* | What sort of medical attention would they need? |
| *Gwyn:* | Helping them to read and write. |

In retrospect I felt that my asking Gwyn to elaborate on what sort of help was needed, and then what kind of medical attention, pushed him too much to come up with some details. I suspect that a younger or less able child would have responded to the more specific question at the end either 'don't know' or some invention to satisfy my questioning. 'Don't know' responses are considered further on.

A different type of prompt used with children with learning difficulties is pictorial cues, either as a prompt card (e.g 'The girl in this picture is happy, but in this picture she is sad . . . which one shows how you would look when . . . ?'). Pictorial cues may also be used as part of a vignette depicting a series of events about which the child being interviewed is asked to comment. Some work (e.g. Begley 2000) has used standard scales using pictorial cues about which the child's response is rated. In other work with children, innovative techniques such as ecomaps or outline faces have been used (Hill *et al.* 1996). These approaches have intuitive appeal but they may be more open to bias, even though the most obvious (e.g. using pictures of a same sex/race/age child) can be avoided by using parallel sets of cards, so that children depicted are from the same groups as the interviewee.

In my current work I am exploring the use of stylised use cards, drawn from script theories about children's storying, to prompt uninterrupted narratives from children with moderate learning difficulties. Children have been trained in the use of the cards and then shown these in turn (with no verbal prompting) to elicit an uninterrupted recall of a series of events. Early results are very promising and the cue cards seem to be effective across a range of events (including, for example, a classroom disturbance, a key school event and routine occurrences). The cards have helped to elicit elaboration of detail of events but have not generated false 'recall'. The approach is interesting from both a methodological perspective (being generalisable across a variety of approaches) and theoretically as being relatively context-free.

### Permitting/encouraging 'don't know' responses

Understanding of complex abstract concepts, such as those associated with religion, may prompt a high proportion of non-responses. Ursula McKenna's work (1998) on children's views about understanding of Christian symbols involved primary age children with learning difficulties. Her questions to them understandably posed many of the children with difficulties. In this extract one suspects that the child needed to give a genuine 'don't know' answer, or to ask for clarification. Instead he and Ursula struggled on, endeavouring to communicate:

| | |
|---|---|
| *Interviewer:* | What work d'you like best in RE? |
| *Danny:* | The Celtics. |
| *Interviewer:* | The Celtics . . . What did you do in that topic? |
| *Danny:* | The Roman Celtics. |
| *Interviewer:* | What did you do when you were doing about them? |
| *Danny:* | They go and kill the Romans. |
| *Interviewer:* | What activities did you do? |
| *Danny:* | Well . . . the Romans kill Julius Caesar. |
| *Interviewer:* | Was that RE work? |
| *Danny:* | Yeh. |
| *Interviewer:* | Was it? |
| *Danny:* | It was this [*showing mosaic picture*]. |

Ceci and Bruck (1995) provide powerful illustrations from courtroom contexts of distortion arising from the interviewer's apparent refusal to believe that a child had forgotten a detail, or had a legitimate reason for not wanting to repeat an earlier remark. While there is less at stake in a research context, their warning about distortion arising from, in effect, disallowing don't know responses or silence, is applicable.

## Providing a résumé

Providing a group of statements in the form of a brief résumé can be particularly valuable with children who have short attention spans. However, doing so may inadvertently distort what was being said, as may have been the case in this example in which 10- and 11-year olds were discussing events that had occurred during a visit from pupils attending a special school:

| | |
|---|---|
| *Wayne:* | 'Cos their playground, their playground is big. |
| *David:* | But there's not many children in it. |
| *Wayne:* | And some of them don't like the loud noises and 'cos . . . 'cos I mean our playground's a lot noisier than theirs. |
| *Tracey:* | Yeh and their playground hasn't got many people in it. |
| *Interviewer:* | You think the noise [in primary school playground] would upset some of them so they wouldn't like it? |

The interviewer's summary here inadvertently introduced the idea that the main-stream pupils were upset by the playground behaviour of pupils from the special school. With hindsight and the benefit of the transcript, we can see that the pupils themselves had not placed this evaluation on the behaviour. Thus the résumé here may have biased after comments by the children, and may also have had repercussions for coding if the résumé was consciously or otherwise used to aid interpretation of the preceding sequence of dialogue.

Another type of résumé occurs in the legal context, when the questioner may be trying to confirm a series of facts leading up to an event (e.g. 'so you were downstairs, there was a knock at the door, the man came in, then what happened . . . ?'). Saywitz (1995) reviews work suggesting that such long compound sentences with embedded clauses are beyond the linguistic comprehension and memory skills of many children under about 8 years old.

## Phrasing of comments by the interviewer

### Modifying terms

Many aspects of specific question wording will influence responses. One category leading to potential bias is the use of modifying terms. Ceci and Bruck (1993) report work in which children's responses reflected a developmental shift in their understanding of marked and unmarked modifiers. Modifiers are adjectives or adverbs, for example, fast/slow, clever/stupid. Marked modifiers have a definite zero, so slow is marked, it contains a possible zero, that is not moving; but fast is unmarked, it is limitless. Children generally acquire unmarked forms, for example fast, before marked forms, for example, slow.

There are also cultural connotations to modifiers that influence response. When asked the question 'How slow/fast was the car going when it hit/smashed into the wall?' the version with 'fast' elicited higher speeds than did 'slow' for all ages from 6 to 14. For 12–14-year olds (but not the younger age groups) there were also faster estimates when 'smashed' not 'hit' was used. So some aspects of wording and hence suggestibility may affect older but not younger children. This is contrary to the usual stereotype that it is young children who will be the more suggestible. These differential effects may, in a similar way, vary with developmental level, so that a 14-year-old with very limited receptive and expressive vocabularies may not give faster estimates for the 'smashed' rather than the 'hit' version of this question.

These two sets of issues concerning the use of modifiers in questions to children have implications for interviews with children in which they are asked to choose (verbally or non-verbally) between polar opposites. For example, a range of research in the integration/inclusion field has asked children to rate peers (or 'photographs/video clips of unknown children) on scales such as 'slow worker'– quick worker'. The developmental work summarised would suggest that younger children might favour the latter ('quick worker') because it had been acquired while understanding of the former ('slow worker') had not.

## Use of pronouns and referents

Another feature of specific question wording that can inadvertently direct children's responses concerns the use of pronouns and referents. 'Did you see THE car?' produced, in both adults and 4–5-year-olds, more affirmatives than did the question 'Did you see A car?' (reviewed in Ceci and Bruck 1933). In an informal context the interviewer may unguardedly switch pronouns in this way, unwittingly leading to a bias in the way the child 'reads' the question:

> Did you like playing THOSE games?
> (> 'yes' response tendency.)
> Do you like working with THESE other children?
> (> 'yes' response tendency.)
> Did you like playing games?
> (> 'no' response tendency.)
> Do you like working with other children?
> (> 'no' response tendency.)

Further, Saywitz (1995) notes that young children (and presumably also children with learning difficulties) often misunderstand referents such as that, they, them, those, here, there. This may be particularly problematic if the researcher is trying to standardise interview questions by using referents, so that the identical question is applicable across respondents, and avoiding use of proper nouns (e.g. not naming the types of game or the children in these examples). If teachers and researchers work with children with, and children without, learning difficulties then the need for more specificity with children with learning difficulties may easily be overlooked.

# Use of context

## *Effect of background information*

The impact of expectations on young children's responses is illustrated by Ceci in work involving a character ('Harry') whose 'clumsiness' was described over a two-month period (reported in Ceci and Bruck 1993). Harry then visited the children's nursery. Children were later told that three toys had been broken and asked about what happened when Harry visited. Only 10 per cent of the children alleged that it was Harry who had broken the toys. When asked presumptive questions (e.g. 'How many toys did Harry break?') children reported more (inaccurate) clumsiness than had occurred. This highlights both the importance of the way in which expectations about people with learning difficulties are presented to children, and the danger of leading questions.

It is not only the language used by the interviewer that shapes the child's responses, it is also the language the child thinks the interviewer would use. This is illustrated well in Eleanor Nesbitt's work (Nesbitt 2000). She interviewed a wide range of children, of different ethnic origins, about their views concerning religion. Although not directly relevant to the SEN context, the specificity of language in that context highlights the less obvious but identical issue when discussing SEN. Eleanor noted, for example, that when talking to her, some children used terms like 'vicar' to describe the person who took the service even though this would not be the child's natural choice for the person (e.g. for a Baptist child, it would be 'minister'; for a Catholic, 'father', etc). The child was not picking up a word Eleanor had used but seems to have used a word that the child thought would be Eleanor's preferred term. The issue is the same but less obvious when a child uses particular terms to describe classmates, for example, 'having difficulties'/'trying hard'.

## *Impact of discussion*

Discussion has been shown to be associated with better subsequent recall of events. In this connection, classroom discussion about key events may assume particular significance. For example, in one integration project (Lewis 1995) 6–7-year-old primary school children regularly discussed the sessions with the teacher after the event. The recurrence of minor misbehaviour by some of the visiting children from the special school was very salient for the primary school children. At this age children are notoriously concerned about rule-keeping and rule-breaking. It was not surprising then that in interviews at the end of a year of link sessions, many of the primary school children recounted incidents of misbehaviour. This echoes in a more naturalistic context Ceci's work on Harry, referred to earlier. In contrast from my observation of the link sessions, special school pupils enjoyed looking at pictures in the books in the primary school classroom. This often occurred but was rarely mentioned by teachers in post-session discussions and was also not repeated by the children when interviewed about events during the sessions.

Post-event discussions will draw attention to particular aspects of the event. They will probably, albeit not wittingly, introduce misinformation. In an interesting study into suggestibility, Bruck and co-workers (1995) explored the association between IQ and suggestibility. The context was the planting of suggestions in children's minds about whether an inoculation had been painful. The 5-year-old children in these studies were classified as resistors or non-resistors (reflecting their susceptibility to misleading information), and statistical analyses were carried out into associations with IQ, memory and stress. In summary, IQ was not a significant factor, thus giving the lie to the popularly voiced notion that children having lower IQ scores will be more prone to being swayed by misinformation after an event.

## Conclusion

My interest in interviewing children about their experiences of integration and inclusion has highlighted the acute ethical and sampling problems. Decisions taken about sampling will clearly have implications for the generalisability of findings. Reliability and validity of the data will be influenced (among other things) by the interviewer's way of initiating dialogue, sustaining that dialogue, particular phrasings and the use made of context.

All researchers, except the small minority using very rigid structured interview schedules, make decisions (mostly intuitively) about these elements of the interview. At the very least, researchers in the inclusion field need to acknowledge the complexities of this process and report in a transparent way the nature of both sides of the interviewer–child dialogue.

## References

Alderson, P. (1999) 'Disturbed young people: research for what, research for whom?' in S. Hood, B. Mayall and S. Oliver (eds) *Critical Issues in Social Research*. Chichester: Wiley, pp. 54–67.

Aldridge, M. and Wood, J. (1998) *Interviewing Children: A Guide for Child Care and Forensic Practitioners*. Chichester: Wiley.

Allan, J. (1999) *Actively Seeking Inclusion: Pupils with Special Needs in Mainstream Schools*. London: Falmer.

Barsby, J. (1990) 'Self evaluation of writing by 7 year old children.' MA thesis. University of Warwick.

Begley, A. (2000) 'The educational self-perceptions of children with Down syndrome', in A. Lewis and G. Lindsay (eds) *Researching Children's Perspectives*. Buckingham: Open University Press, pp. 98–111.

Bruck, M, Ceci, S.J., Francouer, E. and Barr, R, (1995) ' "I hardly cried when I got my shot." Influencing children's reports about a visit to their paediatrician,' *Child Development*, **66**, 193–208.

Bull. R. (1995) 'Innovative techniques for the questioning of child witnesses, especially those who are young and those with learning disability', in M.S. Zaragoza, (ed.) *Memory and Testimony in the Child Witness*. Thousand Oaks: Sage, pp. 179–194.

Ceci, S.J. and Bruck, M. (1993) 'The suggestibility of the child witness: an historical review and synthesis.' *Psychological Bulletin*, **113**, 349–403.

Ceci, S.J. and Bruck, M. (1995) *Jeopardy tub the Courtroom*. Washington DC: American Psychological Association.

Crozier, J. (2000) 'Falling out of school', in A. Lewis and G. Lindsay (eds) *Researching Children's Perspectives*. Buckingham: Open University Press, pp. 173–183.

DES/WO (1994) *Code of Practice for the identification and Assessment of Children with Special Educational Needs*. London: HMSO.

Dent, H.R. (1986) 'An experimental study of the effectiveness of different techniques of questioning mentally handicapped child witnesses.' *British Journal of Clinical Psychology*, **25**, 13–17.

Detheridge, T. (2000) 'Research involving children with severe learning difficulties', in A. Lewis and G. Lindsay (eds) *Researching Children's Perspectives*. Buckingham: Open University Press, pp. 112–121.

DfEE (2000) SEN Code of Practice on the Identification and Assessment of Pupils with Special Educational Needs. *Consultation Document*. London: DfEE.

Dodd, K. and Brunker, J. (1999) ' "Feeling poorly": report of pilot study to increase the ability of people with learning disabilities to understand and communicate about physical illness.' *British Journal of Learning Disabilities*, **27**, 10–15.

Edwards, E. and Mercer, N. (1987) *Common Knowledge*. Buckingham: Open University.

Grieg, A. and Taylor, J. (1999) *Doing Ressearch with Children*. London: Sage.

Gross, M. (1993) *Exceptionally Gifted Children*. London: Routledge.

Hill, M., Layborn, A. and Borland, M. (1996) 'Researching children: methods and ethics.' *Children and Society*, **10** (**2**), 129–144.

Home Office/Department of Health (1992) *Memorandum of Good Practice on Video-recorded Interviews with Child Witnesses for Criminal Proceedings*. London: HMSO.

Kiernan, C. (1999) 'Participation in research by people with learning disability: origins and issues.' *British Journal of Learning Disabilities*, **27**, 43–47.

Le Count, D. (2000) 'Working with "difficult" children from the inside out: loss and bereavement and how the creative arts can help.' *Pastoral Care in Education*, **18** (**2**), 17–27.

Lewis, A. (1992) 'Group child interviews as a research tool.' *British Journal of Educational Research*, **18** (**4**), 413–421.

Lewis, A. (1995) *Children's Understanding of Disability*. London: Routledge.

Lewis, A. and Lindsay, G. (eds) (2000) *Researching Children's Perspectives*. Buckingham: Open University Press.

McKenna, U. (1998) 'Religious understanding in primary age children with learning difficulties.' MA thesis, University of Warwick.

Masson, J. (2000) 'Researching children's perspectives: legal issues', in A. Lewis and G. Lindsay (eds) *Researching Children's Perspectives*. Buckingham: Open University Press, pp. 34–45.

Nesbitt, E. (2000) 'Researching 8–13 year olds' experience of religion', in A. Lewis and G. Lindsay (eds) *Researching Children's Perspectives*. Buckingham: open Universtiy Press, pp. 135–149.

Saywitz, K.J. (1995) 'Improving children's testimony: the question, the answer and the environment', in M.S. Zaragoza (ed.) *Memory and Testimony in the Child Witness*. Thousand Oaks: Sage, pp. 113–140.

Scheurich, J.J. (1985) 'A post-modernist critique of research interviewing.' *Qualitative Studies in Education*, **8**(**3**), 239–252.

# Part IV

## The legal context

# Chapter 18

# Researching children's perspectives

## Legal issues

*Judith Masson*

Including child participants in research, as respondents or interviewers, raises ethical and legal dilemmas about children's rights and the obligations of researchers. Until the 1990s, the research community had been mainly divided into two distinct groups: those, particularly in the fields of education and health, who researched children relying on the consent of their parents or teachers, but who rarely asked the children themselves, and those who excluded children arguing that the issues of competence, consent and risk made children inappropriate subjects or unreliable respondents for research. Both these approaches compromise research legally, ethically and in terms of research findings. Reliance on the consent of others denies the child respondent information which would be thought essential for an adult participating in research, opportunities to clarify the aims of the research, what their role in it might be, and to decide whether or not to participate. The exclusion of children's voices, particularly from research intended to influence policy development, is a flaw which severely (even fatally) undermines the validity of the perspectives and insights gained.

This chapter explores the legal dimensions of children's involvement in research, explaining the current position relating to the rights of children, parents and their carers. It focuses on the law in England and Wales; the position in Northern Ireland and in Scotland is similar. The relevant law is to be found in cases, and in the key statutes, the Children Act 1989 for England and Wales, the Children (Northern Ireland) Order 1995 which is in most respects identical to the law in England and Wales, the Children (Scotland) Act 1995 and the Age of Legal Capacity (Scotland) Act 1991. Those researching in other Common Law countries, for example, the USA, Canada, Australia, New Zealand, will also find that similar concepts have taken root; elsewhere differences are likely to be greater. Wherever the research is to be conducted the researcher must be clear about both law and custom.

Although the relevant law is complex it is not uncertain (Alderson 1995: 74; Ward 1997: 20). Nor should it be seen as a barrier to the participation of children who are competent and willing to do so. To interpret the law in such a restrictive way undermines the rights that it enshrines for children. Although parents have rights because they are parents, there is no recognized tort of interference with parental rights (*F* v *Wirral MBC* 1991). Parents cannot claim damages from a person who has done something with their child of which they do not approve; penalties could of course follow if the activity was against the criminal law. But this would be the case even if the parent's consent had been obtained. Children's capacity to consent may not be clear-cut, researchers who wrongly consider that a child has consented may be acting unethically, but their decisions could be challenged only by a child who had been harmed by the research.

Researchers may owe a duty of care to those they involve in their research and could thus be liable for foreseeable injuries which befall them in the course of the research. Interviewees injured tripping on steep unlit steps as they approached the interview venue or who fell when their chair broke could have a claim.[1] It is also possible to envisage claims by children arising out of their involvement in experiments. Particular care should always be taken that the practical arrangements are suitable; the law generally accepts that children may not be as careful, or as aware of risks, as adults. These are probably unlikely scenarios; usually researchers are not at risk of legal proceedings merely through involving children as respondents to social research. Indeed, unless research is a cover for malign activity, it is difficult to see what proceedings could be brought, or who could bring proceedings, against someone who spoke or corresponded with a consenting child. Including children as interviewers is more problematic in that it raises questions about children's employment and the special care that should be taken of young employees, but many of the precautions which should be taken are relevant to the safety of all interviewees.

There is a close relationship between law and ethics but not everything that is legal is ethical. Frequently law, when used as a tool of regulation, attempts only to set the minimum ethical standard. The aspirations of ethical practice are higher. Having clarified in their own minds that what they propose would be legal, researchers should also consider how it measures up against the ethical standards of their own professional body, of the funding organization and of any other body which is involved in facilitating the research. It can never be appropriate to defend proposed practice solely on the basis that it is legal, nor can it be assumed that those who question the approach taken know or understand the relevant legal or ethical issues.

## 'Gatekeepers'

Children and young people are rarely free to decide entirely for themselves whether or not to participate in research. The enclosed nature of children's lives in families, in schools and in institutions means that they are surrounded by adults who can take on the role of 'gatekeepers', controlling researchers' access and children and young people's opportunities to express their views. Even where they have no power over a child's decision to take part in research, parents, carers and teachers generally control the places, homes and schools that provide the safest and most suitable venues for research interviews with children and young people. Arising from their position as parents, employees or carers, 'gatekeepers' have legal rights and responsibilities to safeguard children's welfare, to follow their employer's directions and comply with the ethical code of their professions. Their legal responsibilities mean that gatekeepers may face disciplinary action, including dismissal or removal of children from their care, if they fail to comply with the standards expected of them. Gatekeepers have a positive, protective function, sheltering children and young people from potential harm and testing the motives of those who want access. Researchers should expect gatekeepers to try to protect children and young people from ill-conceived, valueless or potentially damaging research. They should be able to explain the purpose and value of their research and what steps they will take to minimize any possible risk of harm from participation in it. However, gatekeepers can also use their position to censor children and young people. Researchers need to understand both the source and limits of each gatekeeper's power so that they can negotiate opportunities for children to choose whether to participate in their research.

## Children, childhood and parental responsibility

In England and Wales (and elsewhere in the UK) people under the age of 18 years are legally referred to as children. The use of the same word to cover all young people from infancy to the verge of adulthood may emphasize their incapacity but children are not powerless, nor without legal rights. Children are subject to the control of those who have 'parental responsibility' (see Box text) but parental responsibility itself declines as the child matures. Children are within the protection of the European Convention on Human Rights, now incorporated in the Human Rights Act 1998, and as such have the same rights that are guaranteed to adults.

---

### Who has parental responsibility?

Mother, unless the child has been adopted or freed for adoption
*and*
Father, provided he is (or has been) married to the mother or he has made a parental responsibility agreement with the mother he has a parental responsibility order
*and*
A carer who has obtained a resident order Children Act 1989 (s.12)
*and*
Anyone who has obtained an emergency protection order Children Act 1989 (s.44) very limited duration
*or*
The local authority if the child is the subject of a care order Children Act 1989 (s.33)

Various statutes recognize children's capacity to make specific decisions at particular ages (Childright 1996). The term 'parental responsibility' is used in the Children Act 1989 to encompass 'all the rights, duties, powers, responsibilities and authority which by law a parent has in relation to the child' (s.3(1)). The exact content of this power, the way it can be exercised and its extent are not set out in the Act but have been determined through case law. For researchers a key issue is whether and in what circumstances children can agree to take part in research independently from their parents.

The ethical requirement for the relationship between researcher and researched to be consensual raises the legal question who has the right to consent to research participation by a child. Alderson (1995: 22) has suggested that the 'safest course, though it can be repressive, is to ask for parental consent and also to ask for children's consent when they are able to understand'. The concern for safety here appears to be the safety of researchers lest their actions are challenged in litigation (Alderson 1995: 74). This cautious view is at variance with the current law on parental responsibility which limits the power that parents have over their mature children. Emphasis on respecting children's rights suggests a bolder approach.

The right to make decisions about a child's life is one aspect of parental responsibility. Common decisions for parents relate to the way the child is brought up and include choosing the child's school. The decision whether to participate in research is also included. In Re Z (1996) the court held that a parent who gave confidential information about her child's medical treatment or education was exercising parental responsibility. This case concerned the making of a film about a therapeutic facility where the child who had severe disabilities had received treatment, but the principle applies to providing information orally or in writing. Parents who take part in research and provide information about their child, or who agree to their child participating in research, are exercising parental responsibility. Parental responsibility (the parental right to make decisions) is not absolute but is restricted by the parent's obligation to act in the child's interests and the rights of the mature child to make decisions independently.

Parental decisions are always potentially challengeable but this rarely happens except in the context of the acrimonious relationships of separated parents. A person who wishes to challenge the parent's decision applies to the court, which decides the dispute on the basis of what it considers to be in the best interests of the child (Children Act 1989 s.1).[2] Although the court could override a parental refusal, the only recorded example shows the court taking a paternalistic approach, viewing participation in a television documentary as contrary to the child's best interests. In Re Z (1996) the child's mother wanted her to take part in a television film about the care and treatment she had received in a rehabilitation clinic for children with severe disabilities but her father, who had long been in dispute with the mother, objected to this. The court, applying the principle that the child's welfare is the paramount consideration, barred the girl's participation. The court's view, that 'the welfare of the child would be harmed and not advanced by the publication of this film', was at odds with the view of the mother, who thought that her daughter's confidence and self-esteem would be enhanced by taking part. Research participation will involve far less exposure and thus avoid the adverse consequences of media attention which arose in *Re Z*. However, it may be very difficult to identify a clear benefit to an individual child from having taken part, except those associated with making a contribution or having a say, and thus to show that participation would be in the child's best interests.

Researchers who wish to include young children who are not old enough to decide for themselves about research participation must obtain the agreement of at least one person who has parental responsibility for the child. Although in the absence of court orders to the contrary (Children Act 1989 s.2(8)), the law recognizes separated parents as having equal power to consent, it is not ethical to privilege the view of a parent who is less involved in the child's day-to-day care. Researchers must engage with parents and provide them with the information that allows them to make good decisions about permitting their child's involvement in any proposed study.

Special considerations apply in respect of children who are looked after by a local authority, children in foster homes, residential schools, children's homes or elsewhere. The parents of these children retain their parental responsibility, although their opportunities to exercise it are obviously curtailed. Only where there is a care order does the local authority have parental responsibility for the child (see Box text) and then it holds it together with the parents. If children are only accommodated, the local authority can agree to research with the child only if this is reasonable for the purpose of safeguarding or promoting the child's welfare (Children Act 1989 s.3(5)). Local authorities are required to consult and consider the views of all parents (and children) before making decisions about them (Children Act 1989 s.22(4)(5)). Although this provision often appears to be honoured in the breach, researchers should expect to involve parents even though they do not have day-to-day care of their child.

Parental responsibility is not the determining factor for a child's participation in research where the child is mature. A child who has the capacity to understand fully a decision affecting his or her life automatically has the capacity to make that decision affecting his unless statute law states otherwise (*Gillick* 1986). Competence, the level of understanding required to make decisions, is directly related to the decision to be taken. Thus children are competent and can decide whether or not to participate in a research study, provided that they have a sufficient understanding of what participation entails and how participating may affect them. A considerably higher degree of understanding would be expected before a child could agree to take part in an experiment about the effects of sleep deprivation on exam performance than for a short interview about leisure activities. It is children's level of understanding, not their age, which is important. It cannot be assumed that all children of a particular age are, or are not, competent to decide. Competence can be encouraged by giving the necessary background information and providing oppourtunities to explore it before the issue of research participation is raised. However, this might require permission unless it was part of a normal activity which the child took part in at school, youth club or elsewhere.

Where children have the capacity to make a decision, parents' power over that area of their child's life is ended unless preserved by statute law. Consequently, a parent cannot consent to research on behalf of a competent child. Nevertheless, mature children can explicitly allow parents or other adults to make decisions on their behalf.

Lack of competence to make decisions does not imply the inability to make a contribution through participating in research but it is clearly relevant both to issues of consent and the way the research is conducted. The law uses quite a different standard to determine whether a child can give evidence to a criminal court, a matter which is generally outside either the parent's or the child's control. A child can be a competent witness if he or she understands the importance of accuracy and honesty, and can give a coherent account of an event. Children as young as 4 years old have been accepted as witness in criminal trials, but would probably be called to give evidence only where an alternative source was not available. Views that children are unreliable and untruthful witnesses which dominated legal (and adult) thinking have been challenged by research (Spencer and Flin 1993). Considerable (but probably inadequate) care is now taken to ensure that child witnesses understand what they are being asked to do and that the process does not place too great physical or emotional burdens on them. These changes in criminal proceedings provide useful lessons both for researchers who wish to include children and those who think children's views need not be sought.

## Consent and confidentiality

Having identified who must consent, consideration should be given to the nature of that consent. As far as medical practice is concerned, a concept of 'informed consent' has been developed in a number of countries. Where informed consent is required, only the consent of individuals who were fully informed of the relevant issues before they gave their consent is valid. English law has repeatedly refused to accept the need for informed consent for medical treatment, preferring to accept doctors' views about what patients need to be told. This approach leaves medical staff with considerable scope and frees them from the possibility of facing an action for assault on the basis that the patient's consent was obtained without disclosure of all the possible risks.

Using this approach researchers could argue against the need for informed consent to research. The contrary argument, for higher standards based on ethics rather than law, appears more persuasive. Researchers do not face the risks that informed consent would impose on doctors nor can they claim that their actions are designed and intended to benefit those from whom they seek cooperation. The fundamental importance of consent, freely given, to research participation reinforces the view that the researcher should always explain fully the purpose, process and intended outcomes of research and seek consent on that basis. Where general consents have already been given, for example as part of the arrangements for a child's care or education, these may not be adequately judged against high ethical standards. At the very least, consideration should be given to the possible advantages to both researcher and participant of approaching each new study on the basis that fully informed consent should be obtained.

If consent is to be freely given, care also needs to be taken that children (or other potential respondents) do not feel obliged to participate. Where the person seeking children's participation is in a powerful position over them, as in the case of a teacher or carer, children may feel that they have to agree or, worse still, that they will be penalized if they do not. Researchers need to be alert to such possibilities, particularly where their access is arranged by those who provide services for children.

The notion of confidentiality has a very particular meaning among researchers which needs to be explained and agreed with those participating. Research confidentiality usually entails taking considerable care not to pass information to those connected in any way with the respondent and disclosing information only in ways which protect the identity of those who provided it. The location where the research took place is generally not identified, individuals are anonymized or given pseudonyms, and some facts, which might otherwise identify them, are changed or omitted. All research participants, including children and young people, need careful explanations of research confidentiality when (or before) their consent to participate is sought.

Where children are competent to make decisions, the law allows them the associated confidentiality which it would allow an adult. The confidentiality of younger children, who lack the capacity to consent, also needs to be considered. Although these children may keep secrets from their parents, they are not entitled to confidential relationships automatically. Where arrangements for children's participation have been made with parents or other gatekeepers, these people will of course know that an individual child has taken part, and what the focus of the research is. Natural curiosity and concern for their child may lead them to question the child or the researcher about what was said. This can put pressure on the child. Researchers need to consider this when negotiating access or consent for interviews with children and young people. Where parental consent is needed, it can be sought on the understanding that what the child says will not be passed to parents (Hamilton and Hopegood 1997). In such cases, parents may need to be reassured that certain types of information would be passed to them; where this is the case children should know that this will happen and what parents will be told. Some children may want to give the account of the interview for the researcher but others may prefer the researcher to explain on their behalf.

There are ethical considerations in research (and other work) with children which may mean that the same degree of confidentiality cannot be guaranteed to a child as would be given to an adult. There are two areas of particular concern, where a child discloses that he or she is being seriously harmed or ill-treated, and where the researcher identified a condition, for example, a medical condition or learning difficulty about which the parents could take action. Failure of the researcher to take appropriate action not only might lead to criticism on ethical grounds, but also in some limited circumstances could give rise to legal liability.

In the UK, there is no legal requirement on anyone who knows that a child is being ill-treated to notify social services or the police as there is in some other countries, notably many states of the USA. However, guidance to doctors from the Department of Health (DoH 1994) and lawyers (Solicitors Family Law Association 1995) advises that the confidential nature of the relationship with the patient or client does not provide a justification for failing to pass on information where children are being abused. Researchers should be aware that the promise of confidentiality may have encouraged children to discuss their dreadful circumstances, and may feel betrayed if information is passed on without their knowledge. Where such issues could arise, the researchers need to consider the information and support they can provide for young people. Some young people may prefer the complete confidentiality of ChildLine to disclosure to an interviewer. This is a telephone advice and counselling service for children and young people, particularly those who are abused. Realistically most researchers will be unable to provide the kind of support required by a young person in the throes of a child protection investigation but with forethought they may be able to help them to access local services. In such cases, interviewers may also need support. Employing researchers could even be liable for trauma suffered by interviewers who they knowingly required to conduct distressing interviews.

There will be some studies, particularly those involving the use of diagnostic instruments, where the researcher may obtain information about individual children which would be useful to children or their parents. In addition to any ethical duty to disclose this information, there could be a legal duty to do so, particularly for anyone conducting the research in the course of employment to provide services for children, for example, a doctor or an educational psychologist. It is accepted that doctors owe a duty of care to their patients; a similar duty has been held to apply to educational psychologists carrying out assessments of, or providing advice about, individual children (*Christmas* v *Hampshire CC*; *Keating* v *Bromley LBC* 1995). Although it would be more difficult to establish that a researcher who was not otherwise providing a service owed a duty of care, an education authority which employed the researcher or permitted the research to take place might be held liable. Consequently, researchers need to consider whether and how to provide information about identifiable children. Where young people could take the necessary steps themselves, information should be provided to them directly but the researchers should consider whether they have the necessary maturity to handle it. In the case of younger children, parents should be given the information, as they too may need help to know what steps to take.

## Protecting children participating in research

Current concerns about the victimization of children by those who have gained access to them through employment in schools or care homes, or through organizing children's leisure activities, have drawn attention to child sexual abuse occurring outside the home. Although children are generally at far greater risk of abuse within their families, no one who plans activities involving children and adults can disregard the dangers that some adults pose to children. Legislation requiring those convicted of certain offences against children to register with the police (Sexual Offenders Act 1997) together with new systems to check the criminal records of prospective employees (Police Act 1997) may appear to provide ways of determining that interviewers are appropriate people. However, both detection and conviction for these offences remains extremely low. Making use of the criminal record certificates (Police Act 1997 Pt V) can avoid exposing children only to convicted offenders; for greater care is necessary both in recruitment and the arrangements for research if children are to be safe.

Under the Police Act 1997, prospective employees will be able to obtain criminal record certificates which will disclose to prospective employers whether or not they have criminal convictions. For those whose employment (or voluntary work) involves regularly having sole responsibility for children (or vulnerable adults) it will be possible to have more detailed checks undertaken covering convictions occurring ten or more years previously and even details of offences which did not result in a conviction or a caution. These 'enhanced criminal records certificates' will replace the checking mechanisms available to local authorities and voluntary organizations and should be used for research staff working with children.[3]

Criminal records checks cannot ever replace good recruitment practices which seek to establish the prospective employee's suitability and work history from those who know them. Useful guidance was given to social services departments in the Warner Report (1992).

The arrangements for interviews also need to be considered. Both children and interviewers must feel and be safe during the research. Children may feel more comfortable if they can bring a friend or parent to an interview but this may also inhibit what they say and can make concentration difficult. There are cases where it will be appropriate for the researcher to arrange for chaperones, particularly where the research involves the child travelling to a laboratory or other facility where the research will be conducted. Particular care must be taken both in selection and training if the chaperone is not someone already known to the child. Using large public rooms or corridors allows the interview to be observed but not overheard but may not be practicable. Where children are interviewed at home, interviewers often have little choice about where they see a child. It may be difficult to find a sufficiently quiet place in living areas without disrupting family activities. Bedrooms are not usually suitable places for children to see strangers alone, although they may like to show them to visitors. The garden or the stairs can in some cases provide an appropriate place for an interview.

## Children as researchers

More attention has been given since the mid-1990s to involving children in the research process either as part of advisory groups helping to design and direct studies about things which concern them or as interviewers of other children (Ward 1997). These initiatives raise further legal concerns about children's status and their safety. Children who are engaged as interviewers are working for the researcher and should be accorded no less consideration than adult interviewers. Even under minimum wage legislation, it is likely to be legal to pay children less than adults, but where children possess special skills, such as the ability to obtain good rapport with other children, this should be recognized in the rate of pay as it would be for an adult. The strict regulation of children's work requires additional safeguards to be provided. Interviewers are often not regarded as employees but as sessional workers. However, where there is control over whom they interview and the contents of the interview, as would be the case where children are carrying out fieldwork, it is difficult to argue that they are not employees.

The Children and Young Persons Acts 1933 and 1963,[4] modified by the Children (Protection at Work) Regulations 1998, set out the limitations on work by those below the school leaving age of 16. Children below the age of 14 years may not be employed except in certain categories of light work specified in local authority bylaws. Although these categories may be broadly drawn they will not necessarily cover research work and may vary from place to place. Working hours are also restricted. Children under 15 years may not work for more than 2 hours on any school day or Sunday, or 5 hours on a Saturday. They cannot work for more than 25 hours a week in the school holidays. The Health and Safety (Young Persons) Regulations 1997 impose further safeguards for young people (i.e. those under the age of 18 years) and children (i.e. those below the school leaving age). Before employing anyone below the age of 18 years, employers must assess the risks posed by the work, taking account (among other things) of the immaturity and inexperience of young people. All employees have to be given 'comprehensible and relevant information' about risks and protective measures; where children are employed this information must also be given to a parent.

The concerns about the vulnerability of children being interviewed also apply where children are interviewers. Interviewers are at risk as they travel to interviews; where interviews will take place in private homes they may also be at risk from other household members, about whom little may be known. Those planning the research need to consider these risks with interviewers. Chaperones or drivers who wait outside provide a way of protecting interviewers both on the way to and during an interview but other arrangements such as pairs of interviewers will be more suitable for some studies. As well as physical risks, attention needs to be given to potential psychological harm from hearing disturbing accounts from other children. Young interviewers may well need more training and support than adults: under the regulations this is a legal requirement, not just a professional issue.

## Conclusion

The law's relationship with children is generally protectionist. It seeks to shelter them from exploitation outside the family and control or punish those who would harm them. Protectionism has both advantages and disadvantages for children. It may help to keep them safe although it is often not effective. It has also justified controlling children and can lead to their marginalization. Researchers can help to counteract children's marginalization by involving them in research but in doing so need to take care not to jeopardize their safety nor exploit them. Research with children which does not take on board legal dimensions is likely to harm both children and research.

## Notes

1  This claim would not necessarily be against the researcher. The person responsible for the building would have responsibility as the occupier.
2  In theory anyone may challenge the exercise of parental responsibility but the integrity of the family is protected by requiring those who are not parents, step-parents or long-term carers of the child to obtain the prior permission of the court before making their application (Children Act 1989 s.10).
3  Employers and others seeking to use enhanced criminal records certificates will have to register with the Home Office and countersign each application for a certificate.
4  In Scotland the Children and Young Persons (Scotland) Act 1937 applies.

## Case list

*Christmas* v *Hampshire CC; Keating* v *Bromley LBC* [1995] 2 FLR 276
*F* v *Wirral MBC* [1991] Fam 69
*Gillick* v *West Norfolk AHA* [1986] AC 112
*Re Z (a minor) (freedom of publication)* [1996] 1 FLR 191

## References

Alderson, P. (1995) *Listening to Children*, London: Barnardo's.
Childright (1996) At what age can I . . . ? *Childright*, 128.
Department of Health (DoH) (1994) *Child Protection: Medical Responsibilities – an Addendum to Working Together under the Children Act 1989*, London: HMSO.
Hamilton, C. and Hopegood, L. (1997) Offering children confidentiality: law and guidance, *Childright*, 140, 1–8.
Solicitors' Family Law Association (SFLA) (1995) *Guide to Good Practice for Solicitors Acting for Children*, 2nd edn. Orpington, Kent: SFLA.
Spencer, J. and Flin, R. (1993) *The Evidence of Children*. London: Blackstone.
Ward, L. (1997) *Seem and Heard*. York: York Publishing Services.
Warner Report (1992) *Choosing with Care: The Report of the Committee of Enquiry into the Selection, Development and Management of Staff in Children's Homes*. London: HMSO.

# Chapter 19

# Data protection issues in educational research

*Clare Wood*

## Introduction

'Data protection' refers to issues related to how one collects, stores and manages personal information about other people. It is an important ethical aspect of managing any piece of research, no matter how small scale or informal the project might be. However, it is often neglected, particularly if a researcher is working with a group that they know well, in their workplace, or with very young children. This chapter will explore principles of good practice in relation to data issues, and highlight some potentially problematic situations for educational researchers.

## What constitutes data?

'Data' refers to any information that you collect and store during the course of a piece of research, be it numerical, textual, verbal or observational. This can include specific information about individuals, such as their names, ages, where they live, their occupations, their scores on a test or a task, their responses to a questionnaire or during an interview. It also includes any video recordings, field notes (however informal), photographic evidence, audio recordings or transcripts. All these forms of data need to be handled with appropriate care and sensitivity. Of particular significance in legal terms is 'personal data', which refers to any data 'which relate to a living person who can be identified'. Most research data would be considered 'personal data' in this sense.

## What is the Data Protection Act?

The Data Protection Act was passed in the UK in 1998 and relates to 'the regulation of the processing of information relating to individuals, including the obtaining, holding, use or disclosure of such information'. Research data is exempt from certain aspects of the regulations laid out in this Act, as long as the data is collected and handled according to the principles laid out in the

> Act. The guidance given in this chapter covers these principles. However, if you work in the UK you may find it useful to be familiar with the Act. A copy can be downloaded from http://www.hmso.gov.uk/acts/acts1998/

How data is collected, stored and handled touches on aspects of ethical procedure that should be familiar to researchers. The following section summarises the principles of good practice that influence how one deals with research data.

## Principles of good practice

These principles of good practice are developed from the Data Protection Act guidelines produced by the Open University. The comments illustrate what this principle means in terms of research practice.

1   *Data should be collected fairly and legally.*   Data should always be obtained directly from research participants, with their full knowledge and consent.

2   *Data should be used only for the purposes for which they are collected. The purpose to which the data will be put must be explained to the individuals concerned when the data is being obtained.*   When contacting individuals with a view to conducting a research project, one should clearly explain what the focus of the research will be and how the data collected will be presented in its final form. For example, participants should know whether their data will be pooled and presented as overall group data (which would fully conceal their data and their identity) or whether a case study format might be adopted which might draw directly on data produced by individuals, as is the case when direct quotations are used, or detailed anonymised case information is presented. Equally, having explained the aim of the research and the means of presentation to the participants, it is then unacceptable to adapt or reuse the data to address a substantially different set of research questions. The participants have only consented to participate in the original research study: any substantial amendment to the focus of the study should not be conducted without re-contacting the participants to gain clearance for this new use of their data. The Data Protection Act specifically states that no processing of research data is allowed if the data are used to support decisions made about specific individuals, or if there is likely to be substantial damage or distress caused.

3   *Data should be adequate, accurate, relevant and not excessive: unnecessary data should not be collected.*   It can be tempting when collecting data for research purposes to add in an additional task, or a few more questions on the questionnaire that would collect additional 'interesting' data that you are curious about. You should not do this. Only collect the data that is necessary to address the research questions that you are immediately concerned with answering. It is always a good idea to keep data collection to an absolute minimum and keep it

tightly focussed on the issue at hand. This will mean that your data collection is fast and efficient, it will minimise the inconvenience to your participants, and your data analysis will stay focussed and appropriate to the questions you originally set out to answer.

4   *Personal data should not be kept longer than necessary, and should be kept up to date as necessary.*   This means that data on individuals should be destroyed after it has served its purpose. With respect to student work, all data should be retained until such a time that a mark for a piece of work has been formally awarded and finalised. Once you are confident that you will no longer be asked to produce these data (e.g. for viva or verification purposes), you should take care to destroy these materials appropriately (i.e. shred paper material, wipe video and audio recordings, etc.). Do not be tempted to retain tapes of observations, etc. for nostalgic reasons. It is good practice to advise participants at the outset that their data will be destroyed once the research study has been concluded, and indicate how long it might be retained for before this will occur.

In formal research it is normal practice to retain anonymised data for a period of around five years after the publication of a study (and publication of a study can take several years in itself). This period is to give other academics the chance to scrutinise the data that published claims are based on. Anonymised sets of quantitative data or qualitative material, especially those that relate to published studies, are increasingly stored in national research archives, and such storage is often a condition of some research grants.

5   *Personal data should not be disclosed to third parties.*   This means that information that relates to a person *who can be readily identified from the data* should not be disclosed to other people. Thus one should not give these data to other people, or store such data in a way that other people might intentionally or unintentionally gain access to it. One way of ensuring that accidental disclosure of personal data does not occur is to anonymise each participant with a code number or code name, and use this on all spreadsheets, transcripts, questionnaires, video labels and audio labels. If you do not need to keep a list of the actual names of the people who participated, do not do so. If for some reason you need to retain a list of the names of the people who participated alongside their codes, store this list securely and in a separate location from the coded data.

6   *Data should not be unnecessarily reproduced in any form, or left visible to third parties, however unintentionally.*   You should avoid making copies of personal data – while you should make backups of any data you are working with, this should not extend to photocopying raw personal data or duplicating taped material. Such material should be transcribed and anonymised as soon as possible, and these transcripts stored securely with one backup copy stored equally securely in a different location. Data should not be left lying around on desks or left visible on computer or TV screens.

7   *Personal data should not be given over the telephone or via email. Personal data sent by post should only be sent to validated addresses.*   Avoid transferring data by

unsecured means (i.e. if uncertain that your intended recipient will be the actual recipient of the information, or when you are uncertain if other people have access). This may occur during correspondence with a participant about their data, for example, or if you are working as part of a team of researchers on the same project.

8    *No data relating to a specific individual should be disclosed to anyone unless the individual concerned has given their prior permission.*   This means that you should not 'assume' that it will be OK to discuss data with a third party or give copies of data to a third party without first explicitly gaining consent from the participants concerned. The Data Protection Act states that no processing of research data is allowed if the identity of a participant is given away without consent.

9    *Personal data should be held securely and proper security measures taken for all methods of holding or displaying personal data to prevent loss, destruction or corruption of information. This means that*

   (a)  *Computers that can access personal data should not be left unattended when the data is accessible (e.g. after a password has been entered), and the screen should be cleared of any data after use.*
   (b)  *Individuals must take responsibility for ensuring that personal data is kept away from people who are not entitled to see it.*
   (c)  *Print outs should be stored securely when not in use and shredded when no longer required.*
   (d)  *Passwords should not be easily guessable, should be changed regularly, and not disclosed.*
   (e)  *Removable disks (e.g. floppy disks, zip disks, CD Roms) containing personal data should be removed from the computer after use and stored securely. Similarly, video and audio cassettes and similar media should be removed from equipment and stored appropriately when not in use. They should be reformatted or destroyed when no longer needed.*
   (f)  *Information on hard disks should be password protected.*

Additionally, if you are a researcher who is working in a University setting (e.g. a research student, research assistant/fellow), you should always register any data set with the Data Protection Officer at your institution.

## Appropriate use of data

*The practical implications of good data protection practice are illustrated in the following scenario.*

You have been conducting research with teachers and have audiotaped interviews with them regarding their views on working with 'underachieving boys'. In addition you have conducted observations of some of these teachers working with the boys in the context of their normal lessons. During the course of your analysis you notice a strong theme emerging to do with the teachers' views on punishment and classroom control issues.

(i) During the course of your study the headteacher, from whom you initially got consent to conduct the study in the school, asks if she could watch some of the videos you have made. What should you do?

(ii) You are listening to one of your audio cassettes and you are not quite sure what one of the teachers has just said. What should you do?

(iii) You are typing up your transcripts of the classroom observations late into the night. Your partner offers to take a turn in order to give you a break. What should you do?

(iv) You produce your report as originally outlined. You would like to use stills from the video recordings to illustrate your report/conference presentation. Would this be an acceptable use of the data?

(v) You would like to write the study up for a second report that deals exclusively with classroom control. Would this be acceptable use of the data?

*Comments*

(i) The headteacher gave you permission to conduct your research in her school, however it does not follow that she has the right to 'eavesdrop' on the data you are collecting, however well intentioned her reasons for doing so. You might explain to her that your participants are participating on the understanding that the video material will be confidential to yourself. If she has a strong reason for wishing to view it, you may wish to consult with the teacher and children concerned and gain their consent for the headteacher to view it. However, the participants should be encouraged to view the actual video footage *before* making their decision.

(ii) You should indicate that the section is inaudible using appropriate transcript notation. You should resist the temptation to invite a third party to listen to the tape to 'see what they think it is'.

(iii) You should decline the (very kind) request, but go and have a break/go to bed. When you leave the desk, you should shut down the files you were working on and put away any paperwork and videos in a lockable drawer.

(iv) No. Your participants did not consent for the video material to be used for this purpose, and so it would be inappropriate to do so (and it would also identify them as participants to the research). However, you could go back to the participants concerned and get separate consent to use the stills in this way.

(v) No. Again, your participants did not agree to participate in a piece of research to do with classroom control, they understand the research to be about under-achieving boys. They may not have consented to participate had they known that this issue would be focussed on. You could contact the participants and get separate clearance from them for you to use the data you have collected for this new purpose. Only those people who consent should have their data used in any subsequent analysis.

While these principles may seem very prescriptive in places, they are intended to protect both the researcher and the participants to the research. What may seem 'reasonable' use of the data to you can be seen by a participant as very threatening. This is particularly true of research conducted in educational settings, both with respect to teachers and their pupils. It is worth remembering that the prevailing educational climate is typically one of evaluation, accountability and consequence. Educational research is often perceived by its participants to be concerned with the evaluation of them *as individuals*. As a result, participation in a programme of research can be undertaken with some degree of trepidation and, in some cases, anxiety. The appropriate management of and respect for their data is central to engendering a relationship of trust, as well as conducting a programme of research in a professional manner.

## Withdrawal of consent and ownership of data

One situation that can occur is where an individual withdraws their participation halfway through a programme of research, or even after the project has been completed. Although this is quite rare, a participant is entirely within his or her rights to do so. If this occurs any data that you have obtained from this person should be destroyed with immediate effect and should not be used in any analysis or report.

The participant should always be thought of as 'owning' their data, which they have consented for you to 'use' in a particular, prescribed way. It is, in this sense, not 'your' data to do with as you wish. Your use of it is limited by their consent. Once consent is withdrawn, you no longer have the right to keep it or use it. In some cases a person will leave a study halfway through for reasons other than withdrawal of consent, and will therefore be happy for you to continue to use the data you have already collected. If you are in any doubt you should explicitly discuss this with the person concerned. Following this, if you are still unsure you should err on the side of caution and not use the data.

## Some data protection issues when working with children

Some data protection issues become more complex when working with children, especially when working with children in school contexts. This is illustrated in the following example.

### Collecting data from children in school

You are conducting research in the school in which you normally work. As part of your project you are collecting data from a group of children that you do not teach on aspects of how well they can read and spell. You have obtained consent to conduct the study from the headteacher, the classroom teacher, the children's parents and the children themselves.

(i) After a few days, the classroom teacher makes it clear that she is expecting a copy of the children's reading ages 'in exchange' for her cooperation. What should you do?

(ii) During a session one of the children begins to fidget and shows little interest in the task at hand. What should you do?

*Comments*

(i) When working with children it is a good idea to see both parent *and* child as owning any data generated by the child. Technically schools do have 'loco-parentis' status and see themselves in this way. While they have consented to host the study, they do not own the data you will collect from the children. It is often inappropriate to simply handover data generated by a child to a school teacher. In this situation, the best solution would be to circulate a separate consent form to the parents explaining that the school would like a copy of the children's reading ages for their records, and asking them to sign to indicate their willingness for you to release the data for that purpose. In this example such a request is unlikely to be controversial. However, parents may be reluctant to release other types of research data to a child's teacher (e.g. data about bullying, 'intelligence' scores). The principle here would be to always seek consent from the parents and where possible make the children aware that their teacher will see their work and make sure that they are happy with that situation.

(ii) Fidgeting and this type of reluctant behaviour, especially in very young children, should be taken as an indication that they may wish to withdraw their consent. At school, children are used to 'having to' complete a task that they do not wish to, and are therefore not used to refusing to cooperate in an explicit way. As a result you should abandon this attempt to work with the child and try again on another day, just in case the child is simply feeling tired. If they behave this way on a second occasion, you should assume that consent has been withdrawn.

This example illustrates the ways that data protection issues can be made more complex when applied to educational research. Teachers and parents can see themselves as in a position of seniority over the children in their care. However, care should be taken to ensure that the status of children as research participants is not marginalised as a result of this. Simply because a parent consents for you to collect data from their child, it does not follow that you can do so without the consent of the child too. Similarly, when a parent consents to certain types of disclosure, it is always worth checking that the child understands and is equally happy for you to go ahead. If the child shows any concern, you should not proceed.

Teachers can assume that they have the right to see data generated by children in their care. This is open to question, and as a model of good practice disclosure of an individual's data to their teachers should only occur after the consent of both parent and child has been obtained. However, it should be noted that general patterns and observations relating to the data you have collected as a whole should be fed back to parents and schools during the normal debriefing process. It is the disclosure of individual people's data that data protection issues relate to.

## Good habits and bad practice

A good deal of what is discussed previously is based on a sensitivity to the potential concerns of people who consent to participate in research studies. While as responsible researchers we would not seek to breach any of these principles, many are easily neglected through carelessness, poor planning and problematic time management. To conclude the chapter, the following are offered as 'good habits' to get into, when adopted, should ensure that any data protection issues are dealt with successfully.

(i)   *Being explicit.*   When you are recruiting people to a research study be as explicit as possible about what data you are going to collect and what purpose(s) they are going to be put to. Make it clear who will 'control' your use of the data, and that personal data will be confidential to you. Put this in writing and ask participants to respond with any queries.

(ii)   *Talking to children.*   If you are working with children as research participants, no matter how little the adults around them think they will understand, you should always talk to them about what you are interested in, what you are proposing that they do with you, how that will help you in your work and what you will do with that information when you have finished. Often even the youngest children are interested by this type of talk and enjoy 'working with you' rather than doing what you ask just because you have asked them. Most importantly, check each time you see them whether they are happy to do a given activity with you, and if necessary revisit the chat you have had before about why you are doing it.

(iii)   *Transcribing material quickly.*   If you have to produce transcripts from audio or video material, then bite the bullet and do this straight away. This will mean that the raw personal data (in this case, the audio and video material) is quickly locked away.

(iv)   *Coding data.*   This is a good habit to get into. As far as possible anonymise all data as you obtain it and use codenames or code numbers to refer to research participants. While this can be tedious if you are dealing with data generated from a large number of different people, this will pay dividends in the long run, and is your best protection from unintended disclosure of information.

(v)   *Being tidy.*   Tidiness is something that a lot of us (myself included) struggle with, but when working with data it is a virtue. Being tidy means that transcripts, videos, test sheets and contact details are never left casually on a desktop while you grab a sandwich or are otherwise distracted.

(vi) *Having a safe place.*   This can take some thought and often a bit of re-organisation regarding filing cabinets and desk drawers. If you are conducting research, you will need a place that you can lock precious raw data away in an organised and systematic fashion.

(vii) *Using passwords on the computer.*   Setting up passwords on your personal computer is a really important part of preparing for a piece of research. Where your application programmes allow you to, you should password-protect individual files that contain data.

## Conclusion

Conducting research is a considerable responsibility, and requires careful thought, planning and awareness of issues that will impact not just on the project in hand, but also the participants and the eventual users of the research. Of particular importance is involving participants in a way that respects their interests without compromising those of others who are involved. Research is powerful in its ability to amplify some voices and marginalise others. With respect to data protection, it is important to recognise that we as researchers should see ourselves as managing information that belongs to other people.

# Index